PIONEERS FOR PEACE

Women's International League
for Peace and Freedom 1915–1965

GERTRUDE BUSSEY
MARGARET TIMS

'Not the heroism connected with warfare and
destruction but that which pertains to labour
and the nourishing of human life.'
JANE ADDAMS, *Newer Ideals of Peace*

W I L P F British section: London

First published 1965 by George Allen & Unwin Ltd as
*Women's International League for Peace and Freedom 1915–1965:
a record of fifty years' work.*

Reissued 1980 as *Pioneers for Peace: Women's International
League for Peace and Freedom 1915–1965.*

ISBN 0 9506968 0 3

Printed in Great Britain by the Alden Press, Oxford

Cover design by Gillian Durrant

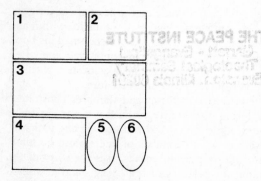

Cover photos:
1 Mission to King of Norway, 1915
2 Disarmament campaign, 1932
3 Hague Congress, 1915
4 Group at Jane Addams House, 1960
5 Jane Addams (from Jane Addams Memorial Collection, University of Illinois)
6 Emily Greene Balch

FOREWORD TO 1980 EDITION

This is the story of a unique group of women during a unique period of history. In a century of unprecedented violence they dared to envision a world free from the ultimate violence of war and oppression and to strive to bring about such a world.

Never numerous, they have exerted an influence well beyond their numbers and stimulated spin-offs into the larger society. They were the first—and remain the only—international women's organization accredited as an NGO to the United Nations with peace as its top priority. They anticipated by sixty years the world community's recognition of the importance of women's work in achieving 'equality, development and peace', theme of the International Women's Decade, 1975–85.

These intelligent and sensitive women first came together in World War I from neutral countries and from countries whose men were slaughtering each other on the battlefield, yet the women warmly embraced as sisters. The symbolism of that moment must never be lost, for the surmounting of artificial barriers in the spirit of reconciliation is the most essential message and the most needed attribute for our time.

Those who met at that first International Congress of Women saw that a permanent peace could be built only on the basis of equal rights, including equal rights between women and men, of justice within and between nations, of national independence and of freedom. This book is a permanent reminder of the thousands of committed and often courageous women who over the years have been associated with the Women's International League for Peace and Freedom.

In the pages that follow, Gertrude Bussey and Margaret Tims tell of the League's activities during its first fifty years. It is a moving and a stimulating story of the struggle for a world without war and violence, for an international order in which conflicts of interest can be minimized and disputes resolved by peaceful means. It is the story of the League's women working for peace against a background of events that shook the established order in Europe and elsewhere, in a period of human history in which violence and destruction reached new dimensions, in which accepted moral and political standards were undermined.

The history of these years was first published in 1965 to celebrate the League's fiftieth anniversary. This second edition is issued to mark the sixty-fifth anniversary of the organization's founding, and in response to the great interest now being shown in the pioneers of the women's movement and the peace movement.

The 1965 Congress was held at the League's birthplace, The Hague, on the theme 'Towards a World without War'. More than 300 attended, making it one of the largest in recent years. The reports and working papers showed how the work of the League had evolved over the years around the United Nations and its family of Specialized Agencies. The long-term goals set by the Congress were the development of strong machinery within the United Nations for the peaceful settlement of international conflicts and the negotiation of treaties on arms control and disarmament. Issues of human rights and economic development to bridge the gap between rich and poor nations were seen as inextricably linked with the fundamental questions of world peace.

When the Jubilee Congress met that year the war in Vietnam was escalating, causing immeasurable suffering and destruction. The WILPF United States section was among the first to oppose its country's military action there, and in this had the support of the entire League with intensive campaigns in all sections to stop the war. The US section's fiftieth anniversary celebration featured Dr Martin Luther King Jr as speaker, who the year before had been awarded the Nobel Peace Prize. In 1968 Coretta Scott King presented a statement at a WILPF news conference calling for negotiations and withdrawal of US troops from Vietnam. Two weeks later the world was shocked by the assassination of Martin Luther King, the apostle of non-violence, leading to widespread rioting in many US cities.

A political thunderbolt struck the 1968 Triennial Congress in Nyborg, Denmark, which gathered just as Soviet tanks rolled into Czechoslovakia. Guest observers from the Soviet Union, Czechoslovakia and other East European states were present. Tempers flared, but the reconciling skills of chairman Dorothy Hutchinson prevented hasty departures and all the women stayed throughout the Congress. A delegation of US women carried out their planned post-Congress visit to the Soviet Union as guests of the Soviet Women's Committee, carrying the Congress resolution deploring such military intervention. The series of US WILPF-Soviet Women's Committee seminars, begun in 1961, continues.

WILPF International sponsored its third conference of Women of the Americas in 1970. A year previously a WILPF delegation had visited several countries of Latin America, resulting in the formation of a group in Chile. In 1973 the world was shocked by the violent overthrow of the democratically elected government of Salvatore Allende, and members of the Chilean section were forced to go underground. A second WILPF mission in 1974 talked to women's groups, prisoners and government officials; its findings were reported to the UN Commission on Human Rights and subsequently published.

The 18th Triennial Congress in New Delhi was memorable for a heart-searching debate on the role of violence in liberation struggles, with some disagreement between absolute pacifists and those who recognized that violence by the oppressed against the oppressors was inevitable, if not justifiable. After the Congress talks were held with Prime Minister Indira Gandhi and early in 1971 a mission went to both North and South Vietnam. Peace treaties were drawn up and signed with women in both parts of that war-torn country and later WILPF raised funds for their maternal and child health centre. Following the imprisonment of Mme Ngo ba Thanh, a leader of the 'third force' in Saigon, WILPF led an international campaign until she was released two years later.

The war in Indo-China raged savagely until 1973 and even today its people do not have peace to reconstruct and develop their nations. In the Middle East open war erupted in 1967 and again in 1973 and peace in that area remains elusive while the fundamental question of the rights of the Palestinians is still to be settled. WILPF sent missions to both Israel and the Arab countries in 1967 and 1975.

Israeli and Lebanese members met together, as in previous Congresses, at Birmingham in 1974. These sessions crackled with tension, but were helpful in promoting understanding of all points of view. As WILPF gathered in Birmingham warfare erupted in Cyprus and a cable urging mediation was despatched to UN Secretary-General Waldheim. Following the Congress an international delegation visited Northern Ireland and proposals for settling the conflict were presented to the British Government. The British section is continuously working on this problem.

The keynote speaker in Birmingham was Helvi Sipilä, Secretary-General of International Women's Year in 1975. That year, as well as participating in major international conferences, WILPF in co-operation with the Women's International Democratic Federation organized the first international Women's Disarmament Seminar at the UN in New York, which was described in the Secretary-General's report as the most important NGO effort of IWY.

This was the era of UN conferences on pressing world problems— food, population, environment—in all of which WILPF actively participated. But the major resources needed for their solution went instead into a relentless expansion of military forces. The decolonizing process that began in the 1950s continued throughout the '60s and '70s, but not always peacefully. Wars of independence raged in Mozambique, Angola, Rhodesia and Namibia, to mention only one continent, while the apartheid regime in South Africa intensified its repression against the majority population.

Violent conflicts in the developing regions of the world were fed by the 'cold war' atmosphere of the '50s and '60s. Europe groaned under the yoke of an arms race unprecedented in history, imposing heavy economic burdens on the populations and in itself posing a dangerous threat to world peace.

The time seemed ripe for intensive work on disarmament, too long diverted by the Vietnam war. The 20th Triennial Congress, held in Tokyo in 1977, declared 'Disarmament and Development' as women's priorities. The theme was poignantly highlighted when delegates made a pilgrimage to Hiroshima for the August 6th Memorial ceremony. The Congress called for steps towards general and complete disarmament with an immediate comprehensive nuclear test ban, cuts in military budgets and more development aid.

Intense pressure by WILPF and other NGOs for a disarmament conference culminated in the UN Special Session on Disarmament in 1978. Members from several national sections attended, some serving as special advisers to their governmental delegations. Productive in many small ways, the session lubricated the negotiating machinery, enunciated the urgent necessity for disarmament and agreed that a second session should be held in 1982. But the failure to conclude any disarmament agreements spread a pall of gloom over the proceedings.

However, in the past fifteen years a number of important treaties and conventions have been signed which provide a solid body of international law, for instance, on bacteriological weapons, use of the sea-bed and outer space. Limited progress has been made in arms control and détente, symbolized in the Helsinki Final Act of 1975 and in evolving a Law of the Sea. Economic, scientific and cultural cooperation has borne dividends. A new spirit of international solidarity has begun to evolve in response to natural disasters, the problem of refugees, and gross violations of human rights, including torture. The International Year of the Child in 1979 focused attention on the need to safeguard the future for children everywhere. The year was appropriately marked by the initiation of a Jane Addams International Book Award for the best children's book promoting ideas of peace and social justice. A series of Nordic seminars have stirred sections in that region to fresh activity. The accident at Three Mile Island in the USA brought home the warnings by WILPF and other groups on the dangers of nuclear power. The League's sections in Europe played a leading role in opposition to the recent NATO decision to deploy new first-strike weapons in that area.

On the other hand, the poor of the world have seen little comfort. Despite the UN Development Decade, five UN Conferences on Trade and Development have made no substantial gains. The call for a New International Economic Order has been virtually ignored, although the report of the Brandt Commission this year underlines the urgency of that need. The problems are compounded by the power of the oil cartel and the economic instability, over-consumption and inflation in the industrialized world. Frustration is increasingly expressed through guerrilla tactics, with seizure of hostages, kidnappings and bombings against which governments seem powerless to act. The shock of events in Iran and Afghanistan reminds us that we live under an insecure, man-made, military-based system. The flames of war and oppression etch the horizon.

Looking back over the years covered by this book, some striking factors emerge. First, the erosion of the dominant Judeo-Christian ethic by the second world war and its aftermath; second, the intensification of the threat to human survival posed by the warfare system; third, the growing irrelevance of strident political polarization to the coming post-industrial society. The old order is crumbling, as alternative lifestyles emerge. Perhaps the watchword for the future is 'technology with a human face'. In this quest we must look to the wisdom of the South and East as well as the North and West, to the feminine values no less than the masculine.

As an organization with world-wide connections surmounting ideological barriers, WILPF is uniquely placed to contribute to the creative revolution of the 1980s. Its work was never more needed. The theme of the 21st Triennial Congress at New Haven, USA, is 'Todays' Women Turn the World towards Peace and Freedom'. The League enters the '80s with a new and urgent determination to make the world safe for people, in the knowledge that with increasing equality and liberation women can and will make a decisive contribution to a more humane future. The challenge ahead is to enable fundamental changes in the making to evolve without violence and avert the threat of a nuclear holocaust. The work of WILPF continues, and will provide material for as fascinating a second volume at its centenary as this history of the first fifty years has revealed.

Pennsylvania, USA,   KAY CAMP
March, 1980.   *International President*

OUTLINE OF MAIN ACTIVITIES 1965–1980

(World events in italics)

1965   *International Co-operation Year*
March   *US marines land in Vietnam, start of massive troops build-up*
May   WILPF 50th anniversary
July   16th Triennial Congress, The Hague:
         'Towards a World without War'
November *Rhodesia declares UDI*

1966
September International seminar on women's education and community
         development, New Delhi. Organized by Indian section.
October Mission to Rhodesia. Frances Murray-Rust (British section).

1967
January *Treaty on Use of Outer Space for Peaceful Purposes*
February *Tlatelolco Treaty for Prohibition of Nuclear Weapons in Latin
         America*
April   Middle East mission to Lebanon, Syria, Jordan and Israel.
         Johanne Reutz Gjermoe (Norway), Ingrid Lindstrom (Sweden).
June   *Six-Day War. Israeli strike against Egypt, Syria and Jordan.*
June   *Civil war in Nigeria following secession of Eastern region (Biafra)*
July   Stockholm Conference on Vietnam (World Peace Council)
October Seminar on human rights, United Nations, New York. Organi-
         zed by US section.

1968   *Human Rights Year*
April   *Martin Luther King assassinated*
May   Jane Addams bust placed in Hall of Fame, New York
July   *Treaty on Non-proliferation of Nuclear Weapons*
August   17th Triennial Congress, Nyborg, Denmark:
             'Peace and Freedom: human rights and responsibilities'
         Soviet invasion of Czechoslovakia

1969
November *Strategic Arms Limitation Talks (SALT I) open between USA and
         USSR*
         International Conference on Chemical and Biological Warfare,
         London. Organized by British section. Over 200 participants
         from 20 countries (see report, 'The Supreme Folly'). Continuing
         committee formed to follow up work.

1970   *International Education Year*
February   Special Disarmament Committee set up by NGOs in Geneva
December / 18th Triennial Congress, New Delhi:
Jan. '71   'Economic and Social Justice: prerequisites for peace and
           freedom'
           Ellen Holmgaard elected International Chairman

1971
January   Mission to North and South Vietnam. Kay Camp, Lois Hamer,
           Sadie Hughes, Patricia Samuel (USA); Marguerite Lorée
           (France); Patricia Shannon (New Zealand).
February   *Treaty on the Sea Bed*
October   *Admission of China to United Nations*
November International Conference on Nuclear Weapons, London.
           Organized by Margaret Curwen (British section) for CBW
           Continuing Committee. Over 300 participants from 18 coun-
           tries.
December   *Indo-Pakistan conflict following secession of East Pakistan
           (Bangladesh)*
           Convention on Bacteriological Weapons signed (ratified 1975)

1972
May   *SALT I Treaty signed*
June   *Conference on Human Environment, Stockholm*: 'Only One Earth'.
           Government representatives from 114 nations, plus parallel
           NGOS Tribune. Two WILPF observers at both conferences.
August   Eleanore Romberg elected International Chairman by Inter-
           national Executive Committee following resignation of Ellen
           Holmgaard
September Disarmament Conference, Geneva, organized by NGOs Special
           Committee on Disarmament. WILPF propose setting up
           machinery for peaceful settlement of disputes.
December   Women's vigils against apartheid organized in several countries

1973
January   *Paris Accords for ceasefire in Vietnam*
March   First visit of Japanese women to People's Republic of China
July   *European Security Conference opens, Helsinki*
August   Women's Conference on European Co-operation and Security,
           Helsinki. Five WILPF representatives.
September *President Allende of Chile shot by military junta*
October   *Yom Kippur War. Egypt and Syria attack Israel.*
           World Congress of Peace Forces, Moscow (World Peace

Council). Over 3,000 participants. Six WILPF delegates and members from seven national sections.

December Conference for Abolition of Torture, Paris (Amnesty International). Three WILPF representatives.

1974

January Mission to Chile. Kay Camp (International Vice-Chairman) and five US members.

July 19th Triennial Congress, Birmingham:
'Peacemaking: key to the future'.
Changes to WILPF Constitution.
Kay Camp elected International President.
Mission to Northern Ireland. Ruth Osborn (Britain); Pat Hughson (New Zealand); Charlotte Dennett (Lebanon); Margaret McCarter, Jean Wagner (USA).
Turkish invasion of Cyprus

August WILPF welcomes appointment of independent working party on slavery by UN Subcommission on Discrimination and Protection of Minorities, after 14 years' pressure by Mary Nuttall (Britain).

November *SALT II talks open*

1975 *International Women's Year*
Special activities in all WILPF sections

April Mission to Middle East. Libby Frank (USA), Edith Ballantyne (Geneva).

June *IWY Conference, Mexico City*
Two WILPF observers at main conference and NGOS Tribune
Mozambique gains independance

August *Helsinki Final Act*

October IWY World Congress, Berlin (WIDF). Seven WILPF delegates and members from eight national sections.

November *Angola gains independance*

1976

March Edith Ballantyne (WILPF Secretary-General) elected President of NGOS at ECOSOC, Geneva.

March/ International Forum on Disarmament, York (International
April Peace Bureau). Over 300 delegates from 50 countries. Organized by Verdun Perl (British section). Call for World Disarmament Conference.

September Northern Ireland Peace Movement started by Mairead Corrigan and Betty Williams

1977
August   20th Triennial Congress, Tokyo:
          'Disarmament and Development: women's priorities'
          Five new sections admitted: Ghana, Jamaica, Mauritius, Mexico,
          Sri Lanka.

1978
June   *Special Session on Disarmament, United Nations, New York*
          Kay Camp special adviser to US delegation. WILPF statement
          presented by Edith Ballantyne.
August   WILPF granted consultative status with UNCTAD.
September *Camp David Agreement for peace between Egypt and Israel*

1979   *International Year of the Child*
          Special activities in all WILPF sections.
March   *Iran becomes an Islamic Republic*
May   *SALT II Treaty signed*
September Conference on a Peaceful and Secure Future for all Children,
          Moscow (Soviet Women's Committee). Nine WILPF represen-
          tatives.
December International Demonstration, Brussels, against deployment of
          medium-range missiles in Europe (Belgian National Committee
          for Action for Peace and Development). WILPF delegation (14
          women from eight countries) received at NATO HQ.
          Soviet invasion of Afghanistan
          President Carter withdraws SALT II Treaty
          Lancaster House Agreement on Rhodesia

1980
April   World Disarmament Campaign lauched in London by Lord
          Philip Noel-Baker and Lord Fenner Brockway to follow up
          recommendations of UN Special Session on Disarmament.
          WILPF a co-sponsor.
April   *Zimbabwe (Rhodesia) achieves independence*
May   WILPF 65th anniversary
July   UN Mid-Decade Women's Conference, Copenhagen:
          'Equality, Development and Peace'
August   21st Triennial Congress, New Haven, USA: 'Towards Peace and
          Freedom'
Note: This summary represents only some of the continuing international
concerns of the League and does not include the work of national sections.
A detailed account of these and other activities must await the publication of a
second volume.

ACKNOWLEDGMENTS

The first acknowledgment for this book must go to the late Professor Gertrude Bussey of Baltimore, USA, who between 1956 and 1961 organized all the preliminary research into the records of the Women's International League for Peace and Freedom covering the period 1915 to 1939. At the time of her death in March 1961 Professor Bussey had completed the draft of twelve chapters, taking the history up to the Prague Congress of 1929. Without this exhaustive groundwork, the present volume could never have appeared. The later stages of the research also owed much to Dr Cornelia Weiss of the British section, to whom Professor Bussey acknowledged her gratitude and to whom the present author is greatly indebted for her ever-helpful advice and friendly guidance.

When I was asked to take over Professor Bussey's papers and continue the history of the WILPF up to the time of its fiftieth anniversary in 1965, it was obvious that a great deal of compression would be required to complete the task in one volume. It was necessary to reduce her material by about half, the remainder being incorporated in the present chapters 1–6. The ensuing chapters 7–14 also owe something to her notes and outline of work. For subsequent chapters I must take full responsibility for the selection and arrangement of the material, and likewise for any errors or omissions.

In the course of this work I have been much indebted to members of the WILPF in many countries who have given freely of their knowledge and advice, supplied photographs, and read the manuscript in part or whole. I must specially thank Gertrude Baer in Geneva, whose fifty years of unbroken service to the League (including 21 years on the Executive Committee and 17 years as International Co-Chairman) give her a unique place in its history; the present International Chairman, Else Zeuthen, and Ellen Holmgaard in Denmark; Andrée Jouve, outstanding in her work for international education since 1919, in France; Marie Lous-Mohr in Norway; Dorothy Detzer Denny, Emerson Lamb, Mercedes Randall and Emily Parker Simon in the USA; Dame Kathleen Courtney, Kathleen Innes, Agnes Stapledon and Nelly Weiss in England.

A legacy to the WILPF from Professor Bussey made this book financially possible; contributions from the British and Swedish sections are also acknowledged with thanks.

The main sources for this history have been the published and unpublished records of the WILPF: Congress Reports, *Pax International* and *Pax et Libertas*, Executive Committee Minutes, International Circular Letters, pamphlets and correspondence. I am most grateful to Elizabeth Tapper, Administrative Secretary in Geneva, for her willing and efficient co-operation in making the archives available and patiently answering many queries. I must also thank Alison Huntley for help in Geneva with the tedious but necessary work of copying.

In addition, I am indebted to Mercedes Randall for allowing me to read some chapters of her then unpublished biography of Emily Greene Balch, *Improper Bostonian* (Wayne, New York, 1964). Outside the WILPF my main reference book has been Mr F. P. Walters' *History of the League of Nations* (Oxford, 1960), to which due acknowledgment is made. I have also consulted the following:

Albrecht-Carrié, R. *A Diplomatic History of Europe.* (London, 1958.)

Bowman, I. *New World.* (Cambridge, 1923.)

Bullock, A. *Hitler: A Study in Tyranny.* (Pelican ed., Harmondsworth, 1962.)

Carr, E. H. *International Relations between the Two World Wars.* (London, 1959.)

Detzer, Dorothy. *Appointment on the Hill.* (New York, 1948.)

Fleming, D. F. *The Cold War and its Origins,* Vols. I and II. (London, 1961.)

Hayes, C. *Contemporary Europe since 1870.* (New York, 1953.)

King-Hall, S. *Our Times, 1900–1960.* (London, 1961.)

Lash, J. P. *Dag Hammarskjold.* (London, 1962.)

Lipson, E. *Europe 1914–1939.* (London, 1945.)

Orwell, G. *Homage to Catalonia.* (London, 1938.)

Russell, B. *Unarmed Victory.* (London, 1963.)

Swanwick, H. M. *The Roots of Peace.* (London, 1938.)

Taylor, A. J. P. *Origins of the Second World War.* (London, 1961.)

Tims, Margaret. *Jane Addams of Hull House.* (London, 1961.)

Wilmot, C. *The Struggle for Power in Europe.* (London, 1952.)

MARGARET TIMS

July 1964

CONTENTS

CHAPTER I

WARTIME PRELUDE

Background to the Hague Congress, 1915—International Suffrage Alliance—Delegates and Proceedings—Mission to Statesmen

———

On April 28, 1915, for the first time in history, women of different nations met together at a time of war to express their opposition and consider ways of ending the conflict. The International Congress of Women which gathered at The Hague in Holland in this ninth month of the First World War included delegations from both Europe and America, from 'enemy' no less than neutral countries.

Inter-governmental peace conferences had been held previously at The Hague—in 1899, convened by the Czar of Russia; and in 1907, with the support of Theodore Roosevelt. A third conference scheduled to take place in 1915 had now been abandoned. Many non-governmental bodies, too, deemed it imprudent to attempt a meeting. As a prominent American delegate, Emily Greene Balch, was to write home from The Hague:

Of all the international gatherings that help to draw the nations together, since the fatal days of July 1914 practically none have been convened. Science, medicine, reform, labor, religion—not one of these causes has been able as yet to gather its followers from across dividing frontiers.

How then had this unique gathering of women come about?

The Hague Congress was the offspring of the International Suffrage Alliance, an already well-established organization with a strong pacifist bias in its leadership. In September 1914 the leader of the Hungarian feminists, Rosika Schwimmer, arrived in the United States of America to lay before President Wilson a plan she had formulated for a mediation conference of neutral nations. She was joined shortly afterwards by the British suffragist Emmeline Pethick-Lawrence and together—although technically 'enemies'—they toured the United States galvanizing the peace sentiment of American women. In January 1915, at a mass gathering in Washington summoned by the President of the ISA, Mrs Carrie Chapman Catt, and Jane Addams, founder of Hull House social settlement, the Women's Peace Party was formed. It adopted a comprehensive policy for peace, including a plan for a conference of neutrals which had been prepared in detail by Dr Julia Grace Wales of Wisconsin University.

Meanwhile, the German branch of the ISA withdrew its invitation for the International Congress of the Alliance to take place, as arranged, in Berlin in June 1915, whereupon Mrs Catt cancelled the international meeting altogether. With this decision the chairman of the Dutch Alliance, Dr Aletta Jacobs—the first woman doctor in the Netherlands—vigorously disagreed. But Mrs Catt remained unmoved, fearing that an attempt to call an International Congress might disturb the harmonious working of the national suffrage groups. In this apprehension she was no doubt right, since many of the suffragists were carried away, like other citizens, by the fervour of nationalism in their own countries. Only the Hungarian Alliance endorsed the holding of a Congress.

Nothing daunted by her failure to obtain official sanction, Dr Jacobs proceeded to call together a group of fellow-workers in Holland and nearby countries: four women from Belgium, four from Germany and five from Britain met at Amsterdam in February 1915. Out of their meeting came the call for a Congress of Women, cutting across national enmities, to gather at The Hague on April 28th—in only ten weeks' time. The detailed arrangements were left to Dr Jacobs and two Dutch associates, Rosa Manus and Dr Mia Boissevain. Another prominent member of the Dutch Alliance, Mme Cor Ramondt-Hirschmann, consented to serve as treasurer, while the British, German and Dutch women agreed jointly to meet all expenses if the Congress should not be self-supporting.

The small preparatory committee was immensely heartened at an early stage of the planning by the consent of Jane Addams to preside at the Congress and to bring with her a strong American delegation. Writing later of her role, Miss Addams remarked with characteristic modesty:

Some have been much too kind to call me the leader of the movement, for I was not that in any sense of the word. It was convened and called by a group of European women and only after all the arrangements were made did we know about it in America and consent to go. They were anxious to have a woman from a neutral country as president and it was safer to have the neutral country as far away as possible, and America was the furthest away. Therefore I was chosen.

While one may question that this was the sole reason for the choice, Jane Addams was right in insisting that the credit of inaugurating the Congress belonged to the group of European women called together by Aletta Jacobs.

But the organizers were soon faced with a serious problem. Would governments permit the delegates to attend? Amongst the most enthusiastic supporters of the Congress were the German suffragists. Some of them set out for The Hague, and were stopped at the Dutch border, but 28 got through. No French or Russian woman was able to attend. The British committee had recruited an imposing delegation of 180, but passports were refused to all but 25; and even as these delegates reached Tilbury, the North Sea was closed to all shipping and they could not sail. Three British women, however, succeeded in reaching The Hague: Chrystal Macmillan, Secretary of the International Suffrage Alliance, and Kathleen Courtney were already in Holland and Emmeline Pethick-Lawrence travelled with the American delegation. This group, too, was delayed on government orders in the English Channel, so that Jane Addams and the other 41 American delegates only reached The Hague just as the Congress was due to open.

The gathering from 12 countries of representatives of over 150 organizations fully justified the hopes and faith of the conveners: in all, 1,136 women participated in the Congress as voting members, together with more than 300 visitors and observers. Too numerous to be accommodated in the Peace Palace, they met in the great hall at the Zoological Gardens. Their purpose was made clear by Dr Jacobs in her opening address:

Those of us who have convened this Congress . . . have never called it a Peace Congress, but an International Congress of Women assembled to protest against war and to suggest steps which may lead to warfare becoming an impossibility.

To certain sections of the world's press and public opinion, the aims of the Congress seemed either laughable or deplorable. The women had been called foolish and naïve; interfering and ill-informed;

irresponsibly feminine, and at the same time boldly unwomanly. The quality of the delegations soon gave the lie to these smear campaigns.

Amongst the influential German delegation was the first woman judge in Germany, Dr Anita Augspurg; and with her a pioneer feminist and trade union organizer from Bavaria, Lida Gustava Heymann. Rosika Schwimmer of Hungary was a striking and powerful woman, with a world reputation in suffragist and pacifist movements. Chrystal Macmillan was a brilliant lawyer. From America came not only Jane Addams, with a national reputation as a social philosopher, but also Emily Greene Balch, Professor of Economics at Wellesley College; Dr Alice Hamilton, a pioneer of industrial medicine; and Julia Grace Wales, whose plan for 'mediation without armistice' had already won approval in the Wisconsin state legislature.

The five delegates from Belgium, arriving a day late after immense difficulties, received an enthusiastic ovation and, at the instigation of the German women, were invited to sit on the platform. Their views were held to be of the utmost importance in drawing up proposals for a just peace. Messages of support poured in from women as far afield as India, Brazil, Spain, Poland, Serbia, Russia and South Africa. In all, more than 300 greetings were sent to the Congress, and about 30 hostile criticisms. Amongst the criticisms was a statement from leading French suffragists, deploring the holding of such a gathering while their country was under invasion; but other Frenchwomen strongly dissociated themselves from this opinion.

The Hague Congress adopted twenty resolutions which laid down the principles and policies of the women's peace movement under six heads: Women and War; Action towards Peace; Principles of a Permanent Peace; International Co-operation; Education of Children; Action to be Taken. The whole future development of the movement stemmed from this comprehensive statement (for full text see Report of the Hague Congress, 1915). Of most immediate importance were Resolutions 4, 19 and 20, namely:

4. *Continuous Mediation:* This International Congress of Women resolves to ask the neutral countries to take immediate steps to create a conference of neutral nations which shall without delay offer continuous mediation. The Conference shall invite suggestions for settlement from each of the belligerent nations and in any case shall submit to all of them simultaneously reasonable proposals as a basis of peace.

This proposal for 'continuous mediation' had formed the original focus of the Women's Congress. It was complemented by two others:

19. *Women's Voice in the Peace Settlement:* that an international meeting of women shall be held in the same place and at the same time as the Conference of Powers which shall frame the terms of the peace settlement after the war, for the purpose of presenting practical proposals to that Conference.
20. *Envoys to Governments:* that envoys shall carry the message expressed in the Congress Resolutions to the rulers of the belligerent and neutral nations of Europe and to the President of the United States.

The idea of personal delegations to governments came from Rosika Schwimmer and aroused much discussion. Jane Addams was at first doubtful of its wisdom; Kathleen Courtney opposed it as impracticable; Chrystal Macmillan proposed a substitute motion that delegates should interview government representatives at The Hague rather than attempt to visit heads of state in their own countries. But this compromise measure failed to win approval and the more ambitious plan was adopted. Thus was initiated phase two of the international women's peace movement.

Once the decision was made, the appointed envoys lost no time in embarking on their formidable mission. During May and June 1915 fourteen countries were visited by two groups of delegates: Jane Addams, Rosa Genoni (of Italy) and Aletta Jacobs were assigned to Austro-Hungary, Belgium, Britain, France, Germany, Italy and Switzerland; Emily Balch, Chrystal Macmillan, Cor Ramondt-Hirschmann and Rosika Schwimmer to the Scandinavian countries and Russia. (In the event, Rosika Schwimmer was prohibited from entering Russia and was replaced by Baroness Palmstierna of Sweden.) In August, Jane Addams obtained an interview in Washington with President Wilson, who had previously received the Congress resolutions: he considered them, he said, 'by far the best formulation which up to the moment has been put out by anybody'.

In October 1915 the envoys from the Hague Congress issued their own conclusions on the achievements of their mission. As a historic document, it is worth reproducing in the original (see Appendix 1). Some well-wishers of the Congress regarded it as a little too optimistic: the women had perhaps been misled by their on the whole friendly reception, had perhaps over-estimated the degree of agreement evinced by statesmen. Others, frankly hostile to mediation at any price, declared they had been 'hoodwinked'. A careful study of the report gives some weight to the charge that the envoys, in their eagerness for action, had over-valued the cautious statements of some ministers that they would 'not oppose' a neutral conference. But Jane Addams was certainly right in maintaining that many statesmen had welcomed their mission, and had perhaps talked more freely just because it was unofficial and non-partisan. There was certainly no question that by this unofficial means much valuable information had been conveyed between countries cut off, by their state of war, from formal communication. Nor was it an overstatement that, because of the women's mission, the calling of a neutral conference for mediation had become a matter of serious discussion by government officials, the press and public opinion in all the countries concerned.

APPENDIX I

MANIFESTO issued by Envoys of the International Congress of Women at The Hague to the Governments of Europe and the President of the United States.

Here in America, on neutral soil, far removed from the stress of the conflict we, envoys to the Governments from the International Congress of Women at The Hague, have come together to canvass the results of our missions. We put forth this statement as our united and deliberate conclusions.

At a time when the foreign offices of the great belligerents have been barred to each other, and the public mind of Europe has been fixed on the war offices for leadership, we have gone from capital to capital and conferred with the civil governments.

Our mission was to place before belligerent and neutral alike the resolutions of the International Congress of Women held at The Hague in April; especially to place before them the definite method of a conference of neutral nations as an agency of continuous mediation for the settlement of the war.

To carry out this mission two delegations were appointed, which included women of Great Britain, Hungary, Italy, the Netherlands, Sweden and the United States. One or other of these delegations was received by the governments in fourteen capitals: Berlin, Berne, Budapest, Christiana, Copenhagen, The Hague, Le Hâvre (Belgian Government), London, Paris, Petrograd, Rome, Stockholm, Vienna and Washington. We were received by the Prime Ministers and Foreign Ministers of the Powers, by the King of Norway, by the Presidents of Switzerland and of the United States, by the Pope and the Cardinal Secretary of State. In many capitals more than one audience was given, not merely to present our resolutions, but for a thorough discussion. In addition to the thirty-five governmental visits we met—everywhere—members of parliament and other leaders of public opinion.

We heard much the same words spoken in Downing Street as those spoken in Wilhelmstrasse, in Vienna as in Petrograd, in Budapest as in the Hâvre, where the Belgians have their temporary government.

Our visits to the war capitals convinced us that the belligerent Governments would not be opposed to a conference of neutral nations; that while the belligerents have rejected offers of mediation by single neutral nations, and while no belligerent could ask for mediation, the creation of a continuous conference of neutral nations might provide the machinery which would lead to peace. We found that the neutrals on the other hand were concerned lest calling such a conference might be considered inopportune by one or other of the belligerents. Here our information from the belligerents themselves gave assurance that such initiative would not be resented. 'My country would not find anything unfriendly in such action by the neutrals', was the assurance given us by the Foreign Minister of one of the great belligerents. 'My Government would place no obstacle in the way of its institution', said the Minister of an opposing nation. 'What are the neutrals waiting for?' said a third, whose name ranks high not only in his own country but all over the world.

It remained to put this clarifying intelligence before the neutral countries. As a result the plan of starting mediation through the agency of a continuous conference of the neutral nations is today being seriously discussed alike in the Cabinets of the belligerent and neutral countries of Europe and in the press of both.

We are in a position to quote some of the expressions of men high in the councils of the great nations as to the feasibility of the plan. 'You are right', said one Minister, 'that it would be of the greatest importance to finish the fight by early negotiation rather than by further military efforts, which would result in more and more destruction and irreparable loss.' 'Yours is the sanest proposal that has been brought to this office in the last six months', said the Prime Minister of one of the larger countries.

We were also in a position to canvass the objections that have been made to the proposal, testing it out severely in the judgment of those in the midst of the European conflict. It has been argued that it is not the time at present to start such a process of negotiation, and that no step should be taken until one or other party has a victory, or at least until some new military balance is struck. The answer we bring is that every delay makes more difficult the beginning of negotiations, more nations become involved, and the situation becomes more complicated; that when at times in the course of the war such a balance was struck, the neutrals were unprepared to act. The opportunity passed. For the forces of peace to be unprepared when the hour comes, is as irretrievable as for a military leader to be unready.

It has been argued that for such a conference to be called at any time when one side has met with some military advantage, would be to favor that side. The answer we bring is that the proposed conference would start mediation at a higher level than that of military advantage. As to the actual military situation, however, we quote a remark made to us by a Foreign Minister of one of the belligerent Powers: 'Neither side is today strong enough to dictate terms, and neither side is so weakened that it has to accept humiliating terms.'

It has been suggested that such a conference would bind the neutral governments co-operating in it. The answer we bring is that, as proposed, such a conference should consist of the ablest persons of the neutral countries, assigned not to problems of their own governments, but to the common service of a supreme crisis. The situation calls for a conference cast in a new and larger mould than those of conventional diplomacy, the governments sending to it persons drawn from social, economic and scientific fields who have had genuine international experience.

As women, it was possible for us, from belligerent and neutral nations alike, to meet in the midst of war and to carry forward an interchange of question and answer between capitals which were barred to each other. It is now our duty to make articulate our convictions. We have been convinced that the governments of the belligerent nations would not be hostile to the institution of such a channel for good offices; and that the governments of the European neutrals we visited stand ready to co-operate with others in mediation. Reviewing the situation, we believe that of the five European neutral nations visited, three are ready to join in such a conference, and that two are deliberating the calling of such a conference. Of the intention of the United States we have as yet no evidence.

We are but the conveyors of evidence which is a challenge to action by the neutral governments visited—by Denmark, Holland, Norway, Sweden, Switzerland and the United States. We in turn bear evidence of a rising desire and intention of vast companies of people in the neutral countries to turn a barren disinterestedness into an active goodwill. In Sweden, for instance, more than 400 meetings were held in one day in different parts of the country, calling on the government to act.

The excruciating burden of responsibility for the hopeless continuance of this war no longer rests on the will of the belligerent nations alone. It rests also on the will of those neutral governments and peoples who have been spared its shock but cannot, if they would, absolve themselves from their full share of responsibility for the continuance of war.

Signed by Jane Addams (United States); Emily G. Balch (United States); Aletta Jacobs (Holland); Chrystal Macmillan (Great Britain); Rosika Schwimmer (Austro-Hungary).

New York, October 15, 1915.

CHAPTER 2

PLANNING FOR THE FUTURE

*International Committee of Women for Permanent Peace
—Work of National Committees—Ford Peace Ship and
Neutral Conference—Second Women's Congress, 1919—
Women's International League for Peace and Freedom—
Envoys to Versailles*

The administrative responsibility for carrying on the work of the new international women's peace movement lay with the International Committee of Women for Permanent Peace which had been set up at the Hague Congress. Its President was Jane Addams, with Aletta Jacobs and Rosika Schwimmer as Vice-Presidents. The central office was in Amsterdam, where Dr Jacobs acted as Secretary and Rosa Manus as Assistant Secretary. In addition, the International Committee included five members from each of the National Committees which delegates to the Congress went back to establish in their own countries. By November 1915, twelve national committees had been formed: Austria, Belgium, Denmark, France, Germany, Great Britain and Ireland, Hungary, Italy, Netherlands, Norway, Sweden and USA. In Australia, a Sisterhood of International Peace had been founded at Melbourne in 1915 and this too became affiliated to the International Committee.

The Committee had two immediate tasks: to consolidate the international links forged at The Hague; and to plan for a second conference to be held, as the Congress had resolved, at the time and place of the Peace Conference. The first instrument for publicizing the new movement was the 323-page report of the Hague Congress, with text in English and German, which was distributed to all organizations and individuals who had sent messages to the Congress. The response from unexpected quarters was heartening. The US Public Affairs Information Service, for instance, cited the report as 'one of the most significant volumes which the Great War has brought forth'. The Committee also started a monthly journal, later reduced to a quarterly. The difficulties of communication, whether written or personal, through closed frontiers, refusal of passports and censorship of mail, caused great hindrance to the international work, and much credit was due to Dr Jacobs and Rosa Manus for keeping the office open throughout the war, maintaining contact with national committees, and reaching out to new groups throughout the world.

The first co-ordinated action of the national committees was to stimulate opinion in favour of a conference of neutrals for continuous mediation. In Holland, Scandinavia and Switzerland mass meetings were organized and governments urged to initiate this step. The Women's Peace Party of America, now the national committee of the international movement, was obtaining the co-operation of other peace organizations for such a step. An alternative proposal canvassed widely in America was that the neutral conference should consist not of government representatives but of lay experts. The idea caught the imagination of Henry Ford, who after hearing a speech in Detroit by Rosika Schwimmer agreed to back the plan; and, in view of President Wilson's continued hesitation, to go ahead immediately without official sanction. As he put it: 'We are going to get behind the work done by the Hague Peace Conference and carry that work forward.'

The International Women's Committee, however, was in two minds about the venture. There had been no international consultation and the European women were largely in the dark, even though Ford himself had suggested that the conference should take place at the Committee's headquarters in Amsterdam and, according to Rosika Schwimmer, promised to donate 200,000 dollars for its work. This sum was never received. Jane Addams, with some misgivings, agreed to travel to the conference on the much-publicized 'Ford Peace Ship', but she cabled to Dr Jacobs: 'Keep the International Committee distinct from the Ford enterprise.' This shrewd advice was soon to prove its worth and may well have saved the International Committee of Women from an untimely disintegration. Rosika Schwimmer, meanwhile, became increasingly impatient with the International Committee, especially when at the last moment Jane Addams withdrew as a delegate to the Ford conference because of serious illness.

The Ford Peace Ship finally set sail in December 1915. The following January an unofficial neutral conference was inaugurated in Stockholm, although by this time Ford had returned to America and Rosika Schwimmer resigned from his group in March. But the neutral committee set up in Stockholm—composed of international lawyers, economists, parliamentarians and civic officials of the countries represented—did much useful work and moves for peace continued to be explored, both unofficially and officially, throughout 1916. In January 1917 President Wilson made his famous 'Peace without Victory' speech, which owed much to the proposals of the Hague Congress, the Ford Conference and other liberal organizations.

But only a few days after Wilson's speech, Germany resumed unrestricted submarine warfare and Henry Ford—no doubt foreseeing the imminent entry of the United States into the war—cancelled his financial backing for the neutral conference and brought its work to an abrupt halt. Fortunately, as it now seemed, the International Committee of Women had not tied its fortunes to the Ford enterprise and could continue independently its long-term planning for peace—even though America's declaration of war in April 1917 ended any hopes for a neutral conference of mediation.

The work of the women's national committees in belligerent countries had of course been more restricted from the start than that of the neutrals. Yet the British committee had continued a vigorous propaganda and educational campaign, with the support of many leading liberals and of organizations such as the Union of Democratic Control which had similar aims. By the end of the war, the women's committee had recruited 4,000 members and established over fifty branches throughout Britain.

Although no French delegates had been permitted to attend the Hague Congress, and although the climate of opinion was distinctly unfavourable, a national committee was quickly organized in France by Madame Gabrielle Duchêne, a wealthy and influential woman and an uncompromising champion of women's and workers' rights. She was supported by Madeleine Rolland and the whole Romain Rolland circle of writers, socialists and pacifists, and by Mme de Saint-Prix, daughter of President Loubet. An appeal to the French Government not to reject any peace proposals out of hand, and to inform the public of all such proposals received, was followed by a search of Mme Duchêne's apartment, the confiscation of papers, and even the imprisonment of some members who continued to write and speak on the need for peace. During the latter part of the war the committee concentrated mainly on women's rights and drew up a comprehensive Women's Charter.

In Italy, the women's committee set up two separate groups in Milan and Rome but governmental opposition hampered their effective working. In December 1916 Rosa Genoni circulated a petition in favour of peace by arbitration which resulted in police action against the Milan group. Nevertheless the group continued to hold weekly lectures at the Popular University and to distribute literature. The group in Rome, under the leadership of Professor Dobelli-Zambetti, turned to social work on behalf of destitute families and was successful in getting a scheme of government allowances started.

The delegates from Germany to the Hague Congress faced a barrage of insults and hostile criticism on returning to their own country; some also were temporarily imprisoned. Yet it is of interest that the German ambassador at The Hague reported back to his Government that the women had won friends by their dignified attitude and had rendered a service to Germany by showing that there were German women ready to stand by their pacifist principles! One wonders how long he remained as ambassador. The general belief in Germany was that no sacrifice was too great for this 'holy war'. It was impossible openly to organize a women's peace movement. Nevertheless, some of the most intensive and courageous post-Congress activity was carried out in Germany, and 29 groups were successfully established in different parts of the country. In 1916 Lida Gustava Heymann was threatened with expulsion from Bavaria if she continued her pacifist propaganda, whereupon the centre of activity was transferred to Hamburg. At the second anniversary of the Hague Congress, in April 1917, appeals were sent to the German Government for a declaration of war aims and a peace without annexation. The women's peace groups were the first to condemn publicly the harsh terms of the Brest-Litovsk treaty with Russia in 1918.

After 1917 the work of the American committee, which had branches in 22 states, became increasingly hampered. Members suffered slanderous attacks, meetings were broken up, and even the national reputation of Jane Addams did not save her from vilification. The American women focused their later efforts on a study of conditions for a just peace settlement and proposals for the creation of a League of Nations. The Scandinavian groups were engaged in similar studies, and in June 1918 sent appeals to their respective governments to take the lead in drawing up proposals for establishing the League.

On November 11, 1918, with Germany's capitulation on the basis of Wilson's 'fourteen points for peace', the opportunity seemed to have come. But as Wilson fought a losing battle for his principles against the secret intrigues and nationalist ambitions of the Allied powers—conceding point after point of his peace terms if only the League of Nations might be saved—it became clear that the hopes of the peace forces everywhere were already in ruins and that the terms of the proposed treaties would lay no foundation for a stable peace in Europe. By the time the International Committee of Women summoned a second Congress in May 1919, the predominating mood was one of disillusionment.

The Congress did not after all meet side by side with the official Peace Conference at Versailles, since its delegates from the Central Powers would not be permitted to enter France. Instead, a neutral location was selected at Zürich, and here the Congress gathered from May 12 to 19, 1919. The number of countries participating had risen since 1915 from twelve to sixteen, the largest delegations coming from Germany, Britain and USA. Amongst the new German delegates was youthful Gertrude Baer from Munich, who held the post of referent on women's rights in the Bavarian Ministry for Social Security; and Frida Perlen, who had attended the preparatory meeting in Amsterdam for the 1915 Congress but was unable to reach The Hague. The American group, in addition to Jane Addams and Emily Balch, included Madeleine Doty, a New York lawyer; Mrs Florence Kelley, founder of the National Consumers' League; and Jeannette Rankin, first woman member of the United States Congress. Mary Church Terrell, first woman member of the Washington Board of Education, represented the coloured women of America.

This time the British delegation had not been prevented from attending. Twenty-five strong, they represented vigorously the convictions of the large British Committee which had been built up during the war. Amongst them were well-known figures in the labour movement like Mrs Philip Snowden, Mrs H. M. Swanwick and Ellen Wilkinson; Catherine Marshall, now secretary of the British Committee, a prominent worker in the suffrage movement and the Union of Democratic Control; and Mary Sheepshanks, editor of *Jus Suffragii* and Vice-Principal of Morley College of adult education.

The Swiss Committee was naturally well represented, including its President Clara Ragaz; Marguerite Gobat, daughter of a leading Swiss pacifist; and Dr Gertrud Woker from Berne University. The strong Scandinavian delegation included Dr Naima Sahlbom, scientist, and Elizabeth Waern-Bugge, noted suffragist, from Sweden; the Norwegian President, Emily Arnesen, with her keen interest in international education; and from Denmark Henni Forchhammer, lecturer and writer, and Clara Tybjerg, International Secretary of the Danish Council of Women.

Among the many vivid personalities in the smaller delegations space permits mention of only a few: the Austrian feminist Yella Hertzka, who had founded the first women's agricultural college in Austria; Vilma Glücklich, Hungarian educational reformer; and the labour leader Louie Bennett from Ireland, which now had its own national committee apart from Britain. The three Australian delegates—Vida Goldstein, Cecilia John and Eleanor Moore—had travelled for ten weeks to attend the Congress.

Because of visa difficulties, only two French delegates were present at the opening of the Congress, Mme Andrée Jouve and Mlle Reverchon. Mme Jouve, a teacher and keen internationalist, was to play an important part in the future educational work of the movement. It was a dramatic moment when, on the final morning, a third delegate arrived at Zürich: Jeanne Mélin, coming from a devastated region of the Ardennes. Spontaneously, Lida Gustava Heymann rose from the platform and embraced her, crying:

A German woman gives her hand to a French woman, and says in the name of the German delegation that we hope we women can build a bridge from Germany to France and from France to Germany, and that in the future we may be able to make good the wrongdoing of men.

Mlle Mélin replied with an impassioned speech, repudiating the statesmen of Versailles and urging the women of the world to unite their forces internationally. Emily Greene Balch rose too and raised her hand in a solemn pledge to work with all her power for the abolition of war. Every woman present at the Congress stood with raised hand and joined her in this pledge. 'I have never', wrote Mrs Swanwick, 'witnessed or imagined so remarkable an affirmation.'

This whole Congress, indeed, was an occasion of powerful emotion. The marks of war were visible for all to see in the faces of the delegates from the defeated countries. Some had been present four years earlier at The Hague, and the change in them was pitiful. Scarred and shrivelled by hunger and privation, they were scarcely recognizable. The American delegates, especially, were deeply shocked. 'Food is a subject that has never left my mind for a day since I came here', wrote Dr Alice Hamilton to a friend at home. The continuation of the Allied food blockade for months after the armistice seemed almost a worse crime against humanity than the war itself. 'What were

CHAPTER 3

POST-WAR TROUBLE-SPOTS

Work at Geneva—First Assembly of League of Nations—Naval Conference 1921—Vienna Congress 1921—WILPF and Non-Violence—Germany, Ireland, USSR—Summer School 1921

———

the wise guidance of Emily Greene Balch the WILPF evolved
utiny and practice its methods and lines of action. Faced with
ger, disease, economic disruption and political violence of post-
rope, how could this small League of women most fruitfully
programme for peace and freedom which had been mapped
e Zürich Congress? The myriad demands of urgent political,
and humanitarian problems clamoured for attention. Not all
met, but the records of the WILPF at this time show how
he international blunders and personal tragedies of the after-
ar came to the notice of the International Secretary: an
a from the 'Fight the Famine' campaign; an exposure of the
dured by Greek and Armenian women and children in
rems; a request from a student for work in Geneva; above
demands for disarmament and for revision of the Treaty
—which, far from securing peace, seemed only to aggra-
left by the war.

of this onslaught Miss Balch held firmly to her conviction
ose of the WILPF was *not* primarily a humanitarian one.
emove the causes of war rather than to allay the suffering
from it—even though this suffering was burnt into the
members both from their own experiences during the
heir journeys in Europe afterwards. They had seen with
half-starved children like pale, reproachful ghosts;
broken-spirited soldiers; old people, bereft of their
evement, filled with bitterness and despair. No women
sympathies could remain indifferent to such sufferings,
maintained that the needs of the victims must be met
F as such, but rather by stimulating the larger relief
more effective action. The WILPF, with its extremely

---

we all about', cried Jane Addams later, 'that such things were allowed to happen in a so-called civilized world?' It was small wonder that the first act of the Zürich Congress was to telegraph President Wilson in Paris demanding the raising of the blockade; immediate relief measures; and, if necessary, food rationing in every country. Wilson cabled back, sympathetically but pessimistically, that the outlook was 'extremely unpromising, because of infinite practical difficulties'. Had women been in conference at Versailles, these 'practical difficulties' might perhaps have been overcome.

But the statesmen were already sowing more bad seed for the future. The Zürich Congress, meeting immediately after the Allied peace terms were made public, was the first international gathering to consider and pronounce on the Treaty of Versailles. Its verdict amounted to an overwhelming indictment of the terms:

This International Congress of Women expresses its deep regret that the terms of peace proposed at Versailles should so seriously violate the principles upon which alone a just and lasting peace can be secured, and which the democracies of the world had come to accept.

By guaranteeing the fruits of the secret treaties to the conquerors, the terms of peace tacitly sanction secret diplomacy, deny the principles of self-determination, recognize the rights of the victors to the spoils of war, and create all over Europe discords and animosities which can only lead to future wars.

By the demand for the disarmament of one set of belligerents only, the principle of justice is violated and the rule of force is continued.

By the financial and economic proposals a hundred million people of this generation in the heart of Europe are condemned to poverty, disease and despair, which must result in the spread of hatred and anarchy within each nation.

With a deep sense of responsibility, this Congress strongly urges the Allied and Associated Governments to accept such amendments of the terms as shall bring the peace into harmony with those principles first enumerated by President Wilson, upon the faithful carrying out of which the honour of the Allied peoples depends.

This resolution, too, was telegraphed to Versailles, but it is doubtful if it even raised a blush.

A more difficult matter for the Congress to agree on was the proposed League of Nations embodied in the Treaty. Although the formation of such a League was warmly approved, the Covenant as drafted was considered unsatisfactory on many points. Certain provisions which were held to be essential for establishing peace were violated or omitted, namely: admission to the League of all countries desiring membership; the right of self-determination in all territorial adjustments; free and equal access to raw materials; abrogation of regional agreements, e.g. the Monroe Doctrine; reduction of armaments of all member-states on the same terms; and provision for easier amendment of the League's constitution. One proviso of the draft Covenant, however, was noted with satisfaction: 'that women should be admitted to all positions in connection with the League'. The undeniable advance in the struggle for the political rights of women seemed to the Congress the one bright gleam in an otherwise gloomy outlook. In the years between 1915 and 1919 partial or complete franchise had been granted to women in Austria, Britain, Canada, Denmark, Germany, Hungary, Iceland, Ireland, Poland, Russia and in many of the American states.

Determined that the gains already made should not be lost, the Zürich Congress adopted a formal constitution incorporating the principles and aims of the international women's peace movement which had grown out of the Hague Congress and been consolidated through the International Committee of Women for Permanent Peace. A League for Permanent Peace was now proposed, but on the suggestion of Catherine Marshall the name was amended to Women's International League for Peace and Freedom. This somewhat unwieldy title of the new organization was soon popularly shortened to Women's International League, or WIL, but may more conveniently and accurately be referred to as the WILPF.

The former national committees now became national sections of the League, which moved its office from Amsterdam to Geneva to coincide with the headquarters of the League of Nations. Each national section was entitled to nominate two 'consultative members' for the International Executive Committee, which was otherwise elected on an individual and not a national basis, thus ensuring a direct representation of the sections centrally and at the same time strengthening international links between them. National sections had a large measure of autonomy, but in policy were bound by the decisions of the International Congresses which were henceforth to take place biennially. Thus the WILPF was from its foundation an international body and not simply a federation of national sections.

The first elected President of the WILPF wa Addams. The two Vice-Presidents were Mrs Hel Britain and Lida Gustava Heymann of Germany. professorship at Wellesley College was termi twenty-five years, in part because of her p accepted the appointment as first International

As in 1915, the Zürich Congress of W personal envoys with recommendations to ferring at Versailles. The selected delega Charlotte Despard, Gabrielle Duchêne, Ro millan and Clara Ragaz. In her report of Macmillan wrote:

Very different views on the [peace] te members who received the deputation. dissatisfied with the failure of the terr what they had hoped, and there were ot Wilson was the best judge of the ap Objection to the secrecy of the nego some members of the Conference s averting war and looked rather to f

None of the women's proposals only Wilson troubled to ackn encouraging outlook for the br WILPF at least had not given up to be concentrated on making force for peace.

limited resources, must concentrate its efforts on its special tasks: the study of political and economic issues; objective fact-finding; personal reconcilation; and the formulation of just and humane policies.

After a few months in a temporary office in Geneva, the WILPF settled in the lovely, eighteenth-century house with its walled garden at No. 12, Rue du Vieux College—appropriately enough, the former home of Zamenhof, the inventor of Esperanto. The house was now named the Maison Internationale, and has been the home of the League ever since. With its library, reception rooms and living accommodation for workers and guests, it soon became a living centre of internationalism in an international city. The new League of Nations was now preparing for its first Assembly in September 1920, and Emily Balch was joined in Geneva by one of the ablest of the British members, Catherine Marshall. Miss Marshall arrived a week before the Assembly opened, when none of the delegates had arrived. She immediately requested a copy of the official papers, and was astonished to be told that she was the first person to ask to see the rules of procedure. The WILPF was concerned about several points, for instance that the agenda for the Assembly seemed to be decided in advance and that its business was to be conducted in private committees with no minutes recorded. These matters were brought to the attention of delegates, resulting in a discussion and modification of the rules of procedure. Thus from the very start the WILPF was able to play some part in determining how the League of Nations should work.

Another development with which the WILPF was dissatisfied was the composition of the League of Nations Council on a big-power basis. The first permanent seats were assigned to Britain, France, Italy, Japan and USA (which never took up its seat). As Catherine Marshall expressed it: 'The people on the Council . . . represent the old order of things and most of them either want the League of Nations to do wrong things or want it to do nothing.' How then could the League be made to do the 'right' things? The WILPF worked in two directions, through its national sections bringing pressure on their governments and through its international office making direct approaches to the delegations. On December 2, 1920, Emily Balch sent to every delegate at the first Assembly a copy of the Hague and Zürich resolutions, together with proposals for necessary steps to be taken by the League of Nations:

1. To admit without delay all nations expressing their desire to be admitted and their willingness to perform the duties of members.
2. To amend the Covenant so as to make both Council and Assembly more directly representative of the peoples, so that they may command the confidence of the world as really international and impartial bodies. (Note: 'The most necessary amendment to the Covenant is to make it more easily amendable. It should in our judgment not be possible, in this matter, for the vote of one single state upon the Council to override the vote of the whole Assembly and all other members of the Council.')
3. To begin, as soon as possible, a general and effective reduction of armaments, as a first step towards the elimination from international relations of the use and threat of force.
   (Note: 'We feel that the first two changes advocated above—admission of all states and amendment—must be accomplished before any substantial progress is likely to be made in disarmament.')
4. To adopt the fullest possible publicity for the proceedings of the Council and the Assembly, in order to enlighten public opinion and win public confidence.

On Point 1, Miss Balch reported that she felt the WILPF had had some influence in securing the admission of Albania as a member-state. The election of China by the first Assembly to replace Greece as a non-permanent member of the Council was also something for which the WILPF worked. Efforts made in co-operation with the Fight the Famine Council to secure an Assembly debate on the economic situation, with a view to calling an International Economic Conference, were, however, frustrated by the negative attitude of the British Dominions and Latin American states.

During the first Assembly also a number of special Memoranda were circulated by the WILPF to every delegation. Two of these documents were printed verbatim in the LON Official Journal, dealing respectively with the use by the League of the weapon of Blockade, against which strong arguments were advanced; and with Violence and Terror—an all too common feature of the post-war world, in spite of the theoretical protection of minorities against atrocities provided for in the Minorities Treaties. The WILPF recommended the appointment of a LON Commission to investigate reports of ill-treatment; and that good behaviour towards minorities should be a condition of League membership. Another memorandum condemned the use of colonial troops in territories under Allied occupation in Europe. Apart from inflaming racial antagonisms, it declared, the practice was an incentive to continued colonialism. Inhabitants of colonial or mandatory territories should not be required to undertake armed service 'other than duties of a strictly police character and that within their own territories only'. This memorandum was officially circulated to all members of the Assembly and subsequently sent by the LON Secretary-General to the governments of all member-states.

On the question of protection of women and children, the WILPF pressed successfully for the setting up of a commission to investigate the condition of women and children deported from Asia Minor and held in Turkey. This success, in face of strong opposition, was due to the persistent work of a Danish member, Henni Forchhammer, who was acting as a technical adviser for her Government at the Assembly. The League of Nations was also urged to appoint a woman member on the Permanent Mandates Commission. It was highly gratifying to the WILPF when Miss Forchhammer was appointed to this Commission the following year.

All this activity on the part of the WILPF took place in the first months of the first assembly of the League of Nations. Close and friendly relations were established with many of the delegates and permanent officials, but this did not blind the WILPF to the defects of the new organization. Ardent advocates of internationalism as they were, the women saw all too well that nations and their representatives were not transformed by their coming to Geneva and participating in the League of Nations. Here, as in all governmental machinery, there was no lack of chicanery and intrigue and a ceaseless struggle for power.

This struggle was nowhere more evident than in the series of inter-war 'disarmament' conferences which began with the Washington conference on limitation of naval armaments called by President Harding in 1921. The disarmament clauses of the Versailles Treaty, whereby Germany alone was kept disarmed, albeit *pour encourager les autres*, had been amongst the most contentious. From its foundation, the WILPF insisted that the only effective disarmament was total and universal. They welcomed the Washington Conference in the hope that it might be viewed as a step in the direction of this larger aim, and national sections were alerted to prepare a vigorous campaign in their own countries. From a large international gathering in Geneva a message was sent to the conference urging that its work be co-ordinated with the League of Nations 'to achieve radical reduction in armaments of every nation by land, by sea and in the air, that ultimately complete disarmament be attained'. Although a courteous acknowledgment was received from Charles Hughes, US Secretary of State, no such steps were taken and the only point on which the conference could reach agreement was a standstill on battleship production for ten years.

Side by side with work for disarmament went pressure for revision of the Peace Treaties which, if they had remedied some of the old evils of Europe, were imposing new stresses that it seemed impossible could endure. Germany's economic problems were insoluble. The break-up of the Austro-Hungarian empire left the new state of Austria unable to support itself. Old conflicts between the Balkan states were only embittered by the re-drawing of frontiers without regard to ethnic groups. Minority problems proliferated, erupting in sporadic civil wars. Hungary, weakened by loss of territory and population, was torn between the extremist factions of Admiral Horthy and Bela Kun. Bulgaria, also deprived of vast territories, was overrun with refugees from Thrace and Macedonia. Border raids by terrorists menaced the Serbs, the Turks and the Rumanians. Greece and Turkey were in conflict over the Treaty of Sèvres, Poland and Germany over the partition of Poland.

To this troubled area the WILPF elected to come for its third International Congress which opened in Vienna on July 10, 1921. Emily Balch had already made an advance tour of the Balkans to encourage the attendance of women from these countries, with good results. National sections in Austria, Bulgaria, Greece, Hungary, Poland and the Ukraine all sent delegates, and a number of observers came from Czechoslovakia, Croatia and Rumania. In all, 222 delegates assembled at the Congress, as well as fraternal delegates and visitors from countries as far away as South America and China. Greece, Poland and the Ukraine were formally admitted into membership, bringing the total of national sections to 21. Before the official business started, a memorial meeting was held in honour of two great Austrian pacifists, Bertha von Suttner and Alfred Herman Fried.

A special session was arranged for members from Eastern Europe to have a full discussion of their special problems. Out of this meeting came a request to the Allied Supreme Council for a just settlement of the Upper Silesian question, signed by both the German and Polish delegations. Other statements dealt with the rights of minorities in Hungary and Croatia and a strong protest was issued against anti-semitic pogroms, particularly in the Ukraine: no state should be admitted to the League of Nations, it declared, which allowed pogroms to take place within its borders. The foundations laid in these joint discussions were consolidated by the WILPF in 1922 by the formation of a Commission for Eastern Europe, with representatives from Austria, Bulgaria, Czechoslovakia, Hungary, Poland and the Ukraine.

Another interesting feature of the Congress at Vienna was a lengthy discussion, lasting over several sessions, on Pacifism in Practice. The WILPF had not been established as a 'pacifist' organization, in the simple sense of adherence to the principle of non-resistance. A motion that the WILPF 'adopts the principle and practice of Non-Resistance under all circumstances' received a simple majority vote but was ruled to be an expression of individual opinion and not binding upon national sections. Already in 1919, there had been divergences of opinion on the attitude the League should take to the movements of violent revolution in Europe. Military interventions by western governments against the revolutionary régimes in Hungary and Russia were condemned by the Zürich Congress, but what about the violence of the revolutionaries themselves? Certain delegates felt that the use of force in the cause of social justice could not be opposed. And yet, an organization which counselled against violence in international conflicts could surely do no other in situations of internal strife? By only one vote, the Congress resolved that the WILPF must maintain its faith in peaceful methods of effecting change, believing that 'it is their special part in this revolutionary age to counsel against violence from any side'.

There were good precedents for this decision in the League's own national sections. Above all in Germany, pacifists had offered heroic examples of pioneering, non-violent action. The successful general strike against the Kapp *putsch* in Berlin in 1920 is perhaps the best known of these. But this was not an isolated case. In Hamburg, Munich, Jena and other cities 'white' Prussian troops were attacking the democratic Weimar Republic, with counter-attacks from the extreme left. In all these disturbances, WILPF members took on an active, and often hazardous, reconciling role. In Munich, Gertrude Baer had led a small mission to negotiate between the white and red forces encamped outside the city, obtaining the promise from both sides that neither would shoot first. Again in Jena, WILPF members pleaded successfully with the Zeiss workers to keep off the streets and close down the factories so that Prussian troops had no pretext to fire. On another occasion, a WILPF member sat with a revolutionary people's court and insisted that no death sentences should be passed; and not one person was so sentenced. For these and other activities in the post-war revolutionary period German members suffered arrest, imprisonment, exile, and even death by shooting.

Somewhat comparable was the situation in Ireland, with increasing violence both by the rebels and the British occupying forces. The severe policy of reprisals inaugurated by the notorious 'Black and Tans' in 1920 caused an outcry in Ireland and protests from British liberal opinion. In October, on the initiative of its Manchester branch, the WILPF British section sent a mission to Ireland to investigate the facts. It included women of the calibre of Dr Catherine Chisholm, Mrs H. M. Swanwick and Miss Ellen Wilkinson. After visiting the main towns in both the northern and southern counties and hearing every point of view from that of the Sinn Fein rebels to Dominion Home Rulers and Ulster Unionists, the delegation reached an uncompromising conclusion: at the general election of 1918 over 70 per cent of votes were cast for Sinn Fein, therefore Dail Eireann ruled by overwhelming consent and the British Government could only 'pretend to govern by force and fraud, leading to the moral injury of Great Britain and the injury of her reputation throughout the world'. The mission advocated an immediate truce and release of Irish political prisoners; armed forces to be withdrawn and government to be placed in the hands of local, elected bodies. The report of the WILPF mission formed the basis for extensive propaganda by the British section, in co-operation with the 'Peace with Ireland' Council. Other national sections were urged to press their governments to support the cause of Irish self-determination. Louie Bennett, President of the Irish section and an unwavering advocate of non-violence, believed that Ireland's struggle for independence offered a unique opportunity for a national campaign of passive resistance, but this way was not taken by the nationalist leaders.

Perhaps the most critical test of the non-violent principles of the WILPF, however, came in its attitude to the Bolshevist revolutions in Russia. Its policy was to urge recognition of the Soviet Government and the resumption of normal trade relations. This did not imply any approval of the excesses and tyranny of the Communist régime, but rather a realization that further violence would do nothing to ameliorate a situation that was itself the fruit of past tyrannies and oppression. The first concern of the WILPF was that the terrible sufferings of the Russian population should be eased. During the great famine of 1921,

Catherine Marshall served as representative of the League on the International Relief Commission convened by the Red Cross. She was instrumental in getting the attendance of Dr Bagotsky, Commissioner of the Russian Red Cross, and Paul Birukoff, secretary and biographer of Tolstoy and a member of the All Russian Famine Relief Committee. But for her efforts, no representative of any official Russian organization would have been present at the conference. She also made two constructive proposals: that the International Commission should act as a channel of correct information on the Russian situation, in consultation with the Russian section of the International Labour Organization; and that national governments should be asked to contribute to the relief fund—but this help was not forthcoming.

On a proposal of the Irish section, the Vienna Congress of the WILPF appointed a commission on passive resistance. It also adopted a resolution from the Swedish section that peace missions should be sent to areas of acute conflict to investigate conditions and seek out local agents of reconciliation. Many members had travelled widely in post-war Europe and were well qualified to undertake such personal, unofficial missions, free from the suspicion of being actuated by any partisan or nationalist interest. Another decision of the Congress was to set up an International Committee on Education, and immediately following the Congress the first international summer school of the League took place at Salzburg. It had been planned by the British section, in co-operation with the Salzburg group, on the theme of Education for Internationalism. More than 300 young men and women from 21 countries came to the school, for which the hosts were the Austrian writer Stefan Zweig and his wife. This successful experiment was only the first of a series of outstanding summer schools held during the next decade. In 1922, the list of participants in the seminar at Lugano on 'The International Idea of Civilization' reads like an international brains trust: Emily Balch, Paul Birukoff, Georges Duhamel, Hermann Hesse, Count Kessler, Romain Rolland, Bertrand Russell, to mention only the best-known names. It was one of the ironies of history that this school was switched at the eleventh hour from Varese to Lugano because of the take-over of the Varese municipality by Mussolini's Fascist militia. The educational campaigns of the WILPF were certainly going to be needed.

CHAPTER 4

A NEW INTERNATIONAL ORDER

*Economic Problems—Conference for a New Peace—
Occupation of the Ruhr—Washington Congress 1924—
Disarmament Campaigns—British Peace Pilgrimage
1926*

The pattern of the post-war world was now beginning to take shape; and so were its most pressing problems. Germany was suffering not only from material destruction but from a deep sense of grievance over the Treaty of Versailles: where were the 'fourteen points' for peace on the basis of which she had offered her surrender? German members of the WILPF openly acknowledged Germany's share of responsibility for the war and recognized that the nationalist and Pan-German extremists in their country would never be satisfied by any treaty revision. Their great fear was that if the worst injustices of Versailles remained unrectified, the young democratic government of the Weimar Republic would not survive; a fear which was all too soon to be realized.

At the meeting of the Reparation Commission in London in 1921, when Germany's liability for reparations was set at £6,600 million, the WILPF (along with other liberal groups) urged that the decisions of the Commission should be guided not merely by considerations of 'justice' but by the more important necessity to create a reconciled and peaceful Europe. Only the British Government was at all disposed towards this view, and the following year Lloyd George called an Economic Conference at Genoa to review Allied policy on reparations, with the co-operation of Briand of France.

Lloyd George had replaced Asquith as Prime Minister in December 1915, and notwithstanding his harsh attitude towards Germany his liberal past had provided some points of contact with the WILPF. The political ability of Catherine Marshall during the women's suffrage campaigns had so impressed him that he was always ready to listen to her—and even to seek her advice. She was summoned to Downing Street in 1921 over the question of the Russian famine and later stayed at Chequers, the Prime Minister's country house, for further discussions both on the economic condition of Europe and on the vexed problem of Irish independence.

The WILPF naturally hoped that Miss Marshall would go to Genoa, but she was unfortunately prevented by illness. Instead, resolutions were sent to the diplomats concerned, reiterating the belief of the WILPF in a system of free trade and condemning the reparations policy as ruinous to the economy of Europe. The French section of the WILPF strongly supported this view, but no amount of pressure could modify the recalcitrant attitude of the French Government, where Briand was now unfortunately replaced as Premier by the far less forward-looking Poincaré.

In January 1921, the WILPF organized a conference in Geneva at which the whole question of economic dislocation and possible remedies was discussed with members of the League of Nations secretariat and the International Labour Office. Other unofficial contacts were also being pursued. In December 1920 Sir George Paish, former economic adviser to the British Government, had written to Emily Balch suggesting that an economic conference should be called in the United States; he further suggested that the person to convene this gathering should be Jane Addams. A great deal of complicated correspondence and discussion ensued with influential sympathizers such as Count Kessler of Germany and Senator Lafontaine of Belgium, and with American business and financial experts. At the request of Miss Balch, Oswald Garrison Villard of *The Nation* went to see the US Secretary of State, Charles Hughes, to probe the American Government's reactions. But still no decisive action was taken.

Finally, as the economic crisis worsened, the WILPF itself decided to summon a Conference for a New Peace. Again, as on the occasion of the first women's Congress, the initiative was taken by Dutch members and the conference met at The Hague from December 7 to 9, 1922. Again, Jane Addams presided. In addition to many leading WILPF members, delegates were present from 111 national and international organizations from 20 countries, estimated to represent a total membership of over 20 million men and women. Sir George Paish and Count Kessler were also amongst those present.

With so large and varied a representation, resolutions were confined to matters of broad principle on which there was common agreement. The conference demanded the convening of a World Congress to draw up new international agreements on which a new, and genuine, peace might be based. Immediate, concerted action was taken by

WILPF sections in the countries concerned to press for a reasonable settlement of reparation claims and for the withdrawal of armies of occupation from the Rhineland. Jane Addams, Catherine Marshall and Jeanne Mélin were deputed to seek personal interviews with statesmen in Britain, France, Holland and Scandinavia, and were received by high officials in all these countries. The following September, at an Executive Committee meeting in Dresden, it was decided to send Gertrude Baer, Aletta Jacobs, Andrée Jouve and Catherine Marshall to Berlin, where they were received by the Minister of Interior; and to Paris, where again they talked with a high government official.

Meanwhile, in the Balfour Note of August 1, 1922, the British Government announced its readiness to cancel all war debts and withdraw all claims to further reparations, if the USA would do likewise. But America refused to link the cancellation of debts and reparations, whereupon in December Britain stated that she would go ahead regardless of the US position. Poincaré, however, remained unmoved by this proposal, since France's reparation claim was greater than her debt to Britain. The Reparation Commission on December 26th declared Germany to be in default; again, British and Italian proposals for a moratorium on payments were rejected by the French; and on January 11, 1923, French and Belgian troops invaded the Ruhr, against the warning of the British Government that the Peace Treaty had given no sanction for such a move.

The WILPF was one of the first bodies to condemn the occupation of the Ruhr and to uphold the passive resistance campaign of the German miners. Gertrude Baer, general secretary of the German section, went to the area to make a personal investigation and reported her conviction that the passive resistance could not be maintained unless the central German Government made a greater effort to meet its financial obligations and reach an understanding with France. This prognosis was proved correct when, after nine months, Chancellor Stresemann was forced to call off the resistance as Germany faced total economic collapse. France, too, was realizing her costly mistake in attempting to enforce reparations. Urged on by Britain, America at last stepped in with the Dawes Plan in 1924, providing for the reorganization of the Reichsbank under Allied supervision and a substantial loan to Germany. Here was one at least of the ill-hatched Versailles chickens coming home to roost. But the material misery of Germany remained 'indescribable', in the words of a Swedish WILPF member, Mrs Beskow, who with a British member Mrs Anneslie also visited the Ruhr, aided by a grant for relief work from the Swedish Save the Children Fund. Nowhere, she said, was there a greater need of reconciliation work and she urged that more workers should be sent to share the hardships, and mitigate the sufferings, of the German population. Unfortunately, as so often happened, this appeal had to go unanswered because of the inadequate resources of the WILPF in both money and personnel to meet the demands made on it.

The decision of the League to hold its fourth International Congress in America was therefore a bold venture, which was only made possible by generous financial assistance from the United States section. But the Americans believed it was of the greatest importance that their members should have some closer contact with the European side of their international sisterhood; for Europeans, too, a transatlantic viewpoint might well offer a creative release from some of their most pressing post-war problems. In spite of the great distances to be travelled, when the Congress assembled in Washington on May 1, 1924, delegates were present from twenty-two national sections, the only absentees being Haiti and New Zealand. Four new sections were welcomed into membership: Belgium, Czechoslovakia, Haiti and Japan. The largest delegations were naturally those of Canada and the United States, with many additional visitors and fraternal delegates. Observers also came from countries in Latin America and the Caribbean, and from Turkey and Liberia.

The theme chosen for the Congress was 'A New International Order', to be considered in its political, economic and psychological aspects. For this purpose the French section had drawn up a memorandum for study by national sections on first steps to be taken; the second part of the programme—steps towards realization of the new order—was left for future consideration. The underlying principles of the French memorandum were (*a*) that all nations are equal in rights; and (*b*) that all nations are interdependent. Political organization was envisaged in terms of a League of Peoples, developing either parallel with or in replacement of the existing League of Nations. The new League would have legislative, executive, judicial and economic powers—but no armed forces and no right of economic sanctions. Economically, the new organization must solve the question of reparations and international debts; institute an international currency; abolish customs barriers and tariffs; and regulate the world supply of foodstuffs and raw materials. In addition, a World Charter of Labour was laid down.

So elaborate and comprehensive a plan for a new world order—no less—might easily have fallen into the pitfall of most such schemes, that of becoming an end in itself. This was not so in the French *cahier*. The place of the individual in the new order was made quite clear:

The ultimate object of every political and economic organization is the safeguarding and perfecting of the individual, who alone is a reality and whose suffering and joy, action and thought, make up the life of the world.

On the individual would rest the responsibility for inculcating the new international spirit—through art and science, through the churches and the press, above all through the reform of education. Without this transformation of the human spirit, any new order would go the way of the old:

As long as men do not recognize that all are subject to this law of disinterestedness and generosity which goes beyond strict justice; as long as they will not work to realize it by a common effort in their inner life and in their private relations, as well as in their public life, the external transformation of the world will not bring the expected benefits.

The care and thought that had been put into the French memorandum must undoubtedly have been of great value in helping the Congress, with all its differing viewpoints, to find common agreement concerning fundamental principles. Immediate political steps advocated by delegates included the democratic control of foreign policy; the outlawry of war; abolition of conscription; and enlargement of the League of Nations. Some time was given to discussion of the desirability or otherwise of a United States of Europe. Those in favour argued that this was a necessary step in eliminating the disastrous rivalries among European countries and in extending the area of free trade and currency agreements. Others felt that to limit such a union to Europe would be a step away from the greater aim of a World Parliament; and that a union of Europe without the participation of Britain and Russia would be just as absurd as was the notion that these two countries would freely give up their own imperial interests in favour of such a union.

The Congress opposed in a resolution the Draft Treaties of Mutual

Assistance which had been presented to the Assembly of the League of Nations by France and referred to governments for consideration, and recommended their rejection. Partial military treaties, it was argued, would undermine the solidarity of the League of Nations and deprive its judgments 'even of the measure of impartiality they now possess', and would be unlikely to bring about any significant reduction of armaments. Other political resolutions urged governments to accept the compulsory jurisdiction of the Permanent Court of International Justice by signing the 'optional clause'; called on the League of Nations to set up a Permanent Commission on National Minorities; and supported President Coolidge's proposal for an international conference on limitation of armaments and codification of international law.

Economic aspects of the new international order were ably dealt with by Marguerite Dumont and Emily Balch. The French delegates strongly denounced the operations of 'international finance' and made recommendations for tariff reductions and control of raw materials. Miss Balch, as usual seeking constructive alternatives, stressed the benefits that would grow from an international control of waterways such as the Dardanelles, Panama Canal and Suez Canal.

In the consideration of psychological factors, the need was expressed for a more enlightened system of education and for training in resistance to mass-suggestion. Dr Anita Augspurg specified the kind of reforms that must lay the foundation for any new social order:

Such change would demand modification in the family, in education in schools, and most glaring of all in the penal system. Capital punishment must be abolished and the whole prison system modified. Education is the best agency in bringing about such a change, but methods of education must be in line with the ends sought.

But the most important single factor in the construction of a new international order, Dr Augspurg believed, was 'the bringing into equilibrium of the influence of men and women'. Women must cease to admire a man with a gun in his hand and must seek to counteract the destructive tendencies in the masculine mentality by what she called 'inner devotion to the right'.

Although the WILPF had always opposed attempts to 'humanize' war, the Washington Congress issued a special condemnation of Chemical Warfare, in the belief that so to publicize its peculiar horrors might arouse opinion against all war. National sections were recommended to appoint special committees to investigate the development and dangers of these new scientific methods. At the same time an International Committee was set up, consisting of Dr Gertrud Woker, Dr Naima Sahlbom and Ester Akesson-Beskow.

Prior to the opening of the Washington Congress a mass youth rally was held at which the main speaker was Senator Borah from Idaho, a good friend of the WILPF. He seized the occasion to strike a blow for freedom of speech, then in some danger in the United States from chauvinist 'patriots', as had been shown in many public expressions of hostility to the Congress. Senator Borah at least did not fear to speak his mind openly and forcefully:

Whether I should agree with those here assembled or disagree with them in their views and in their methods of securing peace, I contend that they have the absolute right under the privileges of the American Constitution to discuss their views at any place they want to. If we have to turn the cause of peace into a fight for free speech, we will have the fight.

This occasion was certainly not the last battle in that particular war.

Some of the European delegates were submitted to humiliations, ridicule and even physical danger immediately after the Congress, when they boarded the 'Pax Special', a railway coach hired by the American Section to take them through various towns and cities on their way to the summer school which was being held at Chicago. Attacks by such groups as the Daughters of the American Revolution and the American Legion, accusing delegates of subversion and 'spying', caused panic amongst local committees and the cancellation of meetings. Nevertheless, successful gatherings with civic, university and church representatives were held in Baltimore, Philadelphia and Pittsburgh. The Dean of Christ Church, St Louis, opened the cathedral to the visitors, but so strong were the fears and suspicions of his congregation that these could only be allayed by a personal assurance from Jane Addams as to the integrity of the delegates. In Detroit, the situation was saved by the labour organization at General Motors, which insisted on meeting the Pax Special with a long line of automobiles placarded with peace slogans—in spite of the opinion of some members of the city council that the train should be derailed and the women 'tarred and feathered'.

In Canada, too, where four delegates travelled on at the invitation of Agnes Macphail, Member of Parliament and herself a delegate at the Congress, there was keen opposition and criticism in some quarters. But here again personal confrontation helped to dispel prejudice and the women were received at the Parliament House, addressing a large gathering under the auspices of the Prime Minister's Council. Nor should it be overlooked, in dwelling on the less hospitable demonstrations, that in Washington delegates to the WILPF Congress were received at the White House by the President of the United States.

Had the journey been worth it? Undoubtedly there was a broadening of outlook from both sides of the Atlantic. If the meeting of American idealism with European disillusion brought some unpleasant shocks of readjustment, this was a necessary part of growth. The Congress marked the tenth year of the women's international peace movement started in 1915. Its progress was surveyed by Lida Gustava Heymann of Germany, one of the WILPF's International Vice-Presidents: an office, she remarked, which was itself a tribute to the spirit of the League at a time when Germany was still excluded altogether from many international organizations. She went on:

At The Hague in 1915 women from 14 nations came together. Today we are connected with 39 nations. Our circle has become world-wide. We can say today: The sun does not set on our League. That is a wonderful feeling, but it gives us the greater responsibility. There is danger that the old spirit, born in a time of deep sorrow, will perhaps not be understood and practised by all. . . . New times demand new deeds and new conditions, new work, and perhaps even new principles. We must not forget that history is evolution. Time must find us ready. We can only conquer if we stand together with the same courage, with the same self-respect and faith in what women have to give to the world, as did the women in 1915.

In her opening address to the Congress Jane Addams had pointed to examples of efforts already being made by some countries to live according to the principles of a New International Order: Austria had freely renounced a piece of Hungarian territory assigned to her by the Peace Treaty; the British Government had abandoned the construction of a naval base at Singapore; the Japanese had withdrawn from the Chinese province of Shantung; Gandhi had been demonstrating in India that self-determination might be won without recourse to violence; and, pressing on governments everywhere, was a rising demand among the peoples of many countries for 'No More War'. In 1924, on the initiative of the first British Labour Prime Minister Ramsay MacDonald, the draft Treaty on arbitration, security and disarmament known as the Geneva Protocol was presented to the Assembly and received unanimous support. Forty-eight states subsequently ratified the Treaty; but with the accession of a Conservative Government Britain drew back owing to pressure from her Dominions, and the Protocol lapsed. Nevertheless, efforts for strengthening peace continued on a wide front. In February 1925 France accepted the German proposal for a Rhineland Mutual Guarantee Pact, on the condition that Germany should join the League of Nations, and in August withdrew her troops from Düsseldorf, Duisberg and Ruhrort. This move was followed in December by the famous Locarno Pact, comprising a series of interlocking treaties of security and mutual assistance. At last, it seemed, the tide had turned in Europe towards a peaceful future. The admission of Germany to the League of Nations, with a permanent seat on the Council, the following September, set the seal on the agreements.

In 1925, too, the League of Nations Disarmament Commission was set up, holding its first meeting the following May. The WILPF seized this opportunity to press still more resolutely its demand for total, universal disarmament. The German section was particularly active in this campaign, but they could not fail to be aware, even under the Weimar Republic, of the powerful forces working against disarmament inside their own country. The smaller but no less vital French section, led by the intrepid Gabrielle Duchêne, maintained its uncompromising stand for total disarmament allied to radical industrial action. Some of the new sections in Eastern Europe found this attitude difficult to understand. Aware of the precarious situation of their own national states, they were reluctant to take the initiative in advocating disarmament unless all the neighbouring states did likewise. The wonder was, indeed, that WILPF members could still be found in these countries who did succeed in surmounting nationalist fears and hatreds and continued to promote the objects of the League. By contrast, the Scandinavian sections enjoyed a good measure of support from their governments and were able to carry out extended public educational campaigns. In the United States, the WILPF obtained the support of other likeminded organizations to secure over 10,000 signatures in favour of a resolution that the proposed International Disarmament

Conference should place on its agenda 'universal abolition of conscription and complete world disarmament'.

Perhaps the most spectacular demonstration for disarmament, however, was made in Britain. In January 1926 a joint council was set up on the initiative of the WILPF, with the support of twenty-eight women's and peace organizations, to plan a national 'peace pilgrimage' under the banner of 'Law not War'. Its objects were twofold: to press for a World Disarmament Conference; and to urge the British Government to sign the Optional Clause of the International Court of Justice (i.e. to accept compulsory jurisdiction in all disputes of a legal nature), to which nineteen states already adhered.

In spite of enormous difficulties caused by the general strike that spring, the Peace Pilgrimage set out as planned in May (the Scottish groups joining a little later) along seven main routes to London from the north of Scotland to Land's End, from East Anglia to South Wales. A thousand meetings were held in towns and villages on the way, and on June 18th the first contingent entered the outskirts of London. The following day the whole pilgrimage assembled at four rallying points around Hyde Park, and from each point a procession set out for the final mass demonstration. An eye-witness described the scene:

Here were women of the Guild House in blue cassocks and white collars, bearing their banners aloft; behind them walked members of the League of Nations Union, with bannerettes representing various countries of the world. Here was a carriage filled with women graduates robed in black and scarlet and purple; there was a group of miners' wives. At the head of each procession rode a woman in a Madonna-blue cloak on a white horse; a notable figure was Miss Sybil Thorndike who carried a banner embroidered with doves.

The pilgrims were met at Hyde Park by a pageant, and from twenty-two platforms speakers from all political parties supported the aims of the demonstration. Simultaneously, Professor Gilbert Murray was broadcasting to the whole country on the importance of arbitration. During the progress of the pilgrimage, special peace services had been held in hundreds of churches. The press had for once shown a favourable attitude to the cause of peace, and more than a thousand press notices were received. The whole enterprise demonstrated an overwhelming sentiment for peace throughout Britain.

The next step was to bring this sentiment to bear on government officials. On July 6th the Foreign Secretary, Sir Austen Chamberlain, received a deputation from the Pilgrimage council. It included such well-known WILPF members as Mrs H. M. Swanwick and Dr Maude Royden. The Foreign Secretary received them sympathetically and listened carefully to their views. In his reply, he pointed out that preparations were already being made for the Disarmament Conference, about which he expressed a hopeful attitude. He was cautious, however, about the possibilities of international arbitration, particularly for Britain with her colonial responsibilities. Clearly, for all the popular support of the Peace Pilgrimage, the British Government would give no such pledge as that demanded. Even the promised Disarmament Conference did not take place for another six years. If left to governments, the New International Order would surely never arrive! The WILPF now began to consider fresh ways of implementing its practical policies for peace.

CHAPTER 5

RECONCILIATION IN PRACTICE

Dublin Congress 1926—Reconciliation in Europe—
Mission to Haiti—Mission to China

Emily Balch had returned to the United States from Geneva at the end of 1922, and was replaced as International Secretary of the WILPF by Vilma Glücklich of Hungary. Miss Glücklich had unfortunately to retire owing to ill-health in 1925, and her death two years later was greatly mourned. She had maintained the flow of international correspondence and political activity initiated by Miss Balch, and had displayed a special concern for the effects of militarism on children. She was followed at the Geneva office by Madeleine Doty, a New York lawyer and wife of Roger Baldwin, secretary of the League for the Rights of Man. Miss Doty did much to develop the monthly journal *Pax International*—in 1926, a circulation of 12,000 was reached in English, French and German editions—and to make the Maison Internationale a live peace centre, particularly during sessions of the League of Nations Assembly.

One of the recommendations of the Washington Congress had been to extend the work of the Peace Missions Committee, and separate centres were established in Sweden and the USA to cover the eastern and western hemispheres. In a sense, the holding of the WILPF's next International Congress at Dublin in 1926 was itself an extended 'peace mission', an example of Jane Addams' concern for 'the propaganda of the deed'. The choice owed something to the courageous stand for non-violence of Louie Bennett and her co-workers, as well as to the tragic situation of Ireland itself. The WILPF, with its support for Irish self-determination, could be sure of a warm welcome. The Congress was in fact the first gathering of an international organization to be held in the Irish Free State since its recognition by Britain in December 1921. It was a tribute to the non-partisan spirit of the League that both Mr Cosgrave, President of the Free State, and Mr de Valera, the Republican leader, were present at the opening of the Congress in the National University on July 8, 1926. Twenty-two countries were represented by delegates from most parts of Europe as well as from Australia, Japan and the USA.

The theme of the Congress, 'Next Steps Towards Peace', represented the second stage in the development of ideas for 'a new international order' which had been discussed at Washington. National sections had been asked to indicate what these steps should be, bearing in mind the particular dangers and tensions in their own countries. These reports were of the greatest interest, serving as a kind of map of the mid-twenties, and no less striking than the diversity of problems in different areas was the unity of principle in approaching them. Most of the European countries showed a resurgence of militarism on the part of governments, due equally to the fear of external attack and of internal revolution. This fear was least in Scandinavia, where there seemed no danger of war except through involvement in a world conflict; it was strong in Belgium, still bitter from its fate in the previous war; and dominant in the newly-independent states such as Poland and Czechoslovakia and the old states like Austria and Hungary which had lost territory by the peace treaties. The great imperial powers added their weight to the forces of militarism by their constant struggle to preserve their own power through new alliances.

A significant development at this time was the marked trend in the socialist parties away from pacifism. Before the war socialism had virtually been synonymous with internationalism and anti-militarism. Now, with the accession of Social Democratic governments in many European states, socialist politicians were faced with problems of 'national defence' which had never concerned them as members of minority opposition parties. In Austria, for instance, the Social Democrats had what amounted to a private army in the Republican Safety League, which they were unwilling to reduce in size in view of threats from Monarchist and Fascist groups, each with their own irregular armed forces. Belgian socialists too believed in the principle of national defence since, as Lucie Déjardin reported, 'they saw their first Ministry go out of office solely for the reason that a group of ex-service men who were socialists had taken as their emblem a broken rifle'. The broken rifle is still the emblem of the War Resisters International.

In confronting this revival of faith in military might, the League advocated yet again that women in particular should further the process, long and slow as it must be, of education for internationalism; that conscription should be abolished; and the authority of the League of Nations strengthened. The British section, in particular, strongly urged that the most important move towards world peace was unconditional acceptance of arbitration as an alternative to the method of war. Poland, on the other hand, believed that arbitration could only become effective when the will to peace already existed; while the German section saw the greatest contribution their country could make as being a voluntary, total disarmament. The Ukrainians, themselves a minority under Poland, felt strongly that the greatest international problem was the condition of national minorities, which had actually worsened since the war. Italy was in the unhappy position of suffering already under an established Fascist régime, and the only hope the struggling section could see was in the re-education of the coming generation. The French section was concerned about Colonialism, pointing to the two French colonial wars in Morocco and Syria as symptoms of worse conflicts to come:

Our section is convinced that if a new policy is not adopted with regard to the countries colonized, protected, or put in tutelage, some day an uprising will break out which may provoke a war, continent against continent, which will imperil modern civilization.

This was certainly no wild prophecy.

One of the most enlightening of the national section reports was given by a distinguished Japanese member, Tano Jodai, of the Japan Women's University, Tokyo. She stressed that the very existence of Japan depended on trade, and warned against a growing Japanese hostility towards America because of US military activity in Hawaii and the Philippines. Nor did Miss Jodai fail to condemn the cult of militarism in Japan, which had been strengthened by the Japanese victory over Russia in the war of 1904. The United States report showed concern for Latin American problems, and in particular for improved relations with Mexico. The section had urged repeal of discriminatory laws against Japanese immigration; and advocated America's accession to the International Court of Justice even though she was not a member of the League of Nations.

Many of the problems raised in reports of the national sections were analysed in greater detail in the three Commissions set up at the Congress to deal respectively with Colonial and Economic Imperialism; Arbitration and Disarmament; and the perennial question of Minorities. The Arbitration Commission drew up recommendations on the development of international law; control of the manufacture and traffic in arms; and urged ratification of the 1925 Geneva Convention on Chemical Warfare. A message was sent from the Congress to the Preparatory Disarmament Commission of the League of Nations urging representatives to work for 'complete and universal disarmament'.

After much discussion of expert papers submitted by Emily Balch, Tano Jodai, Andrée Jouve and Mary Sheepshanks, the Colonial and Economic Commission also made recommendations to national sections for study. It is interesting that in the preamble to two resolutions on colonial and economic imperialism the Congress put forward its belief that 'economic competition and rivalry between states is the chief cause of war'. No such priority had hitherto been laid down by the League. The statement continued:

We hold that raw materials are needed by all nations, and that therefore all have a direct responsibility for the way in which they are produced. We hold that a lasting peace is only possible under an order of society which excludes every kind of imperialism, colonial and economic. The WIL is opposed in principle to the possession of colonies and holding of mandates; but, in view of the fact that colonies do exist, proposes the following safeguards . . .

These safeguards included extension to all colonies of the standard set up in the League Covenant for Mandatory States, and revision of the mandatory system to protect the native from oppression. Economic measures included a proposal for a European Customs Union as a first step towards universal free trade; an International Economic Council under the League of Nations, with representation of producers and consumers; and loans for development through the League of Nations for non-military purposes.

The relations between majority and minority groups had always been a prior concern of the WILPF. The Committee on Minorities pointed out in its report to the Dublin Congress that although the war had ostensibly been fought to free subject groups, the numbers of such people had risen since 1914 from 28 million to between 35 and 40 million. It was recognized that there was no single, or simple, solution to these problems. A special Commission on Minorities under the League of Nations was recommended, to be manned by impartial laymen and not by political representatives of the countries concerned. Since this Congress was enjoying the hospitality of the Irish Free State, a special report on the minority problems of Ireland was presented by the Irish section, which urged the appointment of an international commission to investigate the situation. The section also advocated the complete disarmament of Ireland, which was still sustaining three separate groups of armed forces: the Free State army, the British forces in the north and around the coast, and the illegal Republican army of Sinn Fein.

Many tributes to the spirit and work of the WILPF were paid by prominent Irish citizens. The assistant secretary of the Irish Labour Party, R. J. P. Mortished, while admitting that his country could scarcely claim to have an international or pacifist outlook, was generous in his praise:

The Women's International League has come to us with a magnificent defiance of the destructive power of hate and a magnificent faith in the power of love informed by intelligence. They have come with that incredible but triumphant declaration that the ideal must become real, that what ought to be, will be.

There could scarcely have been a better summing-up of both the aspiration and the achievement of the League: its whole existence was a manifestation that only through 'love informed by intelligence' would the ideal ever become real, and peace be established on earth.

It had been clear from its inception that the WILPF would never be content to rest on its lofty ideals; there was a constant search for means of implementing them through constructive action. It was an accepted principle, on the part of both the International and the national sections, that once an injustice had been verified the injured party must be supported, even where the national interests of sections were affected. Thus the British section which had defended the cause of Irish self-determination was equally firm in upholding the Indian independence movement. The French section in 1925 drew attention to the plight of the Riff people in Morocco, where French forces were suppressing a rebellion, and succeeded in getting medical aid through to them. During the occupation of the Ruhr the section organized 'Fraternal Aid to German Children', by means of which gifts of food and clothing were sent to miners' families. From the other side, the German section in 1923 organized voluntary collections for 'reconciliation-reparations' in a devastated part of France, culminating in a symbolic tree-planting ceremony at Arras in January 1926, on the occasion of the sixtieth birthday of Romain Rolland. (See Appendix 2.)

Two more trouble-spots provided an opportunity for peaceful intervention by the WILPF during these years. In September 1924 members of the Danish and German sections co-operated in setting up a conciliation centre on the disputed Schleswig border. Full cultural autonomy for all minorities along the German-Danish border was advocated, and the German authorities were approached on behalf of the Danish minorities in Germany. As a result of representations to the other side, the teaching of Danish in schools in German-speaking districts ceased to be compulsory. Relations between the Poles and the Germans were also a source of friction, although the Treaty of Locarno in 1925 brought some *rapprochement*. To strengthen these better relations, WILPF members in both countries issued a joint statement of conditions to govern future relations, followed by a conference in Warsaw in 1926 and the setting up of a mixed commission on minority problems.

One of the most effective undertakings of the WILPF in 1926 was a mission to Haiti to investigate the effects of occupation by American marines, who had been sent to the country in 1915 to maintain 'law and order' and remained there ever since. The mission, which was requested by the Haitian section of the WILPF, was composed of two well-known coloured women—Charlotte Atwood, a teacher from Washington, and Addy Hunton, President of the International Council of Women of the Darker Races; Zonia Baber, a former Professor of Geography at Chicago University, and Emily Balch on behalf of the WILPF; Grace D. Watson of the Fellowship of Reconciliation; and Paul H. Douglas, Professor of Industrial Relations at Chicago University (later to become a Senator from Illinois).

Dividing their forces according to their special interests and knowledge, the members of the mission talked to both American and Haitian officials; to agricultural workers, teachers, doctors, lawyers, and many other kinds of people. They spent three weeks in the country and published their findings in a book, *Occupied Haiti*, which was edited and largely written by Emily Balch. The mission recommended that the continued occupation of Haiti was not justified and should be ended forthwith; that full self-government should be restored; that American officials should be replaced as far as possible by Haitians and the administration should be demilitarized; that preventive detention should be ended and freedom of the press restored. It was urged that the United States Government should send an official commission of investigation to Haiti to make a first-hand report; this in fact was done.

Back in Washington the US section's secretary, Dorothy Detzer, followed up the work of the mission with political pressure. She reported progress to Jane Addams:

This morning after a tremendous amount of difficulty, we did get to the Secretary of Latin Affairs for the State Department. . . . We had an interview with Kellogg. My guess is some of the recommendations of Douglas and Balch were acceptable.

In happenings such as the subsequent decisions of the American Government to remove its troops from Nicaragua and Haiti, it is always impossible to claim credit for the work of a single organization, even though in the case of Haiti the US Government's policies were to prove startingly similar to those recommended in *Occupied Haiti*.

The WILPF inevitably found itself in frequent conflict with governmental policies and critical of the actions of statesmen, but the League was realistic enough to recognize that much of its effort would be of little avail unless governments could be influenced and statesmen approached with human understanding. For this reason it was always the policy of the League—a policy that was sometimes open to criticism—to work with rather than against government departments and to maintain cordial relations with official representatives, even where strong disagreement over policy occurred. Such relations were only possible, of course, in democratic states; so indeed was the functioning of the League itself, as future developments in Europe were all too soon to demonstrate.

The success of the Haiti mission in 1926 led to a still more ambitious venture the following year. On the proposal of the Irish Section, the Executive Committee meeting at Liège in 1927 decided to send representatives to Indo-China and China to meet members of the women's movement in these countries and strengthen their links with the League. Those selected for this important and difficult mission were Miss Edith Pye, a British Quaker whose wartime nursing service in France had made her a Chevalier de la Legion d'Honneur; and Mme Camille Drevet, acting secretary of the French section and editor of *La Voix des Femmes*. They were to be joined in China by an American member living in Peking, Mrs Grover Clark, who with her husband was co-editor of the English-language paper *Peking Leader*.

Edith Pye and Camille Drevet sailed from Marseilles on October 28, 1927, accompanied by the Indo-Chinese political leader Wong van Giao. The reactions of some of their fellow-voyagers showed the disfavour with which their eastern friend was regarded by the French Government, even though he belonged to the moderate, constitutional party in Indo-China. In fact, his presence on board caused a diversion of the ship's route, so that the reception which had been prepared for the WILPF mission by a group of Indo-Chinese women did not take place.

The Englishwoman, at least, was struck immediately on arrival both by the immense material benefits which French administration had brought in the way of roads and health services and by the rising nationalism of the Annamites whose sense of the injustice of colonial rule far outweighed their gratitude. The French must realize, Miss Pye noted in her report, that this demand for citizenship and a voice in the destiny of their own country 'is a cry not only of a far eastern race being governed "for its good" but is echoed and repeated by advancing humanity itself, over the whole world'. The education of women, she also noted, was not sufficiently advanced for them to have any widespread interest in things outside the home, although the educated men were most anxious that this lack should be remedied.

The two women stayed three weeks in Indo-China, studying schools, labour conditions, the evils of opium and alcohol, and relations between the Indo-Chinese and the French. Camille Drevet was forthright in her condemnation of bad labour conditions, particularly on plantations in Cambodia and Cochin-China where the 'coolie' had no protection at all; inadequate schooling, covering only one-eighth of the child population; the inferior position of the Annamites in the administration; and restrictions on freedom of expression and association. The opium industry was an entrenched interest which demanded the attention of an international commission. It was essential, she concluded, that the French should take steps to prepare the Annamites for independence by the provision of more schools, freedom to speak and act, and the organization of labour.

From Indo-China, the two-woman mission sailed on to China, arriving at Hong Kong on December 22nd, where they were met by Kathryn Grover Clark. The moment of arrival, in Edith Pye's understatement, was 'unpropitious' owing to the 'very recent disturbances', so that the immediate plan to visit Canton was switched to Shanghai, at that time still an International Settlement. The disturbances referred to by Miss Pye had arisen from the split between the right and left wing of the Kuomintang, hitherto composed of both Nationalist and Communist movements working in co-operation to extend the Republic founded by Sun Yat Sen in 1912 to the whole of China. Now, with the return of Chiang Kai-Shek from Japan to take over leadership of the Kuomintang based on Nanking, a policy of extermination of the left wing began. A Communist rising in Canton had been put down with appalling massacre, and similar atrocities were reported from all parts of China; the Communists in their turn, Miss Pye reported, seemed to have forfeited popular support by their own acts of violence and brutality, and she felt that the Kuomintang, with its promise of stable government, enjoyed a wide measure of popular support. It was not surprising, in the circumstances, that the only section of opinion not encountered by the mission was Communism and that the extreme left wing of the Kuomintang had virtually 'disappeared'. At this very moment, in fact, the future leader Mao Tse-tung was assembling his secret peasant army in preparation for the Long March to the north that was ultimately to bring defeat to the Nationalist Kuomintang.

This absence of Communist representation in 1927 was the more ironic in that the decision eight months earlier by the WILPF Executive Committee to send a mission to China had been partly determined by the desire to make personal contact with Madame Sun Yat Sen—now fled to Moscow. In her place, as Camille Drevet dryly recounted, 'we saw her sister, Madame Chiang Kai-Shek'. The Nationalist leader had recently married one of the famous Soong sisters who had played so important a part in the history of Chinese liberation. Inevitably, the European women made most of their contacts in China through Nationalist officials, who were everywhere friendly and helpful. The Nanking Government seemed anxious to establish better relations with foreign powers, and this may have accounted in part for the warm welcome given to the delegates from the WILPF, the first international organization to send a delegation to China independent of religious or political affiliations.

Following discussions with officials of the National Anti-Opium Association of China, a memorandum was sent by the Association to the WILPF, asking for help in the fight to control the manufacture and importation of narcotic drugs. Stressing the need for international action, the memorandum urged the WILPF to take steps so that the International Opium Conference to be held in Geneva in 1929 should be made effective.

In Nanking the delegates were met by government cars bearing banners of welcome to the Women's International League for Peace and Freedom, and were taken to lunch at the Ministry of Foreign Affairs. The next stage on their journey, north to Peking, found a very different atmosphere. The city was under military rule and no public meetings were allowed. They did, however, meet many different groups of Chinese women, amongst them the YWCA, who implored them to try and stop the sale of arms to China—an important factor in the prolonged civil wars.

Finally, on March 5, 1928, the mission reached Canton. All seemed quiet, the terror had subsided, and there was apparently freedom for all—all, that is, save the absent Communists, who had either escaped to a healthier locality or been shot. It was all the more surprising, therefore, to the WILPF delegates to find that International Women's Day (instituted by the Communists) was still being celebrated on March 8th, thus providing them with an opportunity to address a gathering of over a thousand women. As they had already observed, the feminist movement was far more advanced in China than in Indo-China; and women's organizations were amongst the strongest supporters of the Kuomintang Government. They came to the conclusion that the Nationalist Government should be recognized by foreign powers as the responsible Government of China. As Edith Pye expressed it in her report:

The difference between the Northern and Southern governments seemed to be that, while they were both under the domination of military leaders, Chiang Kai-Shek is definitely working with committees and cabinet and is trying to build up a civil Government to which he is responsible. If recognition of this civil Government as the responsible Government of China is given now by the foreign Powers, we believe that the psychological effect will be a powerful stimulus to those men who are sincerely struggling to bring order out of chaos, and a more stable government would result.

This sensible advice was nullified not by any action of the Western powers but by the Japanese, who from that time on replaced the British and Americans as the chief menace to China's independence. The United States recognized the Nationalist Government in July 1928, the first of the major powers to do so.

The two delegates continued their journey to Japan, where in spite of the growing aggressiveness of the army faction they found a strong anti-militarist movement. They were entertained by Dr Nitobe, an original member of the League of Nations secretariat, and his wife, and met the Christian pacifist leader Kagawa. The Women's Peace Society, as the Japanese WILPF section was called, were eager for friendly co-operation with Chinese women and grateful for the contacts opened to them by the visiting Europeans. They were enthusiastic too about the Kellogg Pact, and promised to try and obtain support for it in Japan.

The problems of the East were brought to western audiences as the delegates travelled back across the United States of America, addressing meetings all the way from California to New York. A public meeting in London, with a Chinese chairwoman, opened a campaign in Europe to follow up the mission to China by international action to check the traffic in opium and arms.

APPENDIX 2

APPEAL issued by WILPF German Section in honour of Romain Rolland and description of voluntary reparation at Arras in 1926. (Recalled by Gertrude Baer in International Circular Letter No. 1, 1945, at the time of Romain Rolland's death.)

'Germany prepares to honour Romain Rolland—Romain Rolland who did not fall a victim to the frenzy of war and victory, Romain Rolland, leader of those between the fronts, guardian of world conscience, interpreter of Young India, advocate of non-violence, creator of Jean-Christophe, synthesis of the French and German spirits.

'German artists and actors, German young people, German broadcasts will honour him, the artist and the man. In all parts of the country the question is raised how best to honour this great European by an act of reconciliation in the spirit of Locarno. The German section of the WILPF will on the day of his 60th birthday give to its French sister section, of which he has been a devoted friend and promoter ever since the outbreak of the war, the first part of a gift designed for the replanting of trees on highways of the devastated areas in Northern France which are still without trees. We cordially appeal to all who want to do homage to Romain Rolland, the artist and man, to contribute to this gift. To honour Romain Rolland means to honour the idea of humanity, to honour Franco-German understanding, to honour our own people.'

This appeal found warm response in the Germany of 1925–26. WILPF local groups, other peace organizations and prominent authors and artists accompanied their contributions with messages of deep appreciation. Nationalists and chauvinists were enraged and packages of insulting letters from them daily found their way into the waste paper basket unread.

On January 29th the first instalment of the gift of voluntary reparations from German women and men was in the hands of the French Section in honour of Romain Rolland and he responded: 'None of the letters I received these days moved me as deeply as that of the German Branch of the WILPF. No present of greater beauty could have been given to me to celebrate my birthday. Your intention of using the gift to plant trees in one of the devastated areas of France is noble and moving. On the 29th a small group of French and foreign friends came to see me. I read them your letter and they were deeply touched by it. Kindly transmit the expression of our profound thanks to the generous contributors. May this fraternal gesture arouse in France a wave of sympathy for the pacifist element in Germany. I trust that the centuries old fight between our two nations is now a thing of the past and that the development of events will in itself lead to bringing them together. I do not underestimate the dangers of the future. But I see them somewhere else. Each day has its concern and its task. Ours will be fulfilled when once we have succeeded in reconciling the two great races of the west.'

A few days later, on February 11th, a gift of 13,000 francs was handed over to the mayor of the town at the City Hall of Arras—a token of voluntary, self-imposed reparation paid for by money from the sale of personal treasures and from the pennies contributed by working women at a time Germany was suffering from run-away inflation, a proof of the desire of German women to do everything in their power to make good the damage done by German troops and to work towards understanding with the French people. Moved by the sincerity of the words of the German delegates, the mayor accepted the contribution and assured them that the trees would be planted on a playground laid out on previous trenches in a section of the town inhabited by the working population. The French press of all political opinions including the official Paris Temps published long and appreciative articles on the reception at Arras, commenting on the speeches made by the French officials and the German representatives. One paper said: '. . . It is not too early for such a gesture of reconciliation. It is never too early for an act of justice and kindness.'

CHAPTER 6

INTERNATIONAL CONFERENCES

*Honolulu Congress 1928—Chemical Warfare—Frankfurt
Conference 1929—London Conference on Minorities 1929
—Vienna Conference 1929—Opium Conference, Geneva
1930*

The Far Eastern links of the WILPF were further strengthened at this
time with the holding of an Interim Congress at Honolulu in August
1928 for the benefit of members who were too far away to attend
European Congresses, but many of whom would then be in Honolulu
for a Pan-Pacific Women's Conference. Jane Addams presided at both
these gatherings, and one effect of her presence was the enrolment of
over a hundred new members in the Honolulu branch of the League
after she had spoken about its work at a public meeting. Delegates to
the Congress from the United States, Australia, New Zealand and the
Far East included Eleanor Moore, secretary of the Australian section
and the president of the Japanese section, Mrs Inoye.

The late 1920s as a whole were marked by a number of international
conferences organized by the WILPF on a more specialized basis than
had hitherto been attempted. They showed a cross-section of the wide
fields in which the League might claim competence to express an
intelligent concern, based upon the knowledge built up through study
and expert consultation over the first decade of its history. One of these
concerns was the development of chemical warfare which, if unchecked, could change the very nature of 'war' as previously known
and bring the battlefield into every civilian home. New threats called
for new efforts to break through the smokescreen of official secrecy
and public ignorance.

Dr Gertrud Woker, Professor of Chemistry at the University of
Berne and a member of the WILPF Committee on Chemical Warfare,
had seen something of the effects of this new research when she
visited the American Gas Armament Center in Maryland, together
with Dr Naima Sahlbom, Professor of Minerology at Stockholm,
whilst attending an international congress of scientists in Washington
in 1924. She was anxious that the WILPF should call together a

conference of experts to discuss Modern Methods of Warfare. On her return journey to Switzerland she consulted members of the French section in Paris, spoke at a large public meeting, and succeeded in enlisting the support of eminent scientists including Dr Paul Langevin, a friend of Albert Einstein. After a further meeting in Berlin in October 1924, a campaign was launched throughout the WILPF national sections appealing to scientists to condemn the misuse of scientific research for war purposes and refuse to serve war with their knowledge.

It was a great disappointment to the Norwegian section when Dr Fridtjof Nansen refused to sign the WILPF appeal on the ground that it was impossible to forbid the use of science in war, or to make rules of warfare, and that the only hope lay in making war itself illegal. The Swedish Red Cross, on the other hand, responded sympathetically, emphasized its opposition to the use of poison gas and urged further steps towards its prohibition.

The League of Nations Conference on Control of Traffic in Arms which took place at Geneva in May 1925 brought fresh opportunities for propaganda. The question of chemical warfare was not on the agenda, but the WILPF Committee on Chemical Warfare sent a memorandum on the dangers of modern armaments to every delegation. Whether this had any influence on the leader of the American delegation, who unexpectedly raised the question later in the proceedings, it is impossible to say. He announced his Government's promise to abstain from the export of chemical munitions or of raw material for their manufacture (although there was no mention of the United States' own well-stocked chemical arsenal). The German delegation then proposed an agreement to prohibit the use of poison gas in war, and a Convention in these terms was adopted by the conference. By the following year twenty-seven states had ratified the Geneva Convention, and WILPF national sections continued their campaigns to urge that all governments should accede to it.

Efforts to convene a conference of experts were also continuing, particularly in Germany, and in January 1929 the WILPF Conference on Modern Methods of Warfare assembled at Frankfurt. It was sponsored by a distinguished international committee which included Lord Cecil, John Galsworthy, Gilbert Murray, Bertrand Russell (Britain); Albert Einstein, Käthe Kollwitz, Otto Meyerhof (Germany); Paul Langevin, Romain Rolland (France); Roger Baldwin, David Starr Jordan (USA); Senator Lafontaine, Paul Otlet (Belgium); Dr Axel

Højer, Selma Lägerlof (Sweden). Other sponsors came from Austria, Czechoslovakia, Denmark, Hungary, Norway and Switzerland. Three hundred delegates from seventy organizations attended the conference, representing nine countries. Amongst the panel of experts participating were the German toxicologist Professor Lewin; Captain C. J. Brunskog of the Swedish Academy of Military Science; the French economist Professor Delaisi; and the head of the Swiss Gas Protection Institute, Dr Steck. Three resolutions were adopted, with only nine dissenting votes:

1. That there is no effective protection against the methods of destruction which science has put at the service of war.
2. That the agreements entered into by the Governments prohibiting these methods do not offer any guarantee of protection because the nations have already morally broken their agreements by preparing the material necessary for this form of war.
3. That the next war in extending its destruction to the civil population will be a war of simultaneous extermination of the people and threatens to destroy all civilization.

It was recommended as an urgent duty that information about the nature of modern warfare should be made known to the peoples of all countries and public opinion mobilized in favour of disarmament. Out of the Frankfurt Conference, it may be surmised, grew the world-wide, popular pressure over the next three years demanding that the Preparatory Disarmament Commission of the League of Nations should fulfil its purpose and summon a World Disarmament Conference. At its sixth session in Geneva in May 1929, the Disarmament Commission adopted a proposal for the prohibition of chemical warfare subject to reciprocity, and the absolute prohibition of bacteriological warfare, and recommended that states which had not yet done so should ratify the 1925 Protocol. It did not agree to the prohibition of preparations for chemical warfare in peace-time. Nevertheless, the organizers of the Frankfurt Conference must have felt satisfied that they had achieved the aim of informing, and to some degree influencing, public opinion about the realities of Modern Methods of Warfare.

Another important area of work during this period concerned the Minority problems of Eastern Europe. At the Dublin Congress in 1926 a Minorities Commission had been appointed and during the three years before the next Congress reconciliation work was undertaken at points of conflict in Germany, Denmark and Poland and in many of the Baltic and Balkan states. A joint German-Scandinavian conference took place at the Schleswig border towns of Flensberg and Søderborg in September 1926. In the spring of 1927 a similar conference was held at the German-Polish boundaries of Kattowitz and Beuthen, as a result of which a mixed border commission was set up. A British WILPF member, Mosa Anderson, spent two months in the Balkans from December 1927 to February 1928, to meet members of the Bulgarian section and if possible to found a new section in Yugoslavia. On her return journey Mosa Anderson stopped in Geneva for talks with League of Nations officials. The heads of the Balkan and South-East European departments of the Minorities section requested copies of her report for submission to the League Council.

This carefully considered and detailed document was of great value in clarifying a highly complex situation. In Yugoslavia, the problem of the status of the Macedonians in Serbia dominated all others. It was alleged that the frequent disturbances amongst the Macedonians were largely due to Bulgarian instigation. There seemed little prospect of friendly co-operation between Yugoslav and Bulgarian women. Their absorption in local and national problems also made it difficult to interest the women in the kind of internationalism practised by the WILPF, although some of them were already familiar with it through attendance at Congresses and summer schools. Mosa Anderson was successful, however, in getting a committee formed in Belgrade and she met interested groups, both Slovene and Croatian, in Zagreb. Other groups in the Hungarian enclave north of the Danube and in Bosnia were also eager to be put in touch with the WILPF.

Bulgaria, too, was dominated by the Macedonian question and by a sense of grievance from her losses to Rumania under the Treaty of Neuilly. Although a large WILPF section existed, with about 7,000 members, Miss Anderson was forced to conclude that the women were mainly concerned to bring their own complaints before the women of other countries and to get support for their cause at the League of Nations. In meetings with both Bulgars and Macedonians, she urged the need to find peaceful solutions and to avoid arousing antagonisms by the use of violence. Their answer to this plea was to point to the case of Ireland, where the use of armed force appeared to have won the freedom hitherto denied! Miss Anderson reported her conviction that unless the Macedonian question could be solved by outside intervention, preferably through the League of Nations, further violence in the Balkans seemed inevitable.

The particular interest of the British section in Minorities questions led to the organization of a conference in London in March 1929 on Minorities and the League of Nations. Its main purpose was to consider the procedure of the League of Nations in carrying out the terms of the Minorities Treaties, which was felt to be quite inadequate. Petitions from minorities were heard by 'committees of three' set up on a rotating system by the League Council, and so great were the number of grievances that 150 committees were appointed between 1921 and 1929. A Committee on Minority Procedure was then set up, to which the London Conference of the WILPF now prepared to make recommendations. It had the advice of specialist lecturers who included Sir Willoughby Dickinson and Philip Noel-Baker of Britain; Mme Bakker van Bosse (Holland); Professor René Brunet (France); and Dr Erwin Loewenfeld (Germany).

The conference recommended that in all cases claiming a breach of the Treaties the minority should be informed of its government's reply; that all petitions dealt with, together with governments' replies and reports of action taken, should be presented to the League Council and published in official documents; and that an advisory committee to the Council be appointed, consisting of men and women with special knowledge of Minority questions from the point of view of both majorities and minorities.

Simultaneously with the London Conference, the WILPF Committee on East European Problems was calling a conference in Vienna of the people most directly concerned—the 'minority' countries themselves. In preparation for this, Camille Drevet spent two months at the beginning of the year travelling in Rumania, Poland and the Ukraine, Lithuania, Latvia and Estonia. No WILPF sections existed in the latter three countries, but in all of them she found interest in the forthcoming Vienna conference and willingness to send representatives. In Rumania, it was encouraging to find WILPF groups which included both Christians and Jews—a form of co-operation which was regrettably rare. In her report Camille Drevet urged the WILPF to draw attention to the dangers of anti-semitism in Eastern Europe. Her general conclusion was that the problems of Eastern Europe could best be solved through a federation of autonomous states, freed from subservience to rival power blocs and linked together by economic and social organizations. But, she pointed out, such a federation could only be formed when dictatorships were replaced by democratic governments.

Thirteen countries were represented at the Vienna Conference in

March 1929 and the main questions under consideration were Polish-Lithuanian, Polish-Ukrainian, Polish-German, Rumanian-Hungarian and Bulgarian-Yugoslav relations. To achieve a subordination of such conflicting national interests in favour of a policy of international understanding might well seem an impossible task. Gertrude Baer reported later, however, that 'owing to the fine spirit which prevailed during all the sessions, the Conference—though sometimes only after long and heated debate—succeeded in each case in finding some solution'. No resolutions were adopted, but a working plan submitted to the delegates was unanimously accepted. It included proposals for facilitation of border traffic; equality of treatment in mixed populations; teaching of the mother language wherever asked for, and teaching in two languages in all border districts; abolition of military training and of compulsory attendance at national demonstrations; amnesty for political prisoners. Whilst these proposals might sound like a counsel of perfection, it was hoped that their definition would provide a focus for bringing together the women concerned in a co-operative effort to remove the sources of friction between them. The Vienna Conference was another step forward in the aim of the WILPF to link the women of Eastern Europe in a common organization.

Meanwhile, the League was following up its previous efforts in yet another field—the enquiry into opium-control which was set in motion by Edith Pye and Camille Drevet in 1927. Miss Pye noted that since their mission the Nationalist Government seemed to have established itself and to be tackling the vast problems facing a united China. Two women had been appointed to the Legislative Council and one, Mme Sun Yat Sen, was a member of the Central Executive. New civil and criminal codes had been enacted: the former embodied equal rights of inheritance for women with men; the latter contained clauses to enforce the complete suppression of opium growing and smoking in China.

Nevertheless, the menace of narcotics was far from obliterated. Although opium-smoking was on the decrease, the illicit traffic in noxious drugs was growing yearly. The League of Nations Advisory Committee on Opium and Dangerous Drugs presented a startling exposure of this traffic in January 1929. One Dutch firm, the Naarden Chemical Co., had over two years exported 955 kilos of morphine, 3,040 kilos of heroin and 90 kilos of cocaine, two-thirds of the total exports going to China. The amount of heroin was roughly equivalent to the medical needs of the whole world for one year. About 60 per cent of the drugs had been bought by the Dutch firm from Switzerland, the other supplies coming from Austria, Britain, France and Germany.

In view of these revelations, and following a second appeal from the National Anti-Opium Association of China in April 1929, the WILPF Executive Committee meeting in Geneva that month decided to hold an international conference on opium the following year. National sections were asked to run campaigns and conferences in their own countries to inform public opinion on the question. The British and German sections both organized successful national conferences in November 1929, and other conferences were held during the winter in France, Holland and the USA.

The International Conference on Opium and Narcotics opened in Geneva on April 28, 1930. Reports were given by the WILPF national sections concerned and by speakers from China, Egypt, India and Japan. Special sessions dealt with medical, political and international aspects of the problem, and in conclusion the whole field was surveyed by Mr A. E. Blanco of the Anti-Opium Bureau in Geneva. Recommendations were sent to the League of Nations Council, requesting an early conference of manufacturing countries to draw up a Convention on Limitation of Manufacture of Narcotics, in consultation with the non-manufacturing countries.

The published report of the WILPF conference, *Opium and Noxious Drugs*, aroused considerable interest both in the press and within the League of Nations. Mr Blanco described the conference as a 'brilliant success'. The resolutions, and one complete paper, were published in the journal of the International Narcotic Education Association in October 1930, with the comment:

The decisions taken by the Council [of the League of Nations] were of the utmost importance and it must be noted that they were favourably influenced by the resolutions adopted by the conference of the Women's International League for Peace and Freedom.

In May 1931 the League of Nations adopted a Convention providing for the limitation of manufacture of narcotic drugs to actual medical and scientific needs. For enforcement purposes a Permanent Central Board and a Supervisory Body were set up. The control of poppy cultivation was not included in the Convention, but the major object of the anti-opium campaigns had been won and the WILPF could justly claim to have played a significant part in this achievement. The League did not now rest on its laurels, however, and consider its job done. This would only be completed when the 1931 Convention was ratified by the requisite number of states, and to this end a further call now went out to national sections to press on their governments the need for ratification.

CHAPTER 7

THE VOICE OF WOMEN

Women at the League of Nations—Nationality of Married Women—Mandates Commission—Progress of the WILPF—'Communist' Allegations—Rosika Schwimmer—Women and the US Navy Bill

---

After the success of the anti-opium campaign, it may be opportune at this point to look again at the relations of the WILPF with the League of Nations, and particularly at the part played by women in the latter organization. Under the stress of pressing international problems since the First World War, it was inevitable that the complementary aim of the WILPF—that women should have freedom to use their gifts in society equally with men—should receive less notice, particularly since the granting of franchise to women in many countries had cut away one of the main planks in the feminist platform. But the battle for women's equal status was far from won—and where could it better be fought than in the new League of Nations? Here, if anywhere, the voice of women must surely be heard in the fashioning of an international order based not upon the old values of power politics but, as Jane Addams used to express it, on 'ministration to human needs'.

In practice, however, the women's voice was no more than a whisper in the assembly of nations. A Danish WILPF member, Henni Forchhammer, had been an adviser for her Government at the League of Nations since the first Assembly in 1920, which boasted also one woman substitute delegate from Norway and one from Sweden, but the increase of representation by women was barely perceptible during the League's first decade. In 1921 the Scandinavian women were joined by a colleague from Rumania, and in 1922 both Britain and Australia sent a woman as substitute delegate. The number then remained stationary until the entry of Germany into the League in 1926 and the appointment of Dr Bäumer as technical adviser to the German delegation. The following year two more countries, Finland and Hungary, included a woman in their delegations. By 1929 there was a grand total of fifteen women attending the Tenth Assembly as delegates and technical advisers, seven of whom were active WILPF members.

In an attempt to remedy this unsatisfactory state of affairs a Joint Standing Committee of women's organizations was set up in 1925, at the invitation of the International Council of Women, for the purpose of securing the appointment of women to the international and expert Committees of the League of Nations. A Council for the representation of women in the League of Nations had already existed in Britain since 1919, and largely owing to this body's efforts the British Government adopted the practice of always sending a woman substitute delegate to the LON Assembly. The Women's International League for Peace and Freedom joined the International Council of Women and six other international organizations on the Joint Committee. Based on 1926 records, the Committee issued a list of League of Nations Commissions showing the proportionate representation of men and women. For example: the Health Committee of 16 members had one woman, Dr Alice Hamilton (WILPF American section); the Mandates Commission of 10 had one woman; the Advisory Committee on Traffic in Women and Protection and Welfare of Children and Young People had three women out of 11 members, although its specialist sub-committees showed approximately equal representation. The legal, financial and political commissions had no woman members at all. It was not until 1929 that for the first time women were appointed to other commissions than the Fifth, dealing with the welfare of women and children: Mrs H. M. Swanwick (WILPF British section) on the Political Commission; Mrs Mary Hamilton, MP, on the Economic Commission; and Miss Agnes Macphail, MP (WILPF Canadian section), on the Disarmament Commission.

In 1926 Mrs Corbett Ashby of the International Suffrage Alliance proposed that the Joint Committee should consider also the position of women in the League Secretariat. A letter was sent to Sir Eric Drummond, head of the secretariat, pointing to the inequality of treatment in the case of an American woman librarian whose contract was not renewed after seven years' service on the grounds that the United States was not a member of the League, while that of a male American in the secretariat was renewed. Indeed, this inequality persisted right through the League's history. Although the Covenant laid down that all positions under the League were to be open equally to women as to men, only one woman ever achieved high office in the secretariat: Dame Rachel Crowdy as chief of the Social section. In

December 1928, when the renewal of Dame Rachel's contract was also in doubt, the Committee again took action and the contract was renewed.

Another task of the Joint Committee was to draw up a panel of suitable women for recommendation as members of the various committees and commissions of the League of Nations, and in this connection an interesting difference of opinion was revealed among the constituent organizations. Catherine Marshall, representing the WILPF, was insistent that such appointments should be made for the correct reasons. She wrote to the secretary of another co-operating body in December 1928:

I see that the point of principle about which I am so keen was not brought forward. I think we should not content ourselves with asking that *a* woman should be appointed on these bodies. If there is no woman adequately qualified I don't want to urge the appointment of '*a* woman' for the sake of having a woman on—I do not think it is sound policy to put anyone on just because she is a woman any more than it is justifiable to keep anyone off just because she is a woman. All these Committees and Commissions should be open to 'men and women' on equal terms, according to individual merit and qualification; and the best judge of anyone's qualification for a particular post is the organization which specializes in that particular work.

She also confided to Madeleine Doty the following June that 'most members of the Committee did not mind what woman, standing for what policy, was on, so long as 'the' woman's point of view (hateful phrase!) was represented', and she deplored the tendency in LON officials to consult women, when they did so at all, collectively in order to ascertain 'The Woman's' view. She continued:

I think this is a way of looking at things which we must guard against. We must teach men that women have just as much right to any number of different opinions as men have, but that they have never seen any one of those opinions completely, with both eyes, until they know how it looks to women as well as to men.

This need for looking at problems 'with both eyes' was surely the real justification for women, as women, to seek to make their voices heard in international affairs.

One matter which was naturally of special interest to women's organizations was the recurring problem of harmonizing the laws of various countries relating to the nationality of married women: in some cases women marrying nationals of other states found themselves with no nationality at all, whereas others had dual nationality. An International Committee of Women was set up (on which the WILPF was represented and of which Chrystal Macmillan was chairman), which addressed a series of memoranda to governments and to the League of Nations, urging the need for an international conference on the matter. After the passing of the Swedish Nationality Law in 1924 the Swedish Government was requested to bring the women's proposal before the League of Nations. This was done the following year and a sub-committee was set up to consider the general question of nationality. But it was made clear in communications received by the women's Committee from the International Court of Justice and the International Law Association that no satisfactory conclusion could be reached while so many different marriage laws existed.

The Dublin Congress of the WILPF had appointed Mrs Kathleen Innes and Catherine Marshall (both of the British section) as referents for League of Nations Affairs. Writing on the work of the Seventh Assembly in *Pax International*, October 1926, Catherine Marshall singled out for the special attention of the WILPF the questions of Arbitration and Conciliation; Disarmament; the proposed International Economic Conference; Mandates; and Minorities. She noted also that the WILPF's own specialist on emigration, Mme Dombska, had represented the Polish Government at the International Conference on Migration which had recently taken place in Geneva.

The British section took action with regard to the Mandates Commission in 1926, following attacks on the Commission by Britain's representative in the League Council, Sir Austen Chamberlain. The British Government violently opposed a proposal of the Commission to issue a detailed questionnaire to mandatory powers and also to hear personal petitions from mandated territories. These proposals were regarded as 'unwarranted interference' on the part of the Mandates Commission. The WILPF British section at once called together a group of experts and a letter of protest at the Government's attitude was published in *The Times* on December 4, 1926. A memorandum was also distributed to Members of Parliament, leading to a debate in the House of Commons on December 14th and an assurance from the Government that Britain would in no way obstruct the work of the Mandates Commission.

The British section was also concerned about the use of forced labour in colonial territories, and organized a conference on the subject in 1927. The matter was taken up internationally by women's organizations, and in May a memorandum was submitted by the International Council of Women to the Committee of Experts on Forced Labour of the International Labour Office. This urged that, pending the total abolition of the system, forced labour for essential public services should only be exacted when voluntary labour was unobtainable; and that the proportion of men taken from any one district should be strictly limited. In the words of the memorandum:

We venture to suggest that the broad principle that the claims of tribal and family life should always dominate, should be the basis of any Convention drawn up to regulate forced labour for public services.

Here was an instance of an obvious women's priority which might well have been overlooked by a body composed entirely of men.

In 1926 the membership of the WILPF was estimated by the Geneva office at 50,000 women in 40 countries. This was an impressive progress in less than ten years of peace, bearing in mind the high intellectual and moral standard of the organization; it had never sought to become a mass movement. But as the influence and size of the WILPF increased, its resources were considerably strained. When Mary Sheepshanks replaced Madeleine Doty as International Secretary in the summer of 1927 she had one assistant secretary, Anne Zeublin; a translator, Blanche Lévy; a part-time book-keeper, Mme Hubert; and a junior assistant, Louisa Jaques, who had joined the office when it first opened in 1919 and was to remain there until after the Second World War. Previously, *Pax International* had also been edited by the International Secretary, but Madeleine Doty on her resignation agreed to continue the editing until she returned to the United States in November 1931. In addition, the Maison Internationale had a Directrice who supervised the domestic and social affairs of the house. Sophie Hattinga-Raven resigned in 1929 after four years as Directrice; she was replaced by another Dutch woman, Mme Henriette Kuipers.

Financially, the Maison Internationale could never have continued to function but for the generosity of Jane Addams, who personally guaranteed a regular sum of 500 dollars a month to Geneva; this sum was made up partly from subscriptions of American international members and partly out of her own resources. In 1930, the US section took over responsibility for the guarantee. It was therefore true to say that, although the WILPF had been born of the travail of Europe, it was nurtured by America. This did not mean, however, that the American influence ever outweighed the European. The international spirit of the League was stronger than its component national parts. The Executive Committee was elected on an individual and not a national basis and its composition was always very mixed: in 1929, for instance, it comprised 2 Americans (including Jane Addams as honorary President), 1 German, 1 Swiss, 2 British, 2 French, 1 Austrian, 1 Canadian, 1 Dutch, 1 Swede and 1 Czech.

There were, of course, always stronger and weaker sections. In Europe, the British, German and Scandinavian groups predominated in numbers and activity. The French section, in spite of its much smaller membership, was a far from negligible influence; Gabrielle Duchêne and Andrée Jouve, for instance, were amongst the leaders of the League for a great many years. The Central European and Baltic sections had a much more difficult time. Austria, with its two separate groups in Vienna and Graz working respectively for humanitarian and political ends, was never a unified section. Poland, influenced by strong nationalist feeling, sometimes found itself in conflict with the international position taken by the League. Czechoslovakia had separate German and Czech groups. Of the East European countries only Hungary—where the WILPF member Anna Kethly was the sole woman in parliament—seemed ready to accept the full programme of the League and to withstand the pressures of nationalism. After the rise of Fascism in Italy in 1922 it was increasingly difficult for Italian women to co-operate with the League except on an individual basis.

It would be absurd to pretend that the WILPF with its wide variety of nationalities, temperaments and opinions did not suffer from clashes over both organization and policy. More or less violent disagreements were a regular feature of life in the League. The brunt of such differences inevitably fell on the shoulders of the International Secretary, which may account in part for the short time in office, averaging not more than two years, of the secretaries during this period. There were of course other reasons. Women like Emily Greene Balch and Mary Sheepshanks, for instance, had heavy responsibilities in their own countries which they could not afford to neglect for too long. The Hungarian Vilma Glücklich, on the other hand, of a sensitive and impetuous nature, suffered deeply from the strains of friction and criticism, which her failing health did not help her to withstand.

Her successor Madeleine Doty, with an American zeal for organization and new methods, was perhaps more likely to voice her own dissatisfaction than to suffer it from others. Mary Sheepshanks at least started her job in Geneva without illusions. She wrote to Madeleine Doty in June 1927:

I left my job last Friday, and on Saturday went to my first WIL meeting and was much concerned at the fresh friction between France and England—the difficulties of international relations are great, and nowhere greater than in a pacifist organization.

If the international spirit of the WILPF survived such stresses, it was due to the exercise of a considerable restraint, devotion and tolerance on the part of the international officers.

Another hazard weathered by the League during these years was the not infrequent accusation that it was a 'communist' organization. In 1928 the 'International Entente against the Third International', a right-wing pressure group in Geneva, included the WILPF in a list of organizations alleged to be directly linked to the Comintern. *Pax International* in December 1928 dismissed the charge as ludicrous:

In May 1927 when a Russian delegation for the first time attended the Economic Commission of the League of Nations, we sent a letter to them inviting the women of the delegation to come and discuss our programme of peace and freedom, but we never received an answer. When the Russians came to Geneva to attend the Disarmament Commission of the League in December 1927, and put forward their peace proposals, we expressed our appreciation.

This is the only connection we have had officially with Russia.

After an exchange of lawyers' letters the Entente withdrew its charges.

Another interesting case arose at about this time, concerning the application for American citizenship of Rosika Schwimmer, whose history since the time of the Hague Congress may here be briefly recounted. In 1918 she had joined Count Karolyi's National Council in the post-war democratic Government of Hungary, and was appointed ambassador to Switzerland—the first woman ambassador in history. This triumph was short-lived, for the Karolyi Government was followed first by a Communist régime, under which she refused to serve, and then by the Fascist white terror. Rosika Schwimmer was obliged to flee to America as a political refugee, but her resettlement there did not end the troubles of this turbulent, gifted and unhappy woman. She resigned from the WILPF in 1927, declaring that the League did not have 'the courage of its convictions'—if, indeed, it had any convictions. The compromising spirit of the WILPF was certainly far removed from Mme Schwimmer's extreme individualism. In October 1927 the Chicago district court rejected her application for citizenship because of her refusal to affirm, as the oath demanded, that she would bear arms in defence of the country. The Illinois Court of Appeal reversed this decision, on the grounds that the question of a woman having to bear arms was purely hypothetical, but when the case was reviewed by the Supreme Court in May 1929 the verdict was again unfavourable.

Chief Justice Oliver Wendell Holmes issued a powerful dissenting opinion, in which he observed that Mme Schwimmer seemed to be 'a woman of superior character and intelligence, obviously more than ordinarily desirable as a citizen of the United States'. Rosika Schwimmer's outspoken statements in court had certainly told against her, as when she declared:

I am an uncompromising pacifist. I am an absolute atheist. I have no sense of nationalism, only a cosmic consciousness of belonging to the human family.

The New York branch of the WILPF, as well as members in other sections, protested strongly against the Court's decision. But it was not until 1946, seventeen years later, that the verdict was quashed and citizenship granted to Rosika Schwimmer.

An example of the power of public opinion, in this instance women's opinion, to influence events occurred in 1928 in connection with the proposed US Navy Bill to authorize the building of 75 cruisers. So great was the public outcry against the Bill that the number of new battleships was reduced to 13, but even this modified measure failed to get through Congress. The WILPF American section, which was in the vanguard of protest, continued to campaign for the total abandonment of the Bill. A tribute to the effectiveness of their campaign came from an unexpected quarter, in a comment by the British *Daily Express* quoted in *Pax International* in June 1929. Referring to the fact that the women of America were blamed for the difficulty experienced at Washington in getting the Cruiser Bill passed, the paper said:

As a portent of the growing power of women in national and international affairs the incident, however it ends, is deeply significant. There is no country where women have the vote in which similar vetoes or obstacles may not be experienced on issues which they conceive to be essentially moral issues; women may then easily work and vote as a sex. Nobody pays much attention to the present League of Nations. But an International League of Women, actively vehement in the politics of all countries, would be a power indeed. It might come very near to abolishing war for ever.

It is interesting that a mass-circulation newspaper should single out for the corporate attention of women 'essentially moral issues', since women are popularly believed to have a less absolute moral sense than men. Whereas a man will live, work, die and if he deems it necessary *destroy* for the sake of a principle, a woman—it is claimed—will always at the critical point hesitate and compromise, sacrificing the principle in favour of more immediate material good. This generalization is probably broadly true, the only point at issue being whether any principle can be regarded as 'moral' which feeds on the blood sacrifice of others. By this criterion the woman's morality is higher than the man's, and the *Daily Express* was surely right in believing that it is on the moral plane of human preservation and betterment, in a spiritual as well as a material sense, that women will one day rise together and sweep away for ever the degradation of war.

CHAPTER 8

THE MACHINERY OF PEACE

Prague Congress 1929—Kellogg Pact—International Disarmament—Internal Disarmament—Economic Commission—WILPF Constitution—Deputation to Austria

The Sixth International Congress of the WILPF took place at Prague from August 23 to 29, 1929. This *venue* was chosen both in order to maintain the links with East European women and because of the 'strategic' importance of this part of Europe, which seemed more and more to be taking on the nature of a bloc against the Soviet Union.

The choice was amply justified by the wide representation of the 209 delegates from 26 countries, as well as three Chinese and two Indian women. Amongst the delegates the WILPF was proud to count six Members of Parliament: Emmy Freundlich (Austria), Lucie Déjardin (Belgium), Ellen Wilkinson (Britain), Agnes Macphail (Canada), Helga Larssen (Denmark) and Margaret Stigmann (Germany). Tributes were paid to two pioneers of the League who had died since the last Congress: Vilma Glücklich and Aletta Jacobs. The Congress was also saddened to receive the resignation of Jane Addams as International President. She had borne the burden of this responsibility for fifteen years and the League could no longer insist that such heavy demands on her time, thought and energy should continue to be made. There was some consolation in her acceptance of the office of honorary life President. It was decided not to attempt to replace her by another working president, but instead to appoint three co-chairmen of equal responsibility. The Executive Committee following the Congress elected Gertrude Baer (Germany), Emily Balch (USA) and Clara Ragaz (Switzerland). Whether this somewhat cumbersome arrangement was the most satisfactory that could be made remained to be seen, but it served as a means of harnessing the best judgments not only of different national groups but of differing lines of opinion within the League—an essential 'safeguard', it was believed, for maintaining full freedom of expression.

The theme of the Prague Congress, 'Renunciation of War—What

Follows?', sprang naturally from the Kellogg Pact of 1928. In her farewell presidential address Jane Addams spoke of the long pacifist tradition among Slav peoples, notably in the Bohemian Church of the Brethren which rejected all violence, and of the famous Czech educator Comenius whose pan-humanist doctrines had won him such renown that he was offered many honours outside Bohemia, including the presidency of Harvard University. She praised the statesmanship of President Masaryk, whose influence in the League of Nations together with Briand, Streseman, Stauning of Denmark, Ramsay MacDonald and President Hoover, offered great hopes of better international relations, and in conclusion quoted Masaryk's remarks on democracy:

In a true democracy, war and revolution will be obsolete and inadequate, for democracy is a system of life. Life means work and a system of work: and work, unostentatious work, is peace.

In this changing world picture the emphasis of the WILPF swung to some extent away from the *personal* solution of violent situations towards the creation of an effective *machinery* of peace. It may be useful at this point to recount briefly the circumstances which led to the signing of the Kellogg Pact.

On April 6, 1927, the French Foreign Minister Briand proposed that France and the United States should sign a treaty mutually 'renouncing war'. The US State Department had a few weeks earlier refused a similar proposal from Switzerland. Now, however, pressure of public opinion—in which the US section of the WILPF played a prominent part, with a petition to the President bearing 30,000 signatures—forced the Government into consideration of the new offer. On August 27, 1928, the Kellogg-Briand Pact for the Renunciation of War was signed in Paris by fifteen countries; all other nations were invited to sign. The Pact had two clauses: the renunciation of war as an instrument of policy; and a pledge that all disputes and conflicts, 'of whatever nature or whatever origin', should be settled by pacific means. It also had two serious omissions: it made no mention of 'defensive' war; and it failed to define 'aggression'.

The opinion of the majority of international lawyers was that the Kellogg Pact appeared to be morally rather than legally binding, and it was clear from the start that the powers were making reservations to their commitment—the USA, for instance, by invoking the Monroe Doctrine; and Britain by retaining the right to act 'as she deemed necessary' in defence of the British Empire. As Mary Sheepshanks commented in *Pax International*, August 1928: 'The test of the genuineness of the pact will be the readiness to disarm of those who sign it.'

The second meeting of the Preparatory Disarmament Commission in November 1927 issued a draft Convention on Disarmament, which did no more than state the points of difference and agreement between the powers, and then adjourned. When it reassembled in March 1928, Litvinoff of Russia flung down his bombshell offer of immediate, total disarmament. The peace movements everywhere rose with joy at what seemed only a natural corollary to the Kellogg Pact. Governments were more suspicious. Was this a genuine breakthrough or a colossal propaganda bluff? Nobody knew, because nobody was willing to find out. Nineteen nations in the Disarmament Commission spoke against the Russian proposal and it was never accepted for discussion.

But public pressure for a World Disarmament Conference was mounting rapidly. In the summer of 1928, on the initiative of the Irish section, the WILPF started an intensive campaign to make the Kellogg Pact a reality and institute measures for disarmament. On September 11th a deputation from the WILPF, representing ten nationalities, was received by the President of the League of Nations Assembly, Herluf Zahle of Denmark. Mr Zahle acknowledged the 'immense and meritorious' work of the WILPF since its foundation, but offered little encouragement for its advancement. On the contrary, he issued a warning:

I fear, ladies, that in advocating solutions of a too positive character, too brusque, too imperfectly adapted to the present-day world, you may add to the difficulties which the men who are responsible for their countries' destinies are trying to smooth away by slow and loyal means. . . .

At least, in this somewhat ungallant reply, the President placed responsibility for the failures of the Disarmament Commission squarely on his own sex, although without apparently drawing the inference that a more 'positive' approach might have helped!

The Ninth Assembly of the League of Nations brought some small encouragement with the approval of the General Act for the pacific settlement of disputes, based on a series of 'model treaties' drawn up by the LON Arbitration and Security Committee. Only two signatures were needed to give the Act the force of a Convention, and by 1931 eighteen states had signed. The WILPF generally welcomed this further evidence of willingness by the powers to bring all disputes to arbitration and continued its world disarmament campaign with new vigour. Amongst the national sections, Australia, Canada and New Zealand were concerned with education for the abolition of conscription; France strongly opposed, and defeated, a Bill for the wartime mobilization of women. The Scandinavian countries, with the aid of a grant from the Nobel Committee, arranged a series of annual study courses on international affairs; lectures were also given in many schools. The German section remained strongly opposed to any return of Germany's former colonies and any steps to rearm their country; on the positive side, the section continued its valuable reconciliation work with France and Poland. The British-American Women's Crusade, linking a number of organizations, pressed for the signing of the Kellogg Pact without reservations. In Britain pressure continued for the signing of the optional clause of the Permanent Court of International Justice and for the Preparatory Disarmament Commission to consider the *reduction* as well as the limitation of arms.

This question of arms reduction immediately came to the fore when the Commission was reconvened in April 1929. No less a person than President Hoover had instructed his representative that the Kellogg Pact was a means to facilitate disarmament. Now Russia stepped in again with fresh proposals, this time for large-scale but not total disarmament: a 50 per cent reduction by the Group I powers and a permanent international control commission. This did not sound like propaganda, and received the backing of a minority which included China, Germany and Turkey, but the majority decision went against discussion of the proposal and the Commission reverted instead to further consideration of the 1927 draft Convention. Another rejected proposal was made by China in the form of a resolution for the universal abolition of conscription. On this issue, a WILPF deputation visited the Chinese Nationalist representative, General Tsiang Tsoping, with a resolution from the Executive Committee in support of his proposal.

In Britain at any rate the peace organizations found fresh grounds for hope in the summer of 1929 with the return of the second Labour Government. The Women's Peace Crusade had campaigned vigorously for a 'Parliament of Peacemakers', under the able leadership of Agatha Harrison—a WILPF member and Quaker who was later to become internationally known for her part in the Indian independence movement. Questions were put to candidates in 300 constituencies as to whether they would support the Kellogg Pact; vote to sign the optional clause; agree to the settlement of disputes by peaceful means; urge a large measure of disarmament; and demand the immediate evacuation of the Rhineland. The Labour Party, reported *Pax International* in July 1929, had promised if they were returned to power to reduce armaments, sign the optional clause, negotiate for naval disarmament and give more active support for the League of Nations. 'This year's assembly of the League of Nations', the paper commented, 'ought to be much more interesting than any meeting since 1924 for England will be helping not blocking progress.' The Tenth Assembly, by all accounts, was the best in the history of the League of Nations and Britain did sign the optional clause in September 1929, together with the Commonwealth countries and eight other states; 25 countries had previously done so.

Meanwhile, on July 24th the General Pact for the Renunciation of War (the Kellogg Pact) came into effect by proclamation of President Hoover and with the adherence of 62 states. Could anything further remain to be done, to usher in the era of peace and progress? The WILPF certainly thought so. Discussion at the Prague Congress fell into two main sections: the machinery of *international* peace and the machinery of *internal* peace, since it was clear that no amount of planning for peaceful relations between countries could hope to succeed if conditions of social justice did not prevail within the national communities concerned.

The machinery of international peace dealt with the related questions of arbitration, security and disarmament. This triple poser was intractable, if not insoluble: How could arbitration be accepted without a feeling of security? How could security be achieved without a measure of disarmament? How, equally, could disarmament be achieved without a visible security? Kathleen Courtney traced the search for security through the Treaties of Mutual Assistance, the Geneva Protocol, the Locarno Treaties and now the Kellogg Pact. The answer had not been found. How, asked Miss Courtney, could security be achieved if not by armed force? That was the crucial question. One could only reiterate: by arbitration, conciliation and judicial methods. The acceptance of these methods, she pointed out, constituted a kind of 'moral disarmament' without which material disarmament would never come about.

On the question of 'internal peace', many members had first-hand experience and information from their own countries. Austria in particular suffered grave risk of civil war from the private armies of the political parties. A Committee for Internal Disarmament was set up by the WILPF Austrian section in November 1927, and an appeal for total, internal disarmament was sponsored by a number of prominent citizens. But the situation remained critical, and at the request of the Austrian section the Congress decided to send a delegation to the Austrian Government and party leaders to plead for the disbanding of private armies.

In dealing with the problems of national minorities, several speakers pointed to the need for acceptance of an 'internal international law'. This meant acknowledgment of the right of self-determination by the majority group; and restraint from the use of violence by the minority. Yella Hertzka proposed that the structure of states with mixed nationalities should be in the form of national federations. The foundation of internal peace, she said, was the absolute equality of all citizens under the law. The dangers of racial conflict were also illustrated by reference to India, China, South Africa and the USA.

The relation between disarmament and economics was never made more clear to the Women's International League for Peace and Freedom than at the Prague Congress. It had the benefit of hearing from Emmy Freundlich, who had been the only woman governmental representative at the World Economic Conference at Geneva in May 1927, and who spoke now on Free Trade and Co-operation. The world war itself, she said, had arisen from the struggle for economic power, and post-war economic nationalism was bringing new dangers in policies of high tariff walls and national self-sufficiency. It was essential to have tariff reductions and greater mobility of labour; she suggested indeed that the International Labour Office should organize 'free emigration' schemes. All countries should ratify the ILO conventions on social welfare, for equality of labour conditions was essential to bring about a general rise in standards of living and thus raise economic productivity. The manipulation of world markets by international cartels and trusts could best be counteracted by strengthening co-operative movements for the democratic control of industry.

These views were confirmed by other speakers. Milena Illóva of Czechoslovakia described the economic nationalism of the Central European and Balkan states, which were still 'fighting the unfinished world war'. Czechoslovakia had taken about 60 per cent of the industry of the former Austro-Hungarian Empire, and in an effort to achieve self-sufficiency Bulgaria, Yugoslavia, Rumania and Hungary had started hundreds of new industries. With strong capitalist governments and low wage-rates, the threat of 'dumping' and cheap imports from these countries caused fresh tariff barriers to be raised, to the detriment of consumers everywhere. She agreed with Emmy Freundlich that a new economic order could only come by international action through the co-operative movement. An interesting proposal for monetary reform came from Mme Léo Wanner of France. She urged the need for a fixed international currency unit, linked to the cost of living, to replace the gold standard: a possibility, she said, which was already under consideration by American and German economists.

The report of the WILPF Economic Commission, which had been appointed at the Dublin Congress, was given by Yella Hertzka. Its main recommendation was for the establishment within the League of Nations of an International Economic Office, comparable in status to the International Labour Office. The Economic Office should include representatives of consumers' as well as producers' organizations, with an adequate representation of women. An Economic Consultative Committee had been set up by the League of Nations after the first World Economic Conference in 1927, and various agreements for tariff reductions had been negotiated. But the Committee had no powers to prevent a reversion to protectionism by any country whenever conditions seemed to warrant it. The failure to create a powerful international agency such as the WILPF proposed was all too soon to become obvious as the economic blizzard from America swept across the world. The Prague Congress resolved that the WILPF would itself organize an Economic Conference in Paris in 1931, with special reference to the recommendations of Emmy Freundlich and Léo Wanner.

In addition to these pressing international questions, the Prague Congress was obliged to look again at the WILPF's own 'machinery of peace', since an amendment to the Constitution was proposed regarding the composition of the Executive Committee. This had previously consisted of nine elected members plus two consultative members from each national section, the latter having the right to vote only once a year at the invitation of the Executive. Now sections demanded that the Committee be increased to twelve and that consultative members should have voting rights at all meetings. The former proposal was carried, but that on voting rights failed to secure the necessary two-thirds majority required for an amendment to the constitution. A comment on this issue from one section which, in view of its great distance from the centres of power in Europe might have been expected to demand the utmost rights for its representatives, provides a worthy example of the international spirit of the League. Writing to Mary Sheepshanks in March 1929, Eleanor Moore of Australia remarked:

With regard to consultative members, it would appear that if they are given full voting powers, they might as well be Executive members straight out. This is not desirable. The very name 'consultative' seems to suggest persons who may give very valuable information or suggestions on some one point in which they have specialized, but who possibly have not that sense of its bearing on the general position which should carry the right to vote on a question of policy. If appointed to be consulted, why can they not be satisfied to be consulted, and let what they have to say influence the Executive on its merits?

Wherever joint action was taken, she wrote, the more the national spirit was made subsidiary to primary human values the better. In Miss Moore's wise advice there seems a lesson which governments might also take to heart!

Recommendations to national sections from the Prague Congress were largely concerned with ways of implementing the Kellogg Pact, but the far-sighted suggestion was also made that a study should be undertaken of 'methods of obtaining international control of waterways, aviation, chemicals, oil and other raw materials, where national control is a source of danger'. This recommendation too might appropriately have been made to governments.

The WILPF deputation to Austria took place in the month following the Congress, its members being Lady Clare Annesley, Emily Balch, Yella Hertzka, Milena Illóva and Dr Naima Sahlbom. The delegates were received by the Federal President; by the leaders of the Christian Socialist, Social Democrat, German National and Peasant parties; and by the general secretary of the Industrial Union. Burgomaster Seitz of Vienna declared that the *Schutzbund* of the Social Democrats would be disarmed immediately if the right-wing Christian Socialists disbanded their *Heimwehr*. The Christian Socialist leader Kunschak denied that his party did not respect the parliamentary system, but demanded alterations to the constitution. Perhaps the most significant comment was that of Dr Wotowa for the German National Party: that it was extremely difficult to maintain the country in a peaceful condition so long as Austria's right of self-determination regarding *Anschluss* was denied by the Peace Treaties.

The party leaders were generally agreed, however, that the principal cause of unrest was the economic situation. The report of the WILPF deputation noted other factors also: the conflict between Catholics and Socialists, and between rural and industrial interests; anti-semitism; and the discontent of many former army officers and imperial officials. Suggestions by the deputation that mediation might be sought from outside the country were, however, resented as 'foreign meddling'. It was pointed out that not only Austria was guilty of harbouring private armies: Germany, Hungary, Italy, Bulgaria and Rumania all had illegal armed organizations. Here was the crux of the matter, and the body to take action on it was the League of Nations. This was the message of Austria to the WILPF deputation:

If only the League of Nations would proclaim that any state that refused to disarm the illegal and extra legal forces within its borders would be exposed to League sanctions!

Another of those 'if onlys' which might have changed the course of history.

In February 1930 Yella Hertzka wrote in *Pax International* that a new constitution for Austria had been peaceably agreed, and that its adoption should result in the complete disarmament of all the illegal military groups—'but so far', she added, 'nothing of the kind has occurred'. Nor was any action taken by the League of Nations to see that it did: 'domestic affairs' were not within the jurisdiction of the League. But, as the WILPF had already perceived, internal disarmament no less than international disarmament was a necessary conditon of peace. And internal violence, if not challenged, would spread inexorably into the international violence of war.

CHAPTER 9

DISARMAMENT AND DEPRESSION

*Five-Power Naval Conference 1930—Traffic in Arms—
Economic Crisis—Disarmament Campaign—WILPF
Economic Conference—Manchurian War—World Dis-
armament Conference 1932*

The drift towards war was hardly checked by the Five-Power Naval
Conference which opened in London on January 21, 1930, with
representatives from Britain and the Commonwealth, France, Italy,
Japan and the USA. On February 6th, the conference received a deputation from the British Women's Peace Crusade, comprising eighteen
organizations including the WILPF. To these were added three Americans, two Japanese and one Frenchwoman. The deputation represented
the largest number of women ever united in this kind of action. The
majority of organizations, however, did not adopt the WILPF stand
for 'total and universal' disarmament, and for this reason the League was
not represented as an international body but only by its British section.

The women were received by the Chairman of the conference,
Ramsay MacDonald, and by delegates from Australia, New Zealand,
Japan and USA. They were introduced by Mrs Corbett Ashby, President of the International Suffrage Alliance. In his reply Ramsay Mac-
Donald stressed the need, as Mme Rudler from France had expressed
it in her speech, 'to unite peace with security'; to which he added that
security was nine-tenths psychological.

On April 22nd a Five-Power Treaty was signed to halt capital ship
building until 1936 and limit the size and armament of aircraft carriers
and submarines. An additional agreement was made between Britain,
Japan and the USA on the amount of tonnage of auxiliary ships, with
a 'safeguard clause' to permit further building if the security of any of
the countries was threatened. The outcome of the conference, as *Pax
International* observed, was 'a great disappointment'.

A subsidiary aspect of the whole disarmament problem was the
widespread traffic in arms, legal or otherwise, which for several
countries provided a substantial export business. The WILPF had been
concerned with this problem for several years, and in 1928 a compre-

hensive report was prepared by Elisabeth Waern-Bugge of Sweden. Her tabulated global analysis of defence budgets and the import and export of arms during the period 1922–27 revealed some startling figures. In 1923, for instance, 31·8 per cent of Britain's arms imports came from Germany, who also supplied Belgium with 33·8 per cent of her arms imports in 1927—although the exporting of arms by Germany was expressly forbidden under Article 170 of the Versailles Treaty. In fact, in 1927 Germany was supplying 24·1 per cent of the total world exports.

Mrs Waern-Bugge commented on the remarkably high proportion of arms and ammunition for 'sporting' purposes which appeared in official statistics and which were undoubtedly a hidden form of war material. A significant factor, too, was the steady increase in arms supplies to colonial territories. There were, as Mrs Waern-Bugge pointed out, obvious anomalies in the figures issued as between exporting and importing countries, which might be partly explained by the frequent re-sale of arms to yet a third country. And she pointed to the rather surprising fact that Holland, with its highly pacific reputation, appeared to be a focal point in the traffic in arms. Nor were the Scandinavians blameless. Sweden exported to Norway, and Norway re-sold abroad, on a quite considerable scale. At the head of the exporters, however, during the six years 1922–27, stood Great Britain who was virtually supplying the whole world with the exception of the USA. The total value of global arms exports during the period amounted to 273,960,000 dollars, and it was only in 1927 that some downfall in the scale of the traffic was detectable.

Of particular interest to the WILPF was the case of China. Germany, Norway and Sweden were all supplying arms on a substantial scale, and virtually the whole of the Japanese arms exports were going into China. The embargo on arms to China which was imposed during 1927-28 did not prevent large-scale smuggling and the trade in arms continued. In April 1930 the WILPF Executive Committee appealed to the International Federation of Trade Unions to use its influence by calling on European workers to refuse to transport the arms. In an extremely sympathetic reply the General Secretary, John Sassenach, reported that he had taken the matter up with the International Federation of Transport Workers as the body mainly concerned, adding: 'We are convinced that the above-mentioned federation will give their wholehearted attention to the very important matter suggested by you.'

The interlocking of disarmament with economic issues was seen to be more and more inextricable. The condition of Germany was a case in point. The death of Stresemann in October 1929 marked the end of a heroic struggle to integrate his country into a democratic community of nations. Stresemann was defeated both by the obduracy of the French in their search for national security and the equally obdurate nationalism of his own compatriots, fed by the economic dislocation that could still be blamed, with some justification, on the Allied powers rather than on the German social order itself. In January 1930 the number of registered unemployed in Germany reached three million, or one-tenth of the industrial population, and it was to rise in the course of the year to five million. Was it mere coincidence that 1930 too saw the rocketing of the National Socialists in the Reichstag from 12 to 107 members? It was perhaps remarkable, in the circumstances, that the Social Democrats still retained 143 seats and the Communists won only 27. But this was the last Social Democratic victory the German Reich was to see.

The final evacuation of the Rhineland by French troops on June 30th removed one cogent German grievance, but this was not followed by any international moves towards general disarmament. The threat of economic collapse not only in Germany but also among the 'victor' nations caused statesmen to shy away from any policy that by reducing production—even arms production—might add one more unit to the unemployment total. This shortsighted policy served merely to postpone the evil day of reckoning: the problems of unemployment and production could clearly only be solved by radical international action. It was to this end that Briand submitted his memorandum to governments in May 1930, proposing a European economic federation of 26 nations. It met with a cool reception, partly due to suspicion of French political motives. The matter was, however, debated at the League of Nations Eleventh Assembly in September and a Commission of Inquiry for European Union was set up. The WILPF Executive Committee meeting in October 1930 received a report on the Briand Memorandum by Gertrude Baer and Gabrielle Duchêne which was critical of the political basis of the proposals. The Memorandum made no attempt to limit national sovereignty; it excluded Turkey and Russia from the proposed Union (they were subsequently invited to join); and it failed to mention either disarmament or the distribution of raw materials.

A subject of related interest with which the League was at this time concerned was the plight of people without nationality—the *'Apatrides'*. A committee to study the problem had been set up at the Prague Congress and in April 1930 the Executive Committee asked Mary Sheepshanks to arrange a Conference on Statelessness at Geneva in September. It was attended by WILPF delegates from Austria, Britain, Germany and Hungary and representatives from the International Council of Women, Society of Friends, International Suffrage Alliance, League for the Rights of Man and League of Nations Union. The size of the problem may be appreciated from the fact that, as a result of the Peace Treaties, the number of stateless people in Austria, Czechoslovakia, Hungary, Italy, Yugoslavia, Poland and Rumania was estimated at over 100,000. Under the Minority Treaties governments were supposed to absorb these residents into citizenship, but this was not being done. The *Apatrides* had no legal rights or protection, no passport to enable them to emigrate, and frequently no work. As Mme Askanazsy of Vienna described it: 'To be stateless means death from starvation.' Only the League of Nations could solve the problem, but it had refused to take action against the governments concerned. Dr Reale, of the League for the Rights of Man, urged that the LON should extend the protection of the 'Nansen passport', which had been issued to fugitives from the Russian revolution, to other classes of refugees.

A resolution from the conference, demanding the appointment of a LON Commission on Statelessness, was presented by a WILPF deputation to three members of the UK delegation who could be relied on to press the matter: Charles Roden Buxton, Mrs Mary Hamilton and Ellen Wilkinson.

The Czechoslovakian and Hungarian sections of the League were particularly concerned with this problem, and a second conference was arranged at Budapest the following May in conjunction with the International Federation of League of Nations Unions. In July 1931 Emily Balch and Mrs Eugenie Meller, on behalf of the WILPF Committee on Statelessness, presented the resolutions of the Geneva and Budapest conferences to the Legal section of the League of Nations, together with detailed proposals for practical ways of dealing with the Stateless problem for so long as it should continue to exist.

Meanwhile, the WILPF Commission on Scientific Warfare, under the chairmanship of Dr Sahlbom, had prepared an appeal for use by national sections in a mass propaganda campaign for universal disarmament. The rate at which this petition snowballed during the next two years was to astonish even the most optimistic of its sponsors.

Under the slogan 'War is Renounced—Let Us Renounce Armaments', the declaration called on governments to instruct their delegates at the forthcoming Disarmament Conference 'to examine all proposals for disarmament that have been or may be made, and to take the necessary steps to *achieve disarmament*'.

The petition started to circulate in Austria, Britain, Czechoslovakia, France, Germany, Holland and USA in May 1930. By January 1931 a total of 33,000 signatures had been obtained—and of these, 10,000 came from the small country of Wales. In February 1931, with ten national sections working for the campaign, the signatures jumped to 240,000. In these first few months the petition was translated into 18 languages, including Arabic.

In September 1930 the women's peace movement was strengthened by the setting up of a Liaison Committee of International Women's Organizations. A development from the earlier Joint Standing Committee, it comprised the International Alliance of Women, International Council of Women, International Federation of University Women, Women's International League for Peace and Freedom, World Union of Women for International Concord and World YWCA. At the opening of the League of Nations Eleventh Assembly, a delegation went to the President, Titulescu, with an Appeal to the World's Statesmen on behalf of more than 40 million women in 56 countries. The deputation was also received by Arthur Henderson, senior British delegate, and Dr Curtius, head of the German delegation. Mr Titulescu, who appeared to listen with great sympathy, promised to circulate the Appeal to all 400 delegates at the Assembly (of whom three that year were women).

In January 1931 the League of Nations Council resolved that the long-awaited World Disarmament Conference should meet in February 1932, and in May 1931 the Council unanimously adopted Arthur Henderson to be its Chairman. This hopeful prospect that at last words might be translated into deeds gave added impetus to the WILPF disarmament petition. In February 1931 the British section organized a mass meeting at the Queen's Hall, London, at which Henderson was the chief speaker. He stressed the importance of public opinion in influencing the conference: 'At the Disarmament Conference as elsewhere . . . the Governments will do what the people want. If the people want disarmament, they can have it.'

A successful tour of Central Europe by Camille Drevet in May spread the disarmament campaign through Greece and Bulgaria,

Rumania, Poland and Hungary. In Canada, the campaign was enthusiastically received in rural communities. In Saskatchewan alone,
nearly 7,000 signatures were collected through women's institutes and
farmers' clubs. The petition was published in the local press and the
United Farmers' Organization sent a copy to each of its branches. The
American section of the WILPF organized a Peace Caravan under the
able leadership of Mabel Vernon which, setting out from Hollywood
in June 1931, travelled nearly 9,000 miles through 25 states to reach
Washington in October, where the petitions collected were handed to
President Hoover. By the end of 1931 the WILPF could report that the
number of signatures to its disarmament petition had passed three
million. By far the largest national total was that of Britain, with just
over a million and a half signatures—although Switzerland, rather
surprisingly, had the highest national ratio: 311,000 signatures out of a
population of four million.

The WILPF petition had been criticized by some other organizations
on the grounds both of vagueness and of pacifist 'extremism', particularly in its French and German translations. Dr Lange, Secretary-
General of the Inter-Parliamentary Union, regarded the demand for
total and general disarmament as 'frankly utopian' and impossible of
attainment. He suggested that the great need was for precise proposals
towards specific aims which governments might accept. 'I regret very
much,' he wrote in February 1931, 'that an organization of so great
importance and influence as your League may possibly destroy the
very object it pursues by over-shooting the mark.' Perhaps in order
to meet these objections, Dr Hilda Clark proposed to the Executive
Committee meeting at Lille in April 1931 that a detailed policy for
disarmament should be issued to national sections for use in conjunction with the petition. The following resolution was adopted:

The WIL as an International organization stands on the basis of total
and universal disarmament as an obligation involved in the Kellogg-
Briand pact but urges as a first step towards this goal, to be taken
within a definite period, that the General Disarmament Conference of
1932 accept a convention for definite and drastic measures of disarmament on sea and land by budgetary and other means, and for international control of civil aviation including the abolition of air warfare.

A further resolution demanded that nations should be represented at
the Disarmament Conference on the principle of equality; and that the
delegations should include both men and women representatives of

peace organizations. National sections were asked to recommend the names of suitable delegates to their governments. The Executive Committee also condemned secret military treaties, such as those made by France with Poland, Rumania and Czechoslovakia, and urged that all treaties should be open and should be registered with the League of Nations.

In September 1931 the Liaison Committee of International Women's Organizations formed a Disarmament Committee to co-ordinate pressure at the League of Nations and propaganda through national sections. It immediately pressed governments to support the Italian proposal at the LON Twelfth Assembly for a one-year standstill on arms production. This proposal was adopted and by November all the major powers had promised their adherence. At the unofficial International Disarmament Congress held in Paris in November 1931 and presided over by Lord Cecil, Gabrielle Duchêne presented a declaration on behalf of the WILPF urging that at the forthcoming World Disarmament Conference national delegations should include representatives of pacifist bodies and should *exclude* all persons having an interest in the maintenance of armaments. So hostile was French right-wing opinion at that time to any plans for disarmament that the Congress was disrupted by organized groups of hecklers.

In spite of the sweeping success of the WILPF petition, prospects for the Disarmament Conference were far from hopeful—not least because of the worsening economic situation in the countries most involved. The slump which had been precipitated in the autumn of 1929 due to the inability of the USA to maintain its loans to Europe, with a consequent drop in purchasing power and fall in prices, was sending up unemployment to dangerous as well as tragic levels. It was against this background that the WILPF Economic Conference which had been planned at the Prague Congress took place in Paris on April 14–16, 1931. The agenda dealt with Rationalization, Unemployment and Markets; Economic and Monetary Stability; and International Economic Organization. Expert speakers from Austria, Hungary, Germany, Czechoslovakia, Holland and France, and from the ILO and International Bank, contributed to the discussions. Calling for the establishment of nationally and internationally *planned* economic systems, the conference recommended:

1. A European Customs Union, of which the first link might be between Germany and Austria, open to all countries and working towards abolition of tariff barriers.

2. Stabilization of the purchasing power of money and rational distribution of credit.
3. Rational economic organization to bring into harmony production, demand and the distribution of purchasing power.

A proposal for a German-Austrian Customs Union had in fact been put before the LON Committee on European Unity in March 1931 by Britain, but was later abandoned due to French hostility.

The first check to the galloping financial crisis came from America, with Hoover's proposal on June 20, 1931, for a moratorium on all war debts for one year. The WILPF sent a telegram to Hoover applauding the moratorium, but pointing out that it must be accompanied by 'binding engagements to reduce military budgets accordingly ... otherwise money saved might merely swell armament expenditure'. No such engagement was made by any power and the benefits of the moratorium were short-lived. Indeed, Britain's financial difficulties worsened with the cutting off of German repayment of loans, and in August the Labour Government was forced to resign and was replaced by a Coalition. On September 21st Britain abandoned the gold standard. The WILPF Executive Committee, meeting at Geneva earlier that month, called on statesmen at the LON Twelfth Assembly to take immediate steps to end 'the present economic anarchy' by concerted action to provide for the international distribution of primary products and foodstuffs. It was nearly a year later before the first moves were made by the League of Nations, following the Lausanne Reparation Conference in June 1932, to summon a World Economic Conference —and by then the time for palliatives had passed. The Executive Committee also reiterated the longstanding WILPF plea for revision of the Peace Treaties and cancellation of war-debts.

But now a new threat to peace arose—not this time in Europe but from the Far East. The anomalous province of Manchuria, remaining outside the control of the Chinese Nationalist Government which had by this time extended its authority as far north as Peking, had long been a source of contention between the rival claims of China, Japan and Russia. After the Russo-Japanese War of 1904 Japan had acquired the right to maintain forces in Manchuria for the protection of the South Manchurian Railway and her troops had been quartered at Mukden ever since. On September 19, 1931, following a minor incident with Chinese soldiers, the Japanese drove out the Chinese provincial government in Mukden and occupied a wide area in the north. By January 1932 the occupation, aided by the use of bombing planes, had spread south to the Chinese border and the whole province was under Japanese control. Here was the first clear case of defiance of the League of Nations Covenant by a Council member. How would the League respond? China had immediately appealed to the Council to take action under Article 11, whereupon the Japanese delegate gave assurances that the military operation was purely for the protection of Japanese lives and property and the troops would be withdrawn into the railway zone when this was secured. The Council adjourned, with relief, for two weeks.

Meanwhile, the WILPF had received an urgent cable from China and promptly telegraphed its Japanese section to use its active influence 'in the spirit of Jane Addams'. A reply was received: 'Co-operating with peace agencies. Shall work for peaceful solution.' Support for China was also sought from the women delegates at the LON. But when the Council reassembled on October 14th it was clear that, far from withdrawing, the Japanese 'police action' was extending into full-scale war. A telegram was sent to the Foreign Minister in Tokyo: 'Having followed statements League Council meeting WILPF urges Japanese Government withdraw troops.' National sections also took separate action. Already on September 19th the United States section had telegraphed the President to invoke the Nine-Power Treaty of 1921 (guaranteeing China's territorial integrity), following this up with an almost daily bombardment of telegrams and letters, deputations and interviews with State Department officials. The Germans appealed to their Government 'to take vigorous steps against all traffic in arms and munitions to the Far East'. Britain urged that the USSR, as a closely interested power, should be invited to assist the League of Nations in its efforts for peace.

Instead, the LON Council called in the United States, which although not a member-state was no less concerned at Japan's flouting of the Kellogg Pact and the Nine-Power Treaty. On October 24th the Council again asked Japan to withdraw her forces under Article 11— but no action could be taken without unanimity, and Japan herself as a Council member was able to veto the resolution! The Council met again in Paris during November and December but could find no effective solution. It did, however, agree that a Commission of Inquiry should be sent to the Far East, under the presidency of Lord Lytton. The proposal for the Commission came from the Japanese Government—itself embarrassed by the excesses of the militarist faction—with strong support from the USA.

Writing from Paris to the national sections in November, Emily Balch clarified the position of the WILPF. Although a 'partisan' attitude was to be deplored, and friendly relations should be maintained with both sides, this did not imply neutrality on the issues involved— namely, whether it was tolerable that governments should secure their aims by armed force on foreign territory; and whether adherence to the League Covenant, the Kellogg Pact and the Nine-Power Treaty was not a categorical promise that all disputes should be settled by peaceful means. There was no doubt of Japan's guilt on these grounds. But, Miss Balch pointed out, other factors could not be overlooked: the operation of economic interests, particularly in munitions, and political intrigues were themselves making for war. These views should be made clear to governments and League delegates, and to the Chinese and Japanese authorities. The possibility of an unofficial peace delegation to Japan should be considered. Above all, the WILPF must support and strengthen those elements *inside* Japan which were working for peace. She referred to a letter by Edith Pye published in the *Manchester Guardian* on November 14, 1931, quoting the pronouncement of a Japanese professor that the League of Nations was in the right and the withdrawal of Japanese troops was an imperative step to peace.

Unfortunately, the voice of reason in Japan was fast being drowned under a hysteria engendered by the guilt and euphoria of a ruthless military success. But the WILPF continued to maintain contact with friends in both China and Japan, as well as to exert pressure on other governments. On November 7th a letter was sent to each member of the LON Council by Camille Drevet, writing now as International Secretary of the WILPF as well as from her personal experience of the Far East, expressing considerable anxiety at the attitude of a section of the press which seemed to be more interested in aggravating the conflict than seeking a settlement. She went so far as to accuse the press of deliberately misleading public opinion by falsification and suppression of news and so 'discrediting one of the countries involved in the conflict for the benefit of the other'. The benefit of which Mme Drevet complained was, of course, going to the 'aggressor' nation, Japan.

The United States section wrote to President Hoover on November 24th again regretting that America had not formally invoked the Kellogg Pact or the Nine-Power Treaty to condemn Japanese aggression, and calling for an embargo on arms shipments to Japan, as was already the case with China. In January 1932 the US Government declared to both China and Japan that it would not recognize any situation brought about by means contrary to the Kellogg Pact, or which impaired American treaty rights in China. The British and French governments were pressed to follow suit, but declined to take any action that might be offensive to Japan. The weakness of the LON Council in failing to deal promptly with the conflict was condemned at a special meeting of the WILPF Executive Committee at Geneva in January 1932, which again urged the prohibition of arms exports to the belligerents and the exertion of diplomatic and economic pressure on Japan to bring about a cessation of hostilities. The Special Assembly called at the request of China in March 1932 resolved that member-states should not 'recognize any situation, treaty or agreement which may be brought about by means contrary to the Covenant of the League or to the Pact of Paris'. This resolution was rendered a little hollow by the almost simultaneous announcement by the Japanese Government of the transmutation of Manchuria into the new state of Manchukuo. No further action was taken by this Assembly, pending publication of the report of the Lytton Commission which was expected in the autumn. The Manchurian question was temporarily shelved, as the world focus again swung back to Geneva.

The first World Disarmament Conference opened at the Salle de la Reformation, Geneva, on February 2, 1932. The largest international conference ever to be held, it included representatives from 60 countries. Its President was Arthur Henderson; its Secretary Thanassis Aghanides, Director of the LON Disarmament Section. War raged in the Far East, unemployment blanketed the USA, Europe shivered on the threshold of new chaos—and as the 'peacemakers' assembled the world held its breath and waited for the words and deeds of hope. What hope was there for success? The hopes of the 'ordinary people' of the world were perhaps of little account. They lay piled in despatch boxes in the library of the conference hall—those millions of petitions, collected during the international disarmament campaigns of the past two years by peace societies and ex-servicemen; by religious and labour organizations; above all by the women, mothers of one slaughtered generation and another now threatened. From the women's organizations alone, eight million signatures were presented at the receiving ceremony on February 6th; and of those eight million, six million came from the campaign of the WILPF—including 173,000 announced by cable from Japan. Under the excitement and anxiety of war the WILPF had not forgotten its primary commitment to long-term work for peace; and now, in the jubilation of a peaceful triumph, it did not forget the sufferings inflicted by war. A group of members marched through Geneva with a poster which read: 'The Disarmament Conference is meeting in Geneva. Japanese bombs are falling on Chinese cities. What will you choose: War or Disarmament?'

After the presentation of its petitions the WILPF received supporting letters and messages from many individuals and organizations, including 96 telegrams from various groups in France demanding general disarmament. These were forwarded to the President of the Conference by Camille Drevet, together with a letter asking that the Conference should set up a plan for total and universal disarmament, in stages, and as an immediate step should take measures to control the private manufacture of arms. In his reply Arthur Henderson wrote on February 22nd:

I need not say that I have examined these telegrams with the utmost interest and that I have read your letter with great sympathy. I have every confidence that the Conference will be able to do something with regard to the private manufacture of arms and materials of warfare.

I will take care that this new manifestation of public opinion which you have brought before me shall be communicated to the members of the Conference by means of the Official Journal.

As I think you know, I have been deeply impressed by the manifestations of public support for the work of this Conference, and I venture to express the hope that you and your friends who are in favour of its success will not relax your efforts until it has brought its work to a successful conclusion.

But it became all too clear, as the statesmen at Geneva unfolded their briefs and expounded their compromises, that no spectacular progress would be made. Even the draft Disarmament Convention so laboriously concocted by the Preparatory Disarmament Commission was now shelved, as France put forward quite new proposals for strengthening security by a standing international force and compulsory arbitration. The plan was tabled by the chief French delegate Tardieu—Minister for War!—and it had the merit of coherence and consistency; its defect was that it was known to be unacceptable to the other major powers. Now Brüning came forward with Germany's plea for equality of treatment; and at this stage Germany still envisaged 'equality' through a qualitative, general disarmament rather than by an increase in her own armaments.

Brüning was followed by Litvinoff, whose appeal for total disarmament once more fell on deaf ears, his only support coming from Turkey. The WILPF wrote congratulatory letters to both delegates and received an appreciative reply from Litvinoff. By the time the Conference adjourned for the Easter recess, the anxiety of the smaller powers for some tangible progress—backed by a vocal world opinion—seemed likely to ensure that agreement might be reached at least on some qualitative arms reductions to meet the German demands. But even these modest hopes were set back by the holding of general elections both in France and Germany, the latter resulting in the replacement of Brüning as Chancellor by the far more reactionary Von Papen. By May 1932, after four months' work, agreement seemed as far away as ever; open sessions were abandoned and discussion was confined to the level of private conversations.

The deadlock was only broken by President Hoover's unexpected proposals on June 23rd for an all-round reduction of one-third in arms expenditure and total abolition of certain offensive weapons. This step was welcomed and immediately approved by no less than thirty countries—but again, big power compromises were at work to circumvent any such action. When the Conference adjourned on July 23rd it adopted a watered-down resolution, proposed by Beneš of Czechoslovakia, which affirmed merely that a 'substantial reduction' in world armaments should be effected by means of a 'general convention'; although with the addendum that its adoption 'in no way prejudges the attitude of the Conference towards any more comprehensive measures of Disarmament'. In addition, a Special Committee should be set up to study the regulation of private arms manufacture (thus vindicating Arthur Henderson's confidence that 'something' would be done in this matter). Forty-one countries, many with reluctance, voted for the resolution; eight abstained; and two—Russia and Germany—voted against. Litvinoff commented: 'I vote for disarmament, but against the resolution.' Germany's reaction was to withdraw her delegates until the principle of German equality was recognized. The first phase of the World Disarmament Conference was over.

CHAPTER 10

THE FATEFUL CHOICE

Grenoble Congress 1932—Mission to Ukraine 1931—
Mission to Palestine 1930—WILPF and India—
Action on Manchuria—End of Disarmament Conference
—World Economic Conference 1933

Meanwhile, the seventh International Congress of the Women's International League for Peace and Freedom took place at Grenoble in France from May 15 to 19, 1932. Its main concern was inevitably the progress of the Disarmament Conference, and the theme of the Congress was 'World Disarmament or World Disaster'. For the first time, Jane Addams was absent from an International Congress. In December 1931 she had been awarded a Nobel peace prize (jointly with Dr Nicholas Murray Butler), and with characteristic generosity she donated the prize money to the international headquarters of the WILPF.

In December 1930 Camille Drevet had replaced Mary Sheepshanks as International Secretary in Geneva. Miss Sheepshanks' resignation, which was greatly regretted, was caused primarily by her strong disagreements over policy with both French and German members of the Executive Committee; disagreements which stemmed from the basic incompatibility between her rational, Anglo-Saxon empiricism and the intense radicalism of the continental 'progressives'. This incipient 'split-mindedness' in the WILPF had already been apparent at the first Hague Congress (between Kathleen Courtney and Rosika Schwimmer, for instance) and continued up to the Second World War.

The reports of the League's twenty-six national sections presented to the Congress showed the usual cross-fertilization of national sentiment and international aspiration. As well as the intensive work in all sections for the Disarmament Petition, a common activity of more than half the sections was to campaign against militaristic education in schools and among youth groups. International education was also continued through the summer schools which had been held at Visigrad on the Danube, at Sofia, and in Alsace and Silesia. New ground was broken in the League's penetration of Latin America with the successful summer school held in Mexico in July 1931, following a visit by Camille Drevet—who in the years under review had also travelled to the Balkans, Denmark, Sweden, Holland, Tunis and Cuba. The US section maintained strong pressure for the withdrawal of Marines from Haiti and Nicaragua, while the British section was now busy with new work arising from the Indian independence campaign. France was deeply concerned with colonialism, particularly in Indo-China and North Africa. The Czechoslovakian section had been re-organized, with more co-operation between the different ethnic groups. Bulgaria, Denmark and Finland all reported large increases in membership. The British section was strengthened by the affiliation in 1929 of the North Wales Women's Peace Council, a hitherto independent body, and soon afterwards by the addition of groups in South Wales; the Welsh women had been stimulated by the Women's Peace Crusade and were intensely active in the disarmament campaign.

Since the last Congress new sections had been founded in Mexico and Tunisia and groups were in formation in Cuba, Yugoslavia, Rumania, Spain and Syria. Italy, alas, had ceased to exist as a national section but contact was continued through Italian women in France and Switzerland. Links were also maintained with women in China, Egypt, India, Palestine, Turkey and the Soviet Union, largely through members travelling in these countries either individually or on behalf of the League.

A section which had experienced special difficulties during this period was the Ukraine. Complaints of atrocities by Poland against the Ukrainian minority in Eastern Galicia were accepted by the League of Nations Council in January 1931 and an investigating committee was set up. News of these atrocities had reached the WILPF in an appeal from the Ukrainian section the previous November. It was accordingly decided to send Mary Sheepshanks, together with an Austrian member, Mrs Helen Oppenheimer, to make an immediate personal investigation both in Galicia and in Warsaw. Their findings bore out the charges made, although it was pointed out that the 'pacification' was only ordered after acts of sabotage by Ukrainians. Writing in *Pax International*, February 1931, Miss Sheepshanks summed up her conclusions:

Several points must be emphasized, that this so-called pacification has been carried out with a ferocity which can only be compared to the previous atrocities carried out in the early nineteenth century by the Bashi-bazouks in the old Turkish territories, and secondly these atrocities were not punishments inflicted for crime but were inflicted without trial and wholesale on an entire population. Thirdly that they were done by command of the Government and were carried out strictly according to plan and were not merely the excesses of subordinates. Fourthly that the victims were denied all medical assistance. Fifthly that every effort has been made to prevent the drawing up of any reports or statistics showing the extent of the repression.

In accordance with the WILPF tradition of hearing both sides of a case, the Polish section was also asked to make a statement. It was typical of the spirit of the League that the member who was most insistent that the Polish case must be heard was Gertrude Baer of Germany—whose country at that time was also in dispute with Poland over the treatment of German nationals in Silesia. The Polish section summarized its findings as follows:

This Section recognizes that during the difficult period when the Polish authorities were trying to suppress the sabotage in the Ukraine, certain acts of abuse and excess occurred. These it regrets and reproves and will do all in its power to see that the culprits are punished. The Section, however, as a pacifist organization deplores the acts of sabotage of the Ukrainian terrorists without which the unhappy incidents would never have occurred. The Polish Section has decided to work with all its power to bring about a fraternal co-operation between the two nationalities in Poland and invites its Ukrainian sisters to collaborate.

Miss Sheepshanks, too, was at pains to make it clear that her strictures were not made in any spirit of hostility to Poland. She stressed this point in letters both to *The Times* and to Arthur Henderson, to whom she wrote on February 20, 1931:

I have submitted my report on my investigations of the treatment of the Ukrainian minority in Poland to the Foreign Office and I believe that it is in your hands. As this report and others of the same nature have been attacked as being anti-Polish propaganda, I venture to inform you that in making known the facts contained in my report I was actuated just as much in accordance with wishes expressed to me by Poles as with those expressed by Ukrainians. While in Poland and more particularly in Warsaw, I saw a number of representative Poles, e.g. a Senator, two ex-Ministers and others and they were emphatic in urging that in the best interests of Poland the true nature of the present military dictatorship in Poland should be made known in Western Europe. Those whom I represent are not in any sense anti-Polish or pro-Ukrainian. Our League has a National Section in Poland and we are just as much concerned for the welfare and interests of Polish subjects of Polish nationality as for that of Polish subjects of the Ukrainian race.

An unsolicited testimonial to Mary Sheepshanks came a few months later from a Canadian Member of Parliament of Ukrainian extraction, Michael Luchkovich, who had received her report from Agnes Macphail. He had quoted this extensively in a debate on the situation in the Canadian Parliament, considering it—he wrote on May 13th—'the most comprehensive and accurate of any I have read to date'. The Executive Committee meeting at Lille in April 1931 sent a resolution to the LON investigating Committee of Three urging that it should consider not only the actual complaints made by Ukrainian petitioners but also 'the causes of friction on both sides underlying the complaints, including the question of granting to the Ukrainian Minority the autonomy which was provided by the law passed in the Polish Seym in September 1922 but which has not yet been put into effect'.

The general conclusions of the Grenoble Congress were incorporated in a comprehensive policy manifesto which was presented to Arthur Henderson at the Disarmament Conference on June 7th. Warning of the great dangers to world peace if the powers continued in their old ways of thinking, the WILPF stated its belief that the first step towards a new era must be 'organized world co-operation' and that the goal of the World Disarmament Conference must be 'total and universal disarmament'. In the meantime, substantial arms reductions would lessen international tension; and arms reduction would be facilitated if the profits were taken out of arms manufacture. The WILPF also put on record its strong opposition to 'the creation of a new form of militarism in the shape of an international armed force in any form', and demanded the establishment of a Permanent Disarmament Commission 'with power to supervise the carrying out of agreements reached'. What this power should be—if not an armed force—was not however specified, and it must be said that this lack of clarification was a general weakness of the peace movement at that time.

Replying to the WILPF deputation, in which twelve national sections were represented, Arthur Henderson pointed out that in his opening speech to the Conference he had declared that total disarmament should be its goal. The deputation was impressed by his sincerity and by his obvious gratitude for all expressions of the popular desire for disarmament. The Manifesto was also sent to every delegate at the Disarmament Conference and to all heads of governments. The Executive Committee meeting immediately after the Grenoble Congress reiterated the League's demand for state control of arms manufacture and total abolition of the armaments prohibited in the Peace Treaties. A resolution on the Far Eastern situation recommended the setting up of a mixed Commission, with American and Russian as well as Chinese and Japanese experts, to draw up new treaties acceptable to both parties.

This Executive Committee received with great regret the resignation of two of the three co-chairmen elected at Prague, Emily Balch and Clara Ragaz. The remaining chairman, Gertrude Baer, was now re-elected and was joined as co-chairman by Edith Pye.

Two new areas of potential conflict were beginning to engage the attention of the WILPF during this period: Palestine and India. Both arose out of British imperialism and so were naturally the special concern of the British section of the League. Britain had acknowledged the Jewish right to a 'national home' in Palestine ever since the Balfour declaration of 1917, but this had not deterred her from also giving encouragement to Arab nationalism when this seemed expedient, and after the granting of the Palestine Mandate to Britain by the League of Nations in 1923 this dual policy soon ran into trouble. After hearing reports on the tense racial situation from Miss Pye, Dr Augspurg and Miss Balch, the WILPF Executive Committee in April 1930 asked Mrs Waern-Bugge of Sweden to go to Palestine and try to establish some co-operation between Jews and Arabs. A Jewish group of the League already existed in Tel-Aviv.

Writing from Palestine in February 1931, Mrs Waern-Bugge was able to report that she had succeeded in forming a group at Ramallah, an Arab village north of Jerusalem, due largely to the interest shown by staff and pupils at an Arab girls' school conducted by the Society of Friends. She also arranged a meeting with Arab Christian, Jewish and European women, but was unable to persuade Moslem women to attend a mixed group. European residents with whom she discussed this problem were astonished, however, that she had even brought together Christian Arabs and Jews. The main difficulty in approaching the Moslem women, of course, was their lack of emancipation as compared with their Jewish and Christian sisters. They could never be reached direct, only through their husbands. To this end, the Swedish consul, Mr Lewis Larson, arranged a meeting for Mrs Waern-Bugge with the Grand Mufti, who expressed great sympathy with the aims and activities of the WILPF, and 'seemed highly to appreciate the telegram sent by the Executive Committee to the British Government urging commutation of capital punishment for political murders during the riots of 1929'.

All in all, the picture was darker than any outsider could imagine possible at that time. The common attitude of the Moslem Arabs was one of 'the most obstinate chauvinism and the bitterest hatred against the Jews', and Mrs Waern-Bugge was obliged to admit that this, combined with their total ignorance of larger international questions, made it impossible as well as unwise to encourage their co-operation with the League. She was more disappointed at the refusal of the Christian Arab women to become permanently attached to a mixed WILPF group, although here again she recognized that their fears of reprisals from the Moslem majority if they associated themselves with Jews were well-founded and that it was best 'not to try to build anything on so frail a ground'. She concluded, therefore, that the main object of her mission had failed—although this was not the view of several eminent Palestinians who assured her that her visit had 'broken the ice' and that nobody previously had tried to spread the idea of peace and reconciliation in that country. As Dr J. L. Magnes, Rector of the Hebrew University, expressed it in his farewell words: 'Do not give up Palestine. Time will show you how much good you have done by this visit.' The Women's International League certainly had no intention of giving up Palestine, and this mission was only the first of many subsequent moves towards the reconciliation of Jew and Arab.

The Indian question was first brought to the notice of the British section of the WILPF by Agatha Harrison, who had been sent to India in 1929 as personal assistant to Miss Beryl Power, the only woman member of the Whitley Commission on Labour. In 1931 Miss Harrison met Rev. C. F. Andrews, biographer of Mahatma Gandhi, and was invited to assist him with preparations for Gandhi's forthcoming visit to London to take part in the second Round Table Conference on the Indian constitution. This was only the beginning of a close collaboration and friendship with C. F. Andrews that was to last until his death in 1940, and which was soon extended to Gandhi himself, to Pandit Nehru and his sister Mrs Vijaya Lakshmi Pandit, and indeed to every personality of note in the Indian independence movement. Agatha Harrison became secretary of the Indian Conciliation Group, founded in 1931 by two well-known Quakers, Carl Heath and Alexander Wilson. Shortly afterwards she helped to form a Liaison Group of four British women's organizations (including the WILPF) as a means of maintaining friendly contacts with the All-India Women's Conference; this was done on the suggestion of Rajkumari Amrit Kaur, later to become first Minister of Health of an independent India.

Agatha Harrison's story has been told elsewhere, in the short biography written by her sister[1] and in the little book of 'Remembrances' published by the British section after her death in 1954. The WILPF was enormously indebted to her for constant counsel and information at every stage of the Indian independence campaign.

After the second Round Table Conference in 1931, Gandhi visited Villeneuve in Switzerland for talks with Romain Rolland. Perhaps because of its close links with Rolland and his sister, the WILPF was called on to organize a public meeting for Gandhi in Geneva. This took place on December 10th, and Gandhi's address on that occasion was printed in full in *Pax International* in January 1932. He referred to the new method adopted by India to gain national independence: 'means that are scrupulously and absolutely non-violent and peaceful'. He then answered a number of questions put to him by the Chairman, Edmond Privat. Many of them dealt specifically with the position of Switzerland as a neutral state, but one point was raised which must be considered by all advocates of non-violence. The questioner asked: Would it not be cowardice for a neutral country to let an army pass through its territory in order to attack another state? Gandhi replied: It would certainly be cowardly. But the army should not be allowed to pass through. Every citizen should obstruct its passage, refuse all supplies, and ultimately offer his own body as a sacrifice:

You would have presented the wall of men, women and children to those armies who dared to cross your country and invited them to walk over your corpses.

In India, Gandhi continued, such acts of non-retaliation had already taken place. The courage required for this kind of action showed the

[1] *Agatha Harrison*, by Irene Harrison (Allen & Unwin, 1956).

strength of non-violence: 'It has never been intended to be an arm for the weak but a weapon for the stronger men.'

This strength was soon to be tested again in India, where the continued civil disobedience campaigns of the Congress Party brought increasingly repressive reprisals by the British. In May 1932 the WILPF Executive Committee protested strongly against the imprisonment of more than fifty thousand Indians, 'guilty only of desiring independence for their country'. It urged the immediate liberation of all political prisoners not guilty of criminal acts; withdrawal of ordinances and a return to methods of law; and the re-opening of negotiations with Indian representatives then in prison. On the initiative of a WILPF member, Mrs Margaret Cousins, an international conference on India took place in Geneva in October 1932, with representatives of 26 organizations from 15 countries. A permanent Committee on India was set up, on which the WILPF was represented by Emmeline Pethick-Lawrence and Madeleine Rolland. Following her return to India, Mrs Cousins was sentenced to one year's imprisonment on December 10th for refusing to promise not to speak in public against the ordinance rule under which India was being governed.

In July 1933, following Gandhi's release, Congress announced the abandonment of mass civil disobedience. This was widely interpreted as a failure of the Indian Congress to win the masses for its policy of non-violence, but as Madeleine Rolland pointed out in *Pax International* in September, the object of the suspension was to prepare for an even greater mass effort in the future. Meanwhile, individual acts of disobedience continued; and so did acts of repression. In August the WILPF British section expressed its deep regret at the bombing of an Indian village by British forces, 'especially in view of the efforts made at the Disarmament Conference to prohibit altogether bombing from the air'.

Meanwhile, that other struggle in the Far East, between China and Japan, was no nearer a non-violent solution. In September 1932 the publication of the Lytton Report brought a clear vindication of China's case against Japan, but with little effect on the reluctance of the major powers to take decisive action. In a last attempt at conciliation, the LON Special Committee of Nineteen in February 1933 asked Japan to accept the autonomy of Manchuria under Chinese sovereignty. Again Japan refused and, faced with an impending threat of sanctions under Article 15 of the Covenent, on March 27th announced her withdrawal from the League of Nations.

Writing in *Pax International* in February 1933, Edith Pye quoted a letter from Manchuria describing the 'reign of terror' under which its people were living and the devastation of the country. And yet, she pointed out, given more enlightened international policies this 'great storehouse of natural wealth' could serve to ease the economic problems of both China and Japan. The WILPF Executive Committee meeting in Geneva in April urged national sections to continue pressure on their governments not to recognize Manchukuo as an independent state and to refuse Japan all assistance in the conflict. An embargo on all arms to the Far East was also recommended. The League of Nations committee set up to watch the situation agreed on non-recognition of Manchukuo and considered the posssibility of an arms embargo; but only Britain made any attempt to apply this and the proposal lapsed. Acknowledging the WILPF resolution, the head of the Chinese delegation wrote:

We are very grateful to your League for its attitude with regard to the Sino-Japanese conflict. It will, indeed, be due to world opinion, where women can play a predominant role, that peace and justice will finally triumph.

The Tangku truce signed between China and Japan on May 31, 1933, hardly qualified as a triumph of peace and justice, but at least it ended hostilities—or rather suspended them. It was only a few years later that fighting was to be resumed in the Far East in a yet more virulent and dangerous form.

Since the adjournment of the Disarmament Conference in July 1932 private negotiations had continued between the European powers and the USA in an effort to meet Germany's demands. On December 11th an agreed formula was reached whereby Germany should be given equality of rights—including the right to a conscript army—in a general system of security. The conclusion of a convention in this sense was to become the chief object of the second year of the Disarmament Conference which opened on January 31, 1933—just one day after the accession of Hitler as Chancellor of the German Reich.

The granting to Germany of the right to conscript an army was hardly the kind of 'equality' for which the WILPF had striven as the basis for a new international order. The French and German sections in particular were dismayed by this unwelcome climax to their fifteen years' work for the reconciliation of their countries. Submitting a joint appeal from the two sections to the President of the Disarmament Conference, Camille Drevet wrote:

The German and French sections have given wholehearted support to your repeated appeals for action towards Disarmament. They will no longer be able to do so, however, if the peoples are not relieved as soon as possible of the menace of any form of military service.

Compulsory military service, she continued, was the quickest way of establishing militarism but would never bring about Disarmament.

Undeterred by this and other warnings from the peace societies of many countries and from the International Peace Bureau in Geneva, the Disarmament Conference continued on its way to disaster. On February 23, 1933, the French proposal for standardized European armies with short-term service was adopted, against a German motion that measures for disarmament should be taken *before* voting on the French plan. But what was needed, as *Pax International* commented, was not a new military system but equality in disarmament. On March 19th a huge demonstration of war veterans in Geneva presented an appeal to Arthur Henderson on behalf of eight million men. This resolution was read out to the assembled Conference, as *Pax International* described it, in an 'icy silence'. No single delegate replied. 'Will the delegates to the Conference', Camille Drevet asked, 'have the strength to deliver their governments from the egoism that is leading us into war?'

Henderson, at least, was trying, and the new draft Convention presented by Ramsay MacDonald on behalf of the British Government on March 16th was adopted by the Conference as the basis for future discussions. But any possible value this gesture might have had was virtually nullified by the almost simultaneous proposal by Mussolini of a Four-Power Pact with Britain, France and Germany. It was inevitable that having opted for rearmament rather than disarmament, the nations would henceforth seek 'security' through power politics rather than by obedience to international law. This return to the pre-1914 system of secret diplomacy was strongly condemned by the WILPF Executive Committee meeting in April.

That same month the WILPF organized in Geneva a study conference on Obstacles to Disarmament which, in two resolutions addressed to the Disarmament Conference, reaffirmed the necessity of total disarmament together with a transformation of the social system, which was described as 'incompatible with peace'. The Disarmament Committee of Women's International Organizations also organized a study conference in May 1933 on the work of the Disarmament Conference, under the direction of Kathleen Courtney. It had plenty to study, with the appeal to heads of state by President Roosevelt on May 16th for acceptance of the British plan, together with further measures of disarmament and a new non-aggression pact; and the announcement by Hitler on May 17th that Germany accepted the draft as the basis for a Disarmament Convention.

Discussion on these points continued in the Disarmament Conference with scarcely a façade of conviction. In June the Conference adjourned with none of the obstacles to disarmament removed: with France demanding more inspection; Japan stalling on naval limitation; and Britain alone among the powers holding out for the retention of bombing planes. Who could say, at this stage, that only Germany was responsible for the coming degeneration into total war?

Nevertheless, events in Germany were revealing a frightening discrepancy between international declarations and domestic policy. Following the general elections in March 1933, when the Nazi representation was increased by 92 seats, repression and persecution became the unconcealed instruments of the German Government. Within months, all other political parties had been dissolved and the ghastly round-up into concentration camps of Jews, left-wing and pacifist sympathizers, and other critics of Nazi policy was well under way. The WILPF Executive Committee in April expressed its horror at the Nazi crimes and sympathy with the victims. A strong protest against anti-semitism was sent to the German Government, followed by similar protests from a number of national sections. The menace of Nazi influence in Austria at this time was also noted, and an appeal was sent to the Second International for combined action in support of Austrian socialists.

Arthur Henderson meanwhile was continuing his thankless task of negotiating between the powers. France put forward amendments to the British plan—proposing a four-year trial period of investigation by the Permanent Disarmament Commission before any actual arms reductions took place—which were accepted by Britain, USA and Italy but not unexpectedly rejected by Germany. When Sir John Simon presented the proposals at the reopening of the Conference on October 14, 1933, they were clearly destined for an early interment. It was, in fact, only minutes after he had spoken that Germany's withdrawal from the Disarmament Conference was announced; and later the same day, her withdrawal from the League of Nations. On October 14th also Hitler made his first public demand for the return of the Saar from France. Not only the draft Disarmament Convention died on that day; with it were buried all hopes of a peaceful political settlement in Europe.

One other way to peace might still have remained open, but for yet another failure in this fateful year of 1933: the way of economic co-operation, long advocated by the WILPF. On June 12th the World Economic Conference opened in London with participation by 64 countries. After nine months of preparation, it was in session for only five weeks. Its failure was largely blamed on the United States, which refused to co-operate in any measures for currency stabilization; and without such stabilization—as the WILPF had pointed out in 1931— no effective international action was possible on any other economic question. Just as international law had been abandoned in favour of power politics, so now international economic planning was abandoned in favour of bilateral, 'smash-and-grab' agreements. The appeal addressed to all governments by the WILPF before the opening of the Conference, that 'the world's necessity should prevail over nationalistic considerations', fell once again on deaf ears. Though this appeal to fundamental reason was to be reiterated for another five years, there was little hope now that, even if listened to, it could have effect in time.

CHAPTER 11

REAPPRAISALS OF POLICY

*Situation in Germany—Case of Camille Drevet—Zürich
Congress 1934—Amendment of Constitution—Split in
British section—The Political Situation*

The year 1934 saw the calling of a special Congress of the Women's
International League for Peace and Freedom, some months before it
was due, for the purpose of considering afresh the policy and constitution of the League in the light of the changed international situation.

The work of the national sections had already been affected by
political developments in several European countries, notably of course
in Germany, where with the consolidation of the Nazi régime it was
no longer possible for the section to function openly at all. Two of its
leading members, Anita Augspurg and Lida Gustava Heymann, fled
to Switzerland early in 1933; other members had also escaped or been
arrested. One of the first proposals for a form of sanctions against
Germany came from Lida Heymann, who in May 1933 suggested a
'travel boycott', coupled with the encouragement of tourism in
Austria which was suffering economically from Nazi restrictions on
German tourists there.

Edith Pye, as joint international chairman of the WILPF, issued a
confidential report to her fellow-officers on April 28, 1933, after a
visit to Germany, describing the impossibility of carrying on peace
propaganda there; only the Catholic Peace Society was still able to
meet. In Berlin the President of the WILPF had been summoned to
police headquarters and warned; in Breslau all pacifist and Jewish
books in the library of the WILPF secretary were removed by local
Nazis. During her stay in Germany Miss Pye made arrangements
whereby any member arrested could at once send a message to the
Geneva office so that her case might be taken up internationally.

In June 1933 Edith Pye appealed directly to Hitler on behalf of
Emma Machenhauer, secretary of the Munich branch of the WILPF,
who was suddenly arrested for no obvious reason—being 'neither
Socialist, Communist nor Jew'. Miss Pye reminded Herr Hitler that
the WILPF had worked since 1919 for the removal of international

injustices, had opposed the post-war blockade of Germany, and had demanded amendments to the Peace Treaties 'in the interest of justice'. She went on:

Our League will continue to work for a right understanding of Germany's present condition, but incidents such as this make it difficult to convince the public in these different countries that the leaders of the great German people adhere to the principles of justice, humanity and freedom which are the only foundations upon which enduring world peace can be based.

Early the following year Miss Pye had to appeal again on behalf of an imprisoned member, this time in Austria, where the Member of Parliament Emmy Freundlich was temporarily arrested following the Dollfuss *coup* in February 1934. She reminded Dr Dollfuss of the WILPF opposition to all violence, which was reaffirmed in a statement of principle issued after the Grenoble Congress in 1932:

This VIIth Congress assembled in Grenoble desires to reaffirm the stand of the Women's International League for Peace and Freedom and all its national groups and sections against violence and oppression of every kind; whether employed between different nations, classes or individuals and whether under the influence of Fascism or Communism or any other system of Government. It declares the League to have no financial affiliation with, nor to be under the domination of any political party, national or international, or any government whatsoever.

This statement of principle had been widely disseminated, not only to strengthen sections suffering under Fascist régimes but also in order to combat the allegations of 'Communism' which continued to be made against the League—not least, at the seat of the international headquarters in neutral, 'liberal' Switzerland.

The campaign against the WILPF by certain conservative elements in the Swiss press, backed by pressure-groups of anti-Soviet exiles in Geneva, came to a head in July 1933 with the threatened expulsion of the international secretary, Camille Drevet, by the federal authorities. The case had wide international repercussions, as the American weekly *The Nation* forcibly commented on July 5, 1933:

The astounding decision of the Swiss government to expel the international secretary of the Women's International League for Peace and Freedom is a challenge to the peace movement that cannot be ignored. Madame Drevet must leave the country before July 14, the government has declared, because she is a 'revolutionary propagandist' and an anti-militarist! Her revolutionary propaganda seems to have consisted mostly in setting before the world the horrible facts of the killing of thirteen workers and the wounding of sixty others by Swiss troops who shot into an unarmed crowd of demonstrators in Geneva on November 9 of last year. But she is also being expelled as an anti-militarist. This can only be because of her connection with the Women's International League. It is obvious that if Madame Drevet can be deported for anti-militarism, no one can safely work for peace in Geneva. (A Swiss citizen would face jail instead of deportation under the same circumstances.) And if the world peace movement is not to be permitted to center its activities in Geneva, the seat of the League of Nations and the disarmament conference, its effectiveness will be immeasurably impaired.

Immediately on hearing the news of the expulsion order the WILPF Executive Committee sent a formal request to the Head of the Department of Justice in Berne demanding the reasons for this action, and stating the full confidence of the League in its secretary:

The political activities of Madame Drevet have been in accord with the policy of the Women's International League for Peace and Freedom in promoting in every possible way disarmament, peace and international understanding, a policy which we have always understood to be in line with that pursued by the Swiss Government itself.

Madame Drevet is the widow of a distinguished French officer who was killed in the 'war to end war', and her devotion to the cause of peace is widely known and greatly esteemed.

The Berne group of the League also intervened and obtained the services of Professor Rennefahrt as advocate for Camille Drevet. The grounds for expulsion given to the chairman of the group were that Mme Drevet had visited the Soviet Union, had had relations with Communists, and had written articles for the journal *Travail*. Professor Rennefahrt, however, stated that if he had found that the WILPF was in any way connected with Communism he would not have taken up the case.

On July 1st Edith Pye had an interview with the Chief of Police in Geneva, Frederic Martin. 'The fury with which M. Martin expressed himself', she reported, 'cannot be described.' He declared Mme Drevet to be a Communist: she had been to Russia and she knew Barbusse (Henri Barbusse, the French revolutionary writer), and that was sufficient crime. Miss Pye attempted to explain that the WILPF worked only for peace and disarmament and was in no sense a revolutionary organization. Whereupon M. Martin threatened to turn the League out of Geneva along with Camille Drevet.

There was a feeling among some members that the WILPF should not wait to be turned out of Geneva but should remove the international headquarters from Switzerland as a gesture of protest. The views of national sections were sought, but majority opinion was against any such move. Support for Camille Drevet continued to pour in, both from members and groups of the League and from wider circles; more than forty outside interventions were made on her behalf. Finally, on July 13th, the expulsion order was suspended, one day before its expiration, and Camille Drevet remained in Geneva. It was regrettable, in the circumstances, that less than a year later, in May 1934, the League was obliged to terminate her employment because of financial difficulties, and the work of the international secretary was temporarily undertaken on a voluntary basis by Emily Balch.

It was in the British section of the WILPF that the demand for a reappraisal of policy first took shape. In March 1934 the section proposed that, in view of the international situation, the International Executive Committee should not pass political resolutions without first obtaining the agreement of national sections. This proposal, if adopted, would obviously hamper the effective working of the Executive Committee. Other sections were also making suggestions for revision of the constitution, and it was therefore decided that an International Congress must be called that year to go thoroughly into the whole matter. As Miss Balch wrote on April 28th to a Japanese member:

Our conception of this Congress is that it will have a rather different character and purpose than others that we have held: that we should not discuss resolutions and manifestos but come to grips with the question in what form and how our work shall be continued in view not only of lessened money resources but, what is more important, of the tense and confused social and political condition of the world.

Preparations for the Congress were left in the capable hands of Gertrude Baer, now resident in Switzerland, and notwithstanding the restricted agenda and difficult situation, 135 delegates attended from 15 countries. There was certainly no lack of interest among its members about the future of the League.

Indeed, the intensity of feeling engendered led to protracted and sometimes stormy discussions, showing strong divisions of opinion on the role of the WILPF in the mid-1930s. The main cleavage ran broadly between the Anglo-American-Scandinavian groups on the one hand, taking their stand on the principles of the 1915 Congress and favouring methods of democratic gradualism; and on the other hand, the Franco-German insistence on more radical action against social injustice and more co-operation with mass movements. In the circumstances of their respective countries, both views were understandable.

Clara Ragaz, President of the Swiss section, in her opening address summed up the crucial areas of dissension:

These differences show most clearly in our attitude toward the transformation of the present economic system, toward violence and, as regards our methods of work, toward the question whether we lay the most weight on our national or our international work.

She recalled that a firm principle of the League had been to unite women from different political camps; this did not prevent members from joining whatever political party they believed most effective. But, she went on,

the justification for the existence of our League is the fact that in the struggle for peace it emphasizes, besides political and economic considerations, ethical and purely human considerations and that it has always considered as absolutely necessary for this struggle its own methods in harmony with the spirit of our League.

This precept at once raised the problem of the use of violence to change a social system which was itself based on violence. Politically, the principles of the WILPF implied the strengthening of democracy; socially, the strengthening of a radical socialism freed from the dogma of class-warfare. It was not the aims of the League that were at present in question, but how to achieve them. A split in the WILPF at this stage, said Clara Ragaz, would be disastrous. She appealed for unity, though not at the cost of honesty:

If we cannot, with a full realization of the differences between us, clasp hands nevertheless then it is better for us to separate for the sake of truth rather than 'for the sake of peace and quiet' to make a pretence of a community which does not exist in reality.

Gertrude Baer spoke of a 'crisis' in the League, which she attributed to three main causes: the changed economic position of the middle-classes, from whom the majority of supporters had been drawn; a failure to attack economic injustice on an international basis; and a failure to win the intellectual co-operation of young people in the techniques of non-violent action.

Kathleen Innes expressed the predominantly British view when she said:

It seems to me that it would mean a turning aside if we worked *first* for a drastic change of the social and economic order. By doing so we should confuse a condition of things with a method of working, and it is an open question whether any given social order would mean peace. So far there are not many signs that it would. It is however not an open question that we stand for peace and against violence under whatever order exists. I want to emphasize that peace is a *method* and not a *state* and that under every system there will be causes for clash unless we remove the psychological causes.

Other points of view were put with equal conviction and Clara Ragaz summed up the discussion under two heads: (1) Aims and purposes of the League: in no circumstances could the League take part in violence, but the majority view showed itself to be 'more indulgent with violent action if resorted to by the oppressed than if by the oppressor'. (2) Work within the League: one school of thought wanted the Executive Committee only to act as a sort of clearing-house for National Sections; the other saw the Executive Committee as the central body, giving out suggestions to be followed by sections.

Then followed the gruelling work of hammering out a Constitution and Statement of Aims on the basis of the amendments submitted by national sections. It was a ding-dong battle in which the chief protagonists were Britain and France, and the main dispute was over the wording of a new paragraph proposed by the French section with German support. In this the 'first duty' of the WILPF was laid down as 'to facilitate and hasten the social transformation' which would inaugurate a new system of social, economic and political equality. The first round of voting saw the adoption of the Franco-German statement 'as a basis for discussion' and the defeat of a British amendment. Put to the vote, the Franco-German statement was carried—but without the two-thirds majority which was necessary for a change in the Constitution. It was left to a Constitution Committee to incorporate further amendments to the statement and present a revised draft for the final vote. This was taken on September 6th—Jane Addams' birthday—and after further agonized discussion the new statement of aims was adopted by 92 votes to 6, with abstentions. Agreement had been won—at a cost which was still to be counted. Wan but triumphant, the Congress despatched a celebratory cable:

The whole Congress united in aims sends best wishes for the birthday of their dear President.

The Statement of Aims voted by the Zürich Congress read as follows and was to remain the official policy of the WILPF for the next 25 years:

The Women's International League for Peace and Freedom aims at bringing together women of different political and philosophical tendencies united in their determination to study, make known, and abolish the political, social, economic and psychological causes of war, and to work for a constructive peace.

The primary objects of the Women's International League for Peace and Freedom remain: Total and universal disarmament, the abolition of violent means of coercion for the settlement of all conflicts, the substitution in every case of some form of peaceful settlement, and the development of a world organization for the political, social and economic co-operation of peoples.

Conscious that these aims cannot be attained and that a real and lasting peace and true freedom cannot exist under the present system of exploitation, privilege and profit they consider that their duty is to facilitate and hasten by non-violent methods the social transformation which would permit the inauguration of a new system under which would be realized social, economic and political equality for all without distinction of sex, race or opinion.

They see as the goal an economic order on a world-wide basis and under world regulation founded on the needs of the community and not on profit.

The work of all the National Sections is based upon the Statements adopted and the Resolutions passed by the International Congresses of the League.

The clauses in the Constitution concerning the powers, duties and composition of the Executive Committee, however, had still to be agreed. The main clash was again between the Franco-German emphasis on the supremacy of the international body and the British desire for the national viewpoints to be represented. A protracted, point by point wrangle resulted finally in adoption of the following rulings:

Between meetings of the Executive Committee the Officers may act on their own authority in international affairs in cases where it is impossible to consult the National Sections provided that the decision is taken unanimously by the Officers.

The Executive and the Officers shall regularly consult the National Sections regarding action on affairs within their respective countries, or on the policy of their country. In emergency when communication is impossible or dangerous, action may be taken without consultation, provided the application of the League principles is clear.

These clauses were incorporated in the Constitution and the whole Constitution was finally adopted unanimously, although there had been abstentions on certain clauses. In view of the controversies over its functions, it is perhaps of interest to give the names of the Executive Committee elected, on an individual and not a national basis, by this Congress: Gertrude Baer, Emily Balch, Dorothy Detzer, Camille Drevet, Gabrielle Duchêne, Yella Hertzka, Lola Hanouskova, Marie Lous-Mohr, Edith Pye, Clara Ragaz, Cor Ramondt-Hirschmann, Naima Sahlbom. Gertrude Baer and Clara Ragaz were elected by the Executive Committee as joint International Chairmen. Emily Balch was asked to continue as honorary International Secretary for another six months.

In addition, the Zürich Congress defined again the requirements which a national group must meet in order to be acceptable as a national section; the minimum membership was set at fifty. One new section was admitted, that for Yugoslavia. With a view to accommodating members driven from their own countries by dictatorship, provision was also made for the formation of a 'World Section' of the League: this must consist of not less than fifty women from at least three different countries. The efforts of the United States section, through its Committee on the Americas, to establish groups in Latin America were warmly welcomed and it was agreed that these groups should be recognized in their own right. The Congress heard with sorrow of the death at Stuttgart in December 1933 of Frida Perlen, one of the organizers of the original Hague Congress; she had been persuaded to leave Germany but returned in spite of the dangers in order to remain with her family. No printed report was issued of the 1934 Zürich Congress, but the minutes record one curious sidelight. Mildred Olmsted moved on behalf of the United States section an amendment proposing 'to have men and women in our League, and to change the name to correspond with this change in membership'. This, the most revolutionary amendment of all, was however withdrawn 'since it is too late to have a full discussion at this Congress'.

Although discussion had been largely limited to the internal affairs of the WILPF, the Congress allowed time for world affairs in the form of emergency resolutions. A telegram was sent to Senator Nye in Washington congratulating him on the first findings of the Nye Commission of enquiry into the manufacture and sale of munitions: an enquiry which might never have taken place but for the persistence of the Executive Secretary of the WILPF US Section, Dorothy Detzer (see Appendix 3). A proposal by the Czechoslovakian section to send a delegation to Berlin on behalf of imprisoned pacifists, together with an appeal to release women political prisoners in Germany, was referred to a special committee for implementation. Other resolutions dealt with equal rights; political prisoners; minorities; concentration camps; Austria. The admission of the Soviet Union to the League of Nations was warmly welcomed.

Nor was the long-term work of the WILPF neglected in these critical times. The problem of the nationality of married women was still being thrashed out in League of Nations committees. The treatment of prisoners in various countries was also taken up, in co-operation with the British Howard League for Penal Reform, with the object of getting a special LON Committee set up to investigate cases of ill-treatment. Miss Sheepshanks again visited the Ukraine in August 1934 and attended the Ukrainian Women's Congress. She found nationalist feeling running high and a strong sense of grievance against the Poles. This situation was not helped by the decision of Poland in September 1934 to refuse any further co-operation with the League of Nations in investigating minority complaints.

The WILPF Colonial Commission in 1933 reported action concerning Cuba, Liberia, Nicaragua, Haiti and the Philippines on the part of the United States section; British recommendations on India; French interventions regarding Syria, Madagascar, and the use of forced labour in Africa; and reconciliation work by the young Tunisian section among Arabs, Jews and Europeans. Due to National Socialist pressure, the long-standing Danish-German co-operation in border districts had to be suspended, but active conciliation was being continued between Sweden and the Baltic states of Finland, Estonia and Latvia. The Dutch section in May 1934 organized a study conference on the causes, nature and means of prevention of war, with emphasis on the psychological factors. As a result, the section was asked to take part in establishing a Peace School in Holland. An appeal was sent from the conference to medical organizations in 35 countries asking them to take up a study of the 'world disease' of war, together with psychologists and sociologists, and governments were urged to collaborate in scientific peace studies.

The first task of the Executive Committee in September 1934, however, was again a matter of internal policy. There was uneasiness among some members at what was regarded as the equivocal attitude of the French section to the use of violence. Clara Ragaz noted that the French delegates had voted against the clause in the new Statement of Aims which repudiated the use of violence under any circumstances, and Gabrielle Duchêne was asked to explain her attitude and that of the section. She replied that the French delegation had merely abstained on this clause in the final vote. The French section detested violence as much as any other, but it did not believe that the social transformation which seemed indispensable to assure peace and justice could be realized without any violence. Mme Duchêne asked the Executive Committee to decide whether the position taken by the French section was inconsistent with membership and could be grounds for expulsion from the League.

Plain speaking was perhaps easier in this small Committee than in the open Congress. Now Edith Pye revealed that it was she who had raised doubts about the French attitude to the fundamental principles of the League and that because of this apparent division in aims she was unable to accept nomination for the chairmanship. Emily Balch confessed that 'she had arrived, with great pain, at the conclusion that G. Duchêne was hampered in her work by her connection with the WILPF and that the WILPF often found its work made difficult by G. Duchêne'. Lida Heymann declared that if the French section were excluded the German section (in exile) would certainly leave the League. Clara Ragaz said there was no proposal to expel the French section and that Mme Duchêne had said she would not retire from the Executive unless the section were expelled. The Germans protested that Mme Duchêne had been elected to the Committee as an international member and not as a representative of the French section. There the matter rested, but Emily Balch added a footnote to the minutes pointing out that some of the discussion seemed to have been based on a misapprehension: 'No one at any time proposed or advocated the exclusion of any person or any group of persons from the Executive Committee or from membership of the League.'

The rupture had been sealed, but not healed. The Executive Committee adopted a proposal by Mme Duchêne to reaffirm its decision taken the previous year that the WILPF should co-operate in demonstrations 'against war and fascism' in so far as this could be done 'without compromising our principles'. But this affirmation did not prevent some strong criticisms, particularly from the Swedish section, of Mme Duchêne's prominent part in organizing the Women's Congress against War and Fascism which had taken place in Paris in August 1934.

In January 1935, the British section was again expressing dissatisfaction and finding itself 'out of harmony with the present actions of the International Executive Committee'. By only a small majority, the Annual Council rejected a motion that it should withdraw from the international organization and agreed to continue working 'to advance the principles it feels essential in the policy of the WILPF as a whole'. Catherine Marshall outlined the main areas of disagreement:

1. The value of the League of Nations in its present form.
2. The value of seeking to influence governments by democratic methods.
3. The desirability of associating with Communist peace movements.
4. The powers of the International Executive Committee to speak for the WILPF as a whole.

As she pointed out, the first three points of division occurred not only between national sections but within them; and occurred also in most other political organizations at that time. This was not at all surprising, in view of the general confusion of values that befogged the international scene.

Contributing to a symposium in *Pax International*, February 1935, Emily Balch summed up 'The Present Political Situation' in the following terms:

Three Powers profess a nationalist-militarist point of view: Italy, Germany, Japan. All three are fascist and are under suspicion of aggressive intentions.

Four Powers may be counted as in a general way seeking stabilization of the *status quo*, or 'security'. Of these England, France and the United States are parliamentary countries, Russia a dictatorship of the proletariat. The means used by all of them are armaments and 'understandings', if not actual alliances. This is especially true of France and Russia who are the most uneasy about possible attack.

Of the lesser European Powers some desire 'revision', some are afraid of it. The desire to enlist their backing leads to endless intrigue among the great Powers. Many of them are also powder-mines for the world through their own feuds, internal and external. These different kinds of tension every now and then coincide in such a way as to create a special danger—as at Sarajevo and Marseilles.[1]

There are also the democratic neutral countries, of which only the Scandinavian countries, Holland and Switzerland are in a position to influence the situation perceptibly.

Centred at Geneva there is the international peace organization. The effectiveness of the League of Nations, in this role, has suffered from the fact that it is neither a military or economic supernational force, nor (what we desire to see it) a universal disinterested moral force.

Since Great Britain and the United States propose not to be involved in European struggles this leaves the direction of policies, in face of the three imperialist Powers, mainly in the hands of France and Russia, and the leadership is with France.

In the light of this analysis, the Franco-British tension within the WILPF can clearly be seen as understandable, if not inevitable. Of the British section Miss Balch said:

[1] King Alexander of Yugoslavia and the French Foreign Minister Barthou were assassinated by emigré terrorists at Marseilles on October 8, 1934.

The members of the English WIL are a great educational force and within certain limits an effective political force. They have a government susceptible to pressure by voters and they have the vote. They have the English tradition of good sense, persistence and democratic activity. They prefer half a loaf to none. They are throwing their force into getting as much as may be possible in the way of a disarmament convention and into preventing the growth of fascism and of instruments of suppression like the sedition law, recently brought into force. Quite particularly in the effort to build up a collective peace system they are laying the greatest stress on support for and development of democratic methods. This means of course that they oppose every kind of dictatorship whatever its ultimate aim.

In France, more closely threatened by the twin dangers of war and Fascism, the priorities were different:

The French section of the WIL considers efforts towards social transformation as the first necessity and regards as its most important service the building up of a great popular movement against war and fascism in common with all elements which are opposing these—a piece of work in which it is being astonishingly successful.

The French attitude was, as ever, logical; the British showed the usual curious union of principle and self-interest. But what of Germany? In Miss Balch's view Germany, for all the sins of its Nazi government, must be brought into the European order, even though this meant recognizing her right to rearm:

The question is whether Germany is more dangerous arming illegally and clandestinely just as she chooses, or arming in public, within agreed limits and under supervision.

A German writer in the same issue of *Pax International* violently opposed this attitude, maintaining that the Hitler rule was sustained by heavy industry and the 'Junkers' and that pacifists bore a heavy responsibility for the rearming of Germany:

Instead of giving their support to those Germans who tried to make a virtue of necessity under the Versailles Treaty and to prepare a new generation for freedom and peace they gave their support, in all good faith and without any knowledge of the facts, to the madmen who under pretext of equality were busy in preparing the intensive rearmament of Germany in all fields.

Clara Ragaz of Switzerland, from a more objective standpoint, reached a similar conclusion:

As pacifists we have every ground to welcome a return of Germany into the community of peoples but it would be disastrous to assume that the present Germany of terrorism and the rule of violence would mean an enrichment of the international life of the peoples. It is our task to strengthen 'the other Germany' and we do not do this by supporting the present Germany and aiding it to attain without repentance or expiation what it set out to attain.

Writers from the smaller European countries—Austria, Czechoslovakia, Hungary and Poland—all tended to agree that Emily Balch, with her 'typical Anglo-Saxon point of view', had failed to appreciate the critical condition of Europe. The only hope these countries could see was in general disarmament and control of arms manufacture—a forlorn hope indeed, as coming events were all too soon to demonstrate.

Whatever the rights and wrongs of Germany's position internationally, the Nazi persecution of the Jews was something which no member of the Women's International League in any country could condone. In September 1935, following a brutal wave of anti-semitism in Germany, the WILPF issued an 'Appeal to the Non-Jews of Europe' that they should not keep silent in face of these crimes:

'Civilized' Europe is silent because it is an accomplice. It is an accomplice because by providing important loans and credits, commodities and raw materials, and thus contributing to Germany's war potential, it strengthens and stabilizes the reign of terror.

'Civilized' Europe is an accomplice when, in order to induce the rulers of Germany to consent to return to the League of Nations and the Disarmament Conference, it glosses over and tolerates their crimes.

The statement concluded:

We appeal to those who still have the courage and the freedom to do so to speak out and to join us in expressing public execration of all pogroms, open or secret, and of the hideous shame to civilization which Hitler has brought upon Europe.

This appeal was widely quoted in the press, being published in full in the *Manchester Guardian*. The WILPF had many differences over the best method of implementing its policies, but its underlying principles remained unshaken. It could not be said that the WILPF ever confused positive peace-making with the appeasement of brute force.

APPENDIX 3

WILPF UNITED STATES SECTION AND THE NYE COMMISSION

Dorothy Detzer was cited by *The Nation* both for her share in persuading the American Government to withdraw its armed forces from Nicaragua and for promoting 'almost single-handed' an enquiry into the munitions industry. John E. Wiltz, a historian, wrote in 1963 (*In Search of Peace*, Indiana University):

No one knows who first thought of a munitions investigation, but a movement for inquiry began in earnest in 1932 when the Annual Convention of the US section of the Women's International League for Peace and Freedom adopted a resolution urging the Senate to investigate the private Munitions Trade. . . .

A detailed account of the campaign to set up the Nye Commission is given in Dorothy Detzer's own record of her twenty years' lobbying on behalf of the WILPF, *Appointment on the Hill*. She concludes:

Unfortunately, however, the careful and important recommendations of the Munitions Committee were not to live. Those recommendations, accompanying the committee's reports to the Senate, were presented in a series of interlocking legislative measures. Together these measures formed not only a comprehensive and far-reaching program for the maintenance of peace, but also supplied bulwarks to safeguard the rights of the American people.

The Neutrality Bill, providing for an embargo on arms and loans to nations at war, was the only legislation even partially enacted into law. But even it was crippled by its 'half-measure' provisions, and was never intended to form an isolated policy plucked from the context of the entire program.

Surely, no Senate committee ever rendered to the American people a more intelligent or important service. It was the nation's loss that it did not comprehend it.

In June 1935 the US section of the WILPF received an award of 3,000 dollars from the Woodrow Wilson Foundation,

for its useful part in informing public opinion regarding the dangers involved in the unregulated private manufacture of the munitions of war, and in the international trade in such munitions, and for the success in helping to focus the influence of that public opinion on the Congress of the United States.

CHAPTER 12

AGGRESSION UNLIMITED

Decline of League of Nations—Ethiopian War—Pressure for Sanctions—Saar Plebiscite—Occupation of the Rhineland—WILPF Policy on Germany—Spanish War

The attitude of the British section of the WILPF to the international body could not unfairly be compared to that of the big powers in the League of Nations which, at every crisis, put national interests before international obligations and so wrecked the first governmental experiment in international organization. Fortunately, matters did not come to this pass in the WILPF; it was not a governmental organization, and there was always the opportunity for goodwill and common sense to rise above national sensibilities. Nor, of course, were its problems comparable to those of the League of Nations; they were only one reflection of the common problems of adjustment to a shrinking world.

But the critical condition of the League of Nations now became startlingly apparent. Japan continued on her expansionist policy in Asia, uninhibited by the formal disapproval of a League to which she no longer owed any allegiance and from whose member-states she obtained the wherewithal for further conquest. The success of this first strong-arm challenge to the embryonic rule of law did not pass unnoticed. Now the second of the 'nationalist-militarist' powers moved up its armour for attack.

The pretext for the Italian invasion of Ethiopia arose from an incident at Wal-Wal in the disputed border area with Italian Somaliland on December 5, 1934. More than one hundred Ethiopians and thirty Italian native troops were killed before the Ethiopians withdrew. Ethiopia appealed for arbitration of the dispute under the Italo-Ethiopian Treaty of 1928, and when this was refused Emperor Haile Selassie asked the LON Secretary-General to bring the matter to the League Council. His request was telegraphed on December 15th. Already on December 13th the WILPF International Chairmen had written to the Secretary-General drawing attention to this new threat to peace—the first communication on the crisis from any international organization. The Geneva Research Centre, noting this fact in a paper on 'Public Opinion and the Italo-Ethiopian Dispute' published in March 1936, described the WILPF as 'one of the most active organizations throughout the dispute, both through its international office in Geneva and also through its national sections in twenty-four countries'. In this matter there was no divergence of policy and the British section was perhaps the most deeply engaged of all.

As the Italian military build-up continued, and no action was taken by the League Council, Haile Selassie appealed again on March 16, 1935, under Article 15 of the Covenant. On March 20th the WILPF again wrote to the Secretary-General. But the Council meeting on April 15th agreed to postpone the question until the next session. Concerned about the increasing truculence of Germany, the powers most directly concerned—Britain and France—were by no means anxious to make an enemy of Italy. In June Anthony Eden, the newly-appointed British Minister for League Affairs, went to Rome with a compromise plan; this was rejected by Italy, with the backing of France. The WILPF Executive Committee meeting in March sent a resolution to the Council, pointing out that Italy was now following the example of Japan—and seemed to be getting away with it: 'It is probable that certain great imperialist countries are disposed to allow her a free hand in exchange for certain advantages.' But, the resolution continued, 'the conscience of the world will be outraged' if the League of Nations remained deaf to Ethiopian appeals. It is of some historical interest that Ethiopia is referred to in this resolution as 'the only great state on the African continent that is still independent', i.e. in a *pre-colonial* state.

At a special Council meeting on July 31st France and Britain were asked to continue direct negotiations with Italy. Discussions were started on August 16th and broke down in three days, with Italy refusing to negotiate any terms for a settlement. Indeed, she attempted to turn the tables by indicting Ethiopia as a 'barbarous state' which, by its practice of slavery, had violated its international obligations. Only Litvinoff was brave or honest enough to declare that this, even if true, was no reason for the big powers themselves to violate their obligations under the Charter. When the League Assembly met on September 9th a majority of states, including Britain and France, pledged themselves to uphold the Covenant, and on September 26th the Council met to consider action under Article 15, namely to investigate the facts of the dispute and make recommendations accordingly. Two days later Haile Selassie, aware of the massing of Italian troops on his borders, announced general mobilization.

On September 10th, the first broadcast to come out of Ethiopia was made by the Empress through the National Broadcasting Company of America. It was an appeal to the women of the world to make their voices heard 'in the firm, united demand that the horrors of useless bloodshed and overwhelming ruin shall not be'. The Empress was speaking at the invitation of the WILPF and was introduced by a New York member, Miss Caroline Singer. The appeal, like so many others before and since, was in vain, and on October 3rd Italian troops crossed the border. In a last, desperate 'women's appeal', Miss Balch telegraphed the Queen of Italy to intervene and stop the war. This move was reported in a BBC news bulletin—the first time, said Edith Pye, that any action of the WILPF had been mentioned in a news broadcast.

On October 5th the League of Nations Council issued a unanimous condemnation of Italy. The Assembly endorsed this verdict four days later and an eighteen-nation Sanctions Committee was set up. Was the League about to redeem itself and expunge its failure over Japan? Export of arms to Italy by member-states was forbidden and indirect financial sanctions were adopted. Britain and France were not lagging this time and Anthony Eden was leading the pressure for sanctions—although not to the point of making them really effective by closing the Suez Canal. At the same time, Britain and France were asked to continue private negotiations with Italy to bring about a settlement. Meanwhile, public opinion in the democracies—including America, with its officially 'neutral' policy—was overwhelmingly in favour of strong action by the League of Nations and pressure was mounting for the extension of sanctions to include an embargo on the most vital war-material, oil.

At last, wrote Kathleen Innes in *Pax International*, the powers were committed to a League of Nations policy. But why were they still hesitating over the oil embargo—surely the first sanction that should have been applied—if not for the sake of vested interests? Scarcely had the ink dried on this article when the answer came. The big powers had *not* renounced their 'vested interets', they were *not* committed to a genuine League of Nations policy. The Sanctions Committee, at the request of France, had deferred consideration of the oil embargo from November 29th to December 12th. On December 8th the reason for the postponement became clear, with the announcement in Paris of the secretly-negotiated 'Hoare-Laval Plan' for a settlement of the dispute. The terms, which Sir Samuel Hoare had been persuaded to accept by the French Foreign Minister Pierre Laval, proposed the virtual annexation by Italy of half Ethiopia's territory, an area of some 160,000 square miles; in return, Ethiopia was offered an outlet to the sea comprising about 3,000 square miles.

The plan was received with shocked indignation by public opinion in all the sanctionist countries. The WILPF British section issued a strong protest on December 10th and called for an immediate oil embargo. This was only the beginning of a national campaign to get the Hoare-Laval Plan rejected. Edith Pye wrote to Gertrude Baer on December 14th: 'I never remember such a universal expression of disgust and fury against the Government.' On December 18th a delegation from four international women's organizations, including the WILPF, delivered a letter to the President of the League Council expressing this overwhelming sentiment:

It is very seldom that we see the nations of the world rising in such spontaneous revolt against a suggested formula for peace, and find them so unanimous in their interpretation of this formula.

It seems to them a prize given to Italy which has been solemnly declared by the Council of the League of Nations to be the aggressor, and to have given her a victory which she had not won by force of arms.

The proposals appear to them to be a betrayal of the countries which, in good faith and loyalty, have applied Sanctions, a betrayal committed by the Great Powers, and a betrayal of Ethiopia which has been the victim of this unqualified attack.

The nations are convinced that only proposals guaranteeing the absolute territorial integrity of Ethiopia and its political independence can provide a solution of the conflict which will re-establish peace in Africa, and ensure peace for the whole world.

In fact, the League Council did not have to reject the Plan: Italy herself did so. But the anger of British public opinion forced the resignation of Hoare and the appointment of Eden as Foreign Secretary.

The Hoare-Laval Plan was dead, but no fresh proposals were made either by the Council which met again on January 20, 1936, or by the Sanctions Committee in February. The decision on an oil embargo, which a panel of experts had unanimously reported to be a feasible proposition, was again postponed until the next meeting in March. In a letter to the Prime Minister on January 15th, Mrs Innes expressed the feeling of the British section: 'while the supply of oil to Italy continues it is to our shame that profits are coming to British citizens, and British-owned petrol is being employed to drive the bombing-planes of the Italian army'. On January 20th the International Chairmen again wrote to the President of the L O N Council, protesting against the resumption of secret diplomatic negotiations by the great powers in violation of the democratic principles of the Covenant. Again, an embargo on oil was demanded.

When the Sanctions Committee met in March, however, France once more asked for postponement of an oil embargo, with British agreement—although now for the first time Eden promised that Britain would support an embargo. Meanwhile, Italy was exploiting her advantageous position with the use of mustard-gas against Ethiopian villages. Militarily, the war was already won, and when the League Council again called for peace talks on March 3rd Mussolini agreed 'in principle' to negotiate. Salvador de Madariaga was deputed by the Council to draft an agreement, but by April 17th was forced to admit the hopelessness of the attempt. The Council met on April 20th, protested against Italy's violation of the Gas Convention of 1925, and ignored Ethiopia's plea for an oil embargo. On May 2nd, with the fall of Addis Ababa imminent, Haile Selassie left his country. A week later, Mussolini announced the incorporation of Ethiopia in the Italian Empire.

By July the attempt to impose sanctions against Italy had officially been abandoned, although popular protests continued to be made. The WILPF British section, protesting against the abandonment of sanctions by the British Government in breach of its election pledges, declared that unless the Italian Government agreed to a settlement acceptable to the League of Nations Italy should no longer remain a member. The International Executive Committee in September requested the League Assembly to submit the Ethiopian question to the International Court of Justice at The Hague. But no further action was taken by the League of Nations. Italy was not expelled from membership. The only expulsion to be considered was that of Ethiopia, since she was no longer an independent state. But at least this final indignity —perpetrated by Britain and France to placate Italy—was resisted by the majority of the Assembly. It was a small gain to have salvaged from the international wreck. The success of this second major defiance of

the League of Nations by an aggressor had already, before its comple-
tion, triggered off a third and set in train the irreversible momentum
towards the Second World War.

But before the third aggressor moved into the spotlight the League
of Nations did score one further modest success. Its supervision of the
Saar Plebiscite in January 1935 was the first, and last, example of a
League of Nations international force operating in a disputed area to
ensure that the inhabitants of that area should determine their own
future. The WILPF sent requests to the Saar Plebiscite Commission in
October 1934 concerning the revision of voting lists and the representation of opposition parties on electoral committees, and these were
approved. In December 1934 an international force was established,
under a British commander, to supervise the elections. It achieved its
task with a minimum of disturbance and was never required to use its
arms. When the ballot-boxes were unsealed on January 14, 1935, the
voting was 90 per cent in favour of reunion with Germany. There was
no reason to doubt that this verdict did represent popular opinion,
and the Saar was handed back to Germany on March 1st, with German
assurances to France that the territory would remain demilitarized. It
seemed as if one potential conflict, at least, had been settled by mutual
goodwill.

But on the very day of the Saar-German reunion, Ramsay Mac-
Donald announced to the British Parliament a vast new programme of
defence expenditure: his first public admission that collective security
had failed, or been abandoned. All the powers were rearming, he
explained—including Germany—and Britain could not lag behind; in
particular, the warlike spirit of Nazism was a menace to peace. The
peace movement, which had seen MacDonald as its only official
spokesman for disarmament, was stunned. As Edith Pye wrote to
Emily Balch on March 7th:

We are all of us here terribly dismayed about the Government's action
in putting out the White Paper and increasing all the estimates. There
is to be a regular campaign, and all the Peace Societies are getting busy.

It seems such absolute madness to issue a statement of that kind
about Germany, just when an attempt was being made to get her back
into the comity of nations. I suppose our German friends are pleased,
but for myself I consider it disastrous, and the defeatism of the disarmament question is almost incredible, a statesman like Ramsay
MacDonald just eating his own words.

The 'German friends' to whom Miss Pye referred were doubtless the exiled WILPF members who, with reason, were more anxious for drastic measures to be taken against Nazi Germany than were the British at that time—although they never advocated rearmament as the alternative to appeasement. It was true that Germany was being wooed back into 'the comity of nations' by Franco-British diplomatic moves towards a general European settlement. But the British announcement gave Hitler the excuse he had been waiting for to settle the Versailles account on his own terms. A fortnight later, on March 16th, the German Army Law was published, reintroducing conscription and providing for a peace-time army of thirty-six divisions. The Peace Treaty, long moribund, was dead. And who could deny that the Allies, by evading their disarmament pledges, had written their own requiem? With the arms race in full swing again, and even the pretence of disarmament abandoned, all that was left to the former victors was a feverish cementing of alliances, old and new. The most decisive was the Franco-Soviet Pact of May 1935 followed in June by the Anglo-German Naval Agreement. A new power alignment seemed to be on the way, which bade farewell not only to Versailles, but to Geneva!

The Disarmament Conference, as *Pax International* pointed out in July 1935, had been 'adjourned but not abandoned'. Its three Special Committees still existed. A draft convention for the regulation and control of the manufacture and trade in arms had been circulated to governments. The Committee on Military Expenditure had prepared a draft convention on the publishing of military budgets. The Air Commission, however, had never even met. The WILPF British section in June had asked the Prime Minister to convene the Commission and make proposals for the reduction of air forces as a step towards their abolition. The British Women's Peace Crusade was at that time campaigning for the complete abolition of military and naval aircraft. The French Ligue Internationale des Mères et des Educatrices, supported by thirty-two organizations, presented a new petition for disarmament to the LON Council in May.

On September 16th the President of the League of Nations Assembly, Eduard Beneš, received a WILPF deputation led by Gertrude Baer. She reiterated the need for total and universal disarmament and urged that the Russian proposals in this sense to the Preparatory Disarmament Commission should at once be seriously discussed: 'If the imminent danger of a new world-war is to be averted there is only one way open—the way of complete and all-round disarmament.' Since disarmament was clearly the one way which would *not* be taken by the European powers, Miss Baer's assertion was never put to the test. Instead, the arms race increased and accelerated, the flouting of the League of Nations by Italy continued, and Hitler in turn saw no reason to lag behind his betters. By the following March, encouraged by Mussolini's success and incensed by the ratification of the Franco-Soviet Treaty in February, he was ready to make the first strike for the recovery of Germany's former 'greatness'.

The occupation of the demilitarized zone of the Rhineland by German troops on March 7, 1936, was a logical start to this crusade. It was accompanied by an offer of fresh pacts of non-aggression and the return of Germany to the League of Nations. All this was in line with normal 'great power' thinking and should not have surprised Hitler's rivals in the field. It was strange, therefore, that France should now at once abscond from her new-found 'security' and turn for help to the despised League of Nations. At her request, a special Council was called hurriedly in London at which France denounced Germany's violation of the Locarno Treaty and called for the imposition of sanctions—a remarkable turn-about from her previous attitude towards Italy. The Council confirmed Germany's violation of Locarno, but could not agree on any further action.

Outside France, it was not difficult to arouse sympathy for Germany's annexation of what was so patently her own territory. In the WILPF it was the occasion for another sharp disagreement between the British section and the international. On March 17th the International Chairmen, Gertrude Baer and Clara Ragaz, wrote to Mr Bruce, President of the LON Council, strongly condemning Germany's action, 'not only as a violation of the Treaties, but as a serious threat to the peace of Europe'. If the League of Nations capitulated before this 'flagrant assault', they declared, its moral standing—already weakened by Italy's aggression—would be destroyed. They urged the League Council to denounce the violation of the Treaties; demand the withdrawal of German troops; and, if the evacuation did not take place by a certain date, recommend to member states the application of economic and financial sanctions. Evacuation of the demilitarized zone should be followed by negotiations to lead to 'simultaneous and controlled disarmament'. Military sanctions were specifically repudiated.

A draft of the letter had previously been circulated to the Executive Committee for approval. Members from the Central European states were unreservedly in favour of the text; Edith Pye of Britain and Cor

Ramondt-Hirschmann of Holland wished to delete the demand for sanctions and ask for further negotiations. The British section invited the Executive Committee to meet immediately in London—a practical impossibility. Accepting the majority view, the Chairmen sent off the letter without amendment, and without consulting the national sections. Its reception was mixed, with even the distant American section showing a sharp division of opinion. Mrs Lola Maverick Lloyd wrote:

Congratulations on our prompt WILPF action in Geneva concerning Hitler's invasion of the Rhineland with his forbidden troops!—The news of your protest was given in today's *Chicago Tribune* on the second page, an accomplishment most unusual for pacifists!

Others, including Emily Balch and Mrs Hannah Clothier Hull, were uneasy that the WILPF had so quickly resorted to an advocacy of 'punitive measures' which might increase the danger of war.

The British section, supported generally by the Scandinavians, remained firmly opposed to the letter. It was not entirely clear whether their objection was primarily against the inclusion of 'sanctions' in the Chairmen's letter, or against their 'unconstitutional' action in sending it to the League of Nations without prior consultation with national sections. But it was only because of disagreements over policy that the constitutional issue arose.

When the Executive Committee met at Prague in April 1936 the British view was expressed in an emergency resolution asking for an assurance from the Chairmen that in future 'action in such cases be taken only with the agreement of *all* sections'. This was clearly an impossible undertaking to give, if the WILPF was to retain any effective freedom of action as an international organization. The resolution was defeated but the Chairmen, in view of the British lack of confidence in their judgment, announced their decision to resign. Edith Pye, on the other side, offered her resignation from the Executive Committee, which seemed to her to have endorsed the 'undemocratic' and 'autocratic' behaviour of the Chairmen. These drastic steps were only averted by the co-option of Cor Ramondt-Hirschmann as a third International Chairman and an agreement that no action was to be taken in future without the unanimous approval of all three.

In addition, the Executive Committee adopted a resolution on Sanctions which it was hoped would clarify the policy of the WILPF. This recommended the application of moral, diplomatic, financial and economic sanctions in the event of a treaty-breaking government refusing to accept *a priori* the decision of a judicial tribunal or court of arbitration; it rejected both military sanctions and the weapon of food blockade. Another resolution recommended the refusal of financial loans to Germany:

The Executive Committee of the Women's International League for Peace and Freedom would consider any loans or financial assistance strengthening the present German régime as an international catastrophe and as seriously increasing the danger of war.

The wisdom of this resolution, although it had been proposed by Catherine Marshall and carried unanimously, was also later disputed by the British section. Consciously or otherwise, the British section of the WILPF was echoing the policy of its own Government in maintaining the fiction of reasonable 'negotiation' between Nazi Germany and the democracies. Lida Gustava Heymann spoke for the exiled German group when she declared to the Executive Committee: 'in three years it may be proved that all the states of Europe ought to have made front against Hitler instead of negotiating with him'. It was not three years, but only three months before the next salvo was fired, this time as a combined operation of the Fascist and Nazi dictators with supporting action from that other dictatorship 'of the proletariat', as Emily Balch had described it—Soviet Russia.

The so-called 'civil war' in Spain was an international conflict from the first day of General Franco's armed insurrection against the Republican Government, when his forces landed from Morocco on July 18, 1936, under cover of German and Italian planes. On the other side, the Republican Government was receiving aid from the Soviet Union, primarily to put down internal revolts fomented not by Fascists but by dissident anarchist and socialist groups. Here were the ingredients for an all-out confrontation not only of old-style power politics but also of the new ideologies. Alarmed at the danger of a world war for which nobody was yet prepared, governments moved in quickly to set up a Non-Intervention Committee, with the object of prohibiting the supply of war material to either side, while popular opinion rallied behind the 'democratic', anti-Fascist forces supporting the Republic.

On grounds of legality alone, the sympathies of the WILPF were inevitably on the side of the Republican Government, as the victim of yet another Fascist violation of the rules of international morality.

This was especially so after it became clear that 'non-intervention' was operating entirely to the benefit of General Franco, whose supplies from his Fascist backers continued to flow in unchecked. But the first concern of the WILPF was to restore peace by the withdrawal of foreign troops rather than to ensure a Republican victory by redressing the unfair balance on that side. Already in August 1936 Louie Bennett was writing to Gertrude Baer on the possibility of mediation by President de Valera of Ireland. Emily Balch, too, had written to the Joint Chairmen in August on the need for a truce. She also foresaw the dangers of a quick victory for the Left:

It will mean, I fear, an internecine feud between anarchists, syndicalists, socialists, communists and Republicans, instead of a post-war conflict between the different groups of Rightists which will tend to disintegrate *them*.

This only fell short of the truth in that the Leftist disintegration came even without the victory. By November Italy and Germany had recognized Franco's headquarters at Burgos as the legitimate government of Spain, and the special League of Nations Council, called at the request of the Republican Government in December, could do no more than reiterate that 'non-intervention' must be strictly enforced.

The WILPF Executive Committee meeting at Geneva in September 1936 had protested against the 'unilateral neutrality' which 'constitutes in effect a sort of blockade of Republican Spain, and may give neutrality the character of complicity', and demanded an independent body under the League of Nations to enforce genuine non-intervention on both sides. On December 23rd the International Chairmen wrote to the governments represented at the League Council proposing the withdrawal of foreign troops fighting on the side of the rebels, under effective control, to be followed by withdrawal of volunteers fighting for the Republicans. The following February, on a proposal from the Netherlands section, the Chairmen asked national sections to press their governments to set up an International Commission for Spain. Names of suggested commissioners included Judge Michael Hansson (Norway), of the Nansen Office for Refugees; Sean Lester (Ireland); Louie Bennett and Edith Pye from the WILPF; and Carl Heath of the Society of Friends.

Following the Executive Committee meeting in April 1937, a deputation from the WILPF presented a resolution to Mr Quevedo, President of the LON Council, again pointing out the 'flagrant violation' of Article 10 of the Covenant and demanding the immediate evacuation of all foreign troops fighting with the rebels. The Executive Committee also issued a strong protest against what it called 'the recent massacre in the Basque country of a defenceless population'. This referred to the bombing attacks on open cities, notably Guernica, by German planes—a form of warfare which could still, in 1937, shock public opinion. In the resulting terror and chaos, many thousands of Spanish children were evacuated from their homeland to camps in France and England. Edith Pye, who was actively engaged in relief work for the British Joint Refugee Committee, described this exodus of children as 'a new phenomenon in human history'. She watched fifteen hundred child refugees arrive in France, and wrote in *Pax International*, June 1937:

Seen together in a mass they looked woefully pale and undernourished, but they were full of gay courage, dainty and fresh; they were excited and keen to see a new country. . . . The one question they asked when they were told they would be sent on into the country was 'Will there be enough bread?'

This tragedy, she predicted, was 'a foretaste of what mankind may expect if a way is not found out of the nightmare of conflict and rearmament. . . . By its illustration of what modern warfare means, it should serve to increase the efforts of all who are working to do away with it.'

The upsurge of a popular peace movement was, in fact, a notable feature of the last pre-war years. The abdication of the great powers from the League of Nations, and the failure of power politics itself to offer any alternative system of international security, left a vacuum which could only have been filled by the one remaining unused source of power—'the power of the people'. Had this power remained solidly welded on the side of 'peace and freedom', it is conceivable that even yet the coming war might have been averted. But peace and freedom were not yet seen, by the general public, as one indivisible unity. Even within the WILPF itself, the stress of maintaining this unity was considerable. The peoples of the world were overwhelmingly for peace; but they were fatally divided in the means to its achievement. The schisms which had already shaken, but not shattered, the WILPF were now becoming obvious on a wider national and international scale.

CHAPTER 13

UNITING FOR PEACE

British Peace Ballot 1934—People's Mandate Campaign—International Peace Campaign—USA and Neutrality—League of Nations Reform—WILPF Twentieth Anniversary—Death of Jane Addams—Luhacovice Congress 1937—Sino-Japanese War

---

If the British section of the WILPF appeared to be dragging its feet in the international organization during the 1930s, this did not mean that there was any sluggishness in its work at home. The section was always one of the most vigorous, and represented a positive educational force in British public opinion. It was amongst the most active of the thirty-eight organizations co-operating in the national 'Peace Ballot' organized by the League of Nations Union in June 1934. The ballot was virtually a referendum on foreign policy in the form of the following questions:

1. Should Great Britain remain a member of the League of Nations?
2. Are you in favour of an all-round reduction of armaments by international agreement?
3. Are you in favour of the all-round abolition of national military and naval aircraft by international agreement?
4. Should the manufacture and sale of armaments for private profit be prohibited by international agreement?
5. Do you consider that, if a nation insists on attacking another, the other nations should combine to compel it to stop by (*a*) economic and non-military measures? (*b*) if necessary, military measures?

This questionnaire was put to the British electorate by a vast army of half a million voluntary canvassers, tramping from door to door throughout England, Scotland and Wales. Eleven and a half million replies were collected, representing about 40 per cent of the electorate. Of this 40 per cent, an overwhelming majority said Yes to the policy advocated by the questions, viz: (1) 96 per cent, (2) 90·7 per cent, (3) 82·6 per cent, (4) 90·2 per cent, (5a) 86·8 per cent, (5b) 58·6 per cent. The crucial question was of course 5(b), and even here a small majority was in favour of 'collective security' to the point of military sanctions.

The Peace Ballot, however, was no more and no less than an expression of opinion. It carried no obligations and made no recommendations for future action, although the very fact of this united public opinion undoubtedly strengthened the voice of the British Government in calling for economic sanctions against Italy in the autumn of 1935. It also led indirectly to two international campaigns which demanded not only promises but action from both governments and peoples to save the peace. The first of these was initiated by the WILPF on the proposal of an American member, Lola Maverick Lloyd, who wrote to the US section's President Hannah Hull in April 1935 that she got the idea for 'a People's Mandate to Governments' while studying 'the unsatisfactory English peace questionnaire circulated this winter by their League of Nations Union'. The People's Mandate was adopted by the International Executive Committee that same month and recommended to national sections as their major work for the coming year. It took the form of a demand to governments for common action, in fulfilment of their pledges under the League of Nations Covenant and the Kellogg Pact, 'to meet the present threat of complete world chaos' by the following four steps:

Stop immediately all increase of armaments and of armed forces.
Use existing machinery for peaceful settlement of present conflicts.
Secure a world treaty for immediate reduction of arms as a step toward complete world disarmament.
Secure international agreements founded on recognition of world interdependence to end the economic anarchy which breeds war.

By November 1935 Camille Drevet, European secretary of the Mandate Committee, was able to report active co-operation for the campaign in Czechoslovakia, France, Holland, Hungary, Sweden and USA. The American campaign, energetically organized by Mabel Vernon, grew so rapidly that in February 1936 the WILPF relinquished its control to a combined People's Mandate Committee for the Western Hemisphere and the Far East, under the chairmanship of Mrs Carrie Chapman Catt. In March the People's Mandate Committee, having obtained one million signatures, sent a delegation to President Roosevelt to present its first demand: Stop immediately all increase of armaments and of armed forces. The delegation was introduced by Congresswoman Caroline O'Day, who expressed her 'enthusiastic support' for the Mandate, and the chief spokeswoman was Dr Mary Woolley, President of Mount Holyoke College and a former US delegate to the World Disarmament Conference.

The start of the British campaign was postponed until after the Hoare–Laval crisis and general election of November 1935, but by April 1936 the Mandate had been endorsed by twenty-eight national organizations including trade unions, peace societies, and religious and women's groups. The campaign had also spread to Australia, Austria, Ceylon, Denmark, Egypt, Greece, India, Ireland, New Zealand, Norway, Rumania, Spain, Tunisia and Yugoslavia.

The question whether the People's Mandate should be introduced into Fascist countries provoked considerable discussion. The WILPF Executive Committee in April 1936 agreed to try and send a deputation to Hitler, and possibly also to Mussolini, to explain the purpose of the campaign, but subsequently two of the International Chairmen, Clara Ragaz and Gertrude Baer, were found to be strongly opposed to the suggestion. Even Cor Ramondt-Hirschmann, who accepted the proposal in principle, did not wish to participate personally, and after further consultation with national sections the idea was dropped. The British and Scandinavians, however, felt quite strongly that such an attempt should have been made. It was the old question again, whether a Fascist dictatorship could be appealed to in the name of reason or must be utterly resisted.

The problem was well stated in a letter to Camille Drevet from Professor G. Ferrero, the exiled Italian social historian, in December 1935. He was a sympathetic supporter of the WILPF but declined to sign the Mandate because, he said, these 'general appeals' were useless and might even compromise the cause of peace by making pacifist propaganda seem unrealistic. The only way to peace, he believed, lay in the overthrow of Fascism. This was also the view of the mass Movement Against War and Fascism, with which the French section of the WILPF was so actively associated; although this did not prevent the section from contributing to the People's Mandate the collective assent of over three and a half million members of twenty-eight organizations—by far the largest of any national total.

By the end of August the European Committee, working in twenty-five countries, had amassed over 10 million declarations, both collective and individual, in favour of the People's Mandate. Several countries had already sent deputations to their national governments in support of the Mandate: Britain with a million and a quarter adherents, Holland with 100,000 and Hungary with nearly 13,000. Though the Hungarian mandate was comparatively small numerically, it was presented by a Committee of Honour which comprised an Archbishop, a Bishop of the Reformed Church, the Chief Rabbi of Budapest, the former Minister of Education György Lukacs, the Member of Parliament Anna Kethly, the writer Mihaly Babits and the Duchess of Odescalchi. The deputation was introduced in the name of the WILPF by Mrs Eugenie Meller, and it was stated that many more signatures could have been obtained but for 'intimidation'. Hungary was perhaps the nearest to a Fascist state in which the Mandate circulated, and had been indicted by the League of Nations in December 1934 for acts of 'political terrorism' against Yugoslavia—although the deputation was now assured of the Hungarian Government's desire for 'peace with justice'. In these circumstances, the backing received for the Mandate campaign was no small achievement.

By the time of the presentation of the Mandate to the League of Nations on September 26th, deputations to governments had also taken place in Czechoslovakia, Denmark, Finland, France, Norway, Sweden, Tunisia and Yugoslavia. The book of signatories was handed to Dr Saavedra Lamas, President of the Assembly, by Camille Drevet together with representatives from Australia, Czechoslovakia, France, Norway and USA. The deputation was presented by Princess Radziwill of the LON Secretariat, with whom the WILPF had a long and friendly association. The 10 million national endorsements of the People's Mandate now presented did not include the 3 million members represented in five international organizations supporting the campaign. In addition, the American Committee presented over a million signatures to Dr Lamas in the Argentine the following March. A pleasing postscript in September 1937 was the receipt by the British section of nearly 6,000 signatures on behalf of the women of Nigeria from the Lagos Women's League.

In her final report to the Executive Committee in April 1937 Camille Drevet estimated that the total number of adherents to the People's Mandate in Europe was over 14 million: a popular vote for peace far outstripping that shown by the World Disarmament Petition in 1932. She urged that this achievement should not be the end of the campaign, but only the preface to a renewed demand for total and universal disarmament.

148 *Women's International League for Peace and Freedom*

In fact the People's Mandate had already been overtaken by another International Peace Campaign, which was the second international movement to grow out of the British Peace Ballot. This 'Rassemblement Universel pour la Paix', as it was first called, was started in the spring of 1936 by an Anglo-French group led by Lord Cecil, Philip Noel-Baker, Norman Angell, Edouard Herriot, Léon Jouhaux and Pierre Cot. Its broad aims were to stop the arms race, take the profit out of arms manufacture, and restore the authority of the League of Nations. So rapid was the growth of the International Peace Campaign that by the summer of 1936 it had established an office in Geneva and was preparing for its first international Congress to take place in Brussels from September 3rd to 6th. In France, where the formation of the Popular Front Government in July 1936 gave fresh impetus to the peace forces, the RUP was a genuinely national movement, solidly supported by the trade unions, co-operative societies, and feminist and ex-service organizations. By September national committees for the International Peace Campaign were working in 48 countries, claiming to speak for 400 million people. The organizing secretary for the Congress was Rosa Manus, who as one of the founders of the WILPF had assisted Dr Aletta Jacobs in organizing the first International Women's Congress at The Hague in 1915.

Before the Brussels Congress a special Call to Women was issued on behalf of seven international women's organizations, and a one-day conference of representatives of women's organizations preceded the Congress on September 2nd. Their findings were presented to the Congress by Gabrielle Duchêne and Mary Dingman, secretary of the Peace and Disarmament Committee of Women's International Organizations, and included a demand for more women representatives in League of Nations bodies and in the International Peace Campaign itself. Only one place on the IPC Council was allocated to a woman representative of three major organizations, on a rotating basis, the seat going in the first instance to Gertrude Baer on behalf of the WILPF. In all, about five thousand delegates attended the Brussels Congress, representing 22 international organizations and 48 countries. Describing the Congress in *Pax International*, November 1936, Kathleen Courtney wrote:

There are those who say that this Congress comes too late, that it is ten years behind time; but ten years ago such a Congress could not have been organized, and those who witnessed the enthusiasm and determination of the delegates at Brussels will not easily believe that peace cannot yet be saved if the peoples of the world unite in its support.

The peoples, alas, did not unite, which was perhaps not surprising since the peace movement which should have led them was itself badly split. The WILPF Executive Committee, endorsing its support of the International Peace Campaign in September 1936, expressed reservations about the imposition of military sanctions in the name of 'collective security'. This was no mere quibble, but a deeply-held difference of principle as to the use of military force in any circumstances and for any purpose. Because of this difficulty, two of the most energetic WILPF sections, Australia and the USA, felt unable to affiliate to their national IPC committees.

Eleanor Moore, of Australia, pointed to other weaknesses in the IPC, notably the fact that it was 'one-sidedly European'. Three-quarters of the human race, she wrote to Clara Ragaz, lived outside Europe, and 'if by neutrality policies and regional pacts they can keep peace among themselves, that will go far towards making world peace a reality'.

The question of neutrality was at this time a burning issue in the United States, following the passing of the first Neutrality Act on August 31, 1935. In America too the peace movement was divided between those who advocated peace-keeping by collective security and those whose first aim was to keep America out of all wars. The latter group, amongst which the WILPF was to be counted, was not 'isolationist' in the accepted sense of the word—wrote Dorothy Detzer in *Pax International*, January 1936—but stood for 'an internationally organized world divorced from any military obligations'. The WILPF therefore welcomed the Neutrality Act and supported the fresh neutrality bills introduced at the beginning of 1936. These, Miss Detzer pointed out, were essentially *embargo* measures and did not imply any neutrality of principle:

None of this is new to the United States section of the Women's International League. For eight years we have been working for an embargo law on munitions, and for six years for an embargo law on loans and credits. . . . The so-called neutrality bills contain provisions which for years we have been wishing to secure.

The US National Council for Prevention of War, of which the WILPF was a participating organization and Emily Balch was a vice-chairman, published President Roosevelt's speech at Chautauqua on August 14, 1936, concerning the second Neutrality Act and US foreign policy, with an explanatory letter from its Executive Secretary Frederick J. Libby. It was important for Europeans to understand, he wrote, that Roosevelt was expressing 'with great accuracy' the general attitude in America when he said: 'We are not isolationists except insofar as we seek to isolate ourselves completely from war.' Whether or not it was desirable, such lofty isolationism was certainly not possible inside Europe, seething as it was with conflicting ideologies and divided loyalties both within and between its national boundaries. Lacking both the will and the basis for unity, pacification could only come by imposed force or by voluntary submission to an impartial authority. Could a reformed League of Nations still save the peace?

The League itself had acknowledged the necessity for revision of the Covenant by setting up a special Committee at the 1936 Assembly to consider proposals for reform submitted by member-states. These were mainly concerned with separation of the Covenant from the Peace Treaties; universality of membership; means of war-*prevention*; means of effecting peaceful change; and establishment of regional treaties. With the exception of the last, these steps had long been advocated by the WILPF. It had set up a Committee for Revision of the League of Nations in April 1936 and at the Executive Committee in September Mrs Thora Daugaard of Denmark presented a memorandum incorporating proposals from Austria, Britain, France, Holland, Hungary, Sweden and USA. The Swedish and Netherlands sections in particular had worked on this question, and prepared virtual blueprints for a new Covenant. There was general agreement that universality of membership was desirable, and equally that membership should carry certain privileges which would encourage a more positive attitude to the League by member-states. But any real reform was conditional on a complete change of outlook from nationalism to internationalism. As the Executive Committee expressed it:

The WILPF believes that no external reform of the Covenant, however it might contribute to tiding over the present crisis, can avail to secure the proper functioning of the League of Nations today, unless its members rise to the level of a truly independent international outlook, disarm, and willingly abandon their sovereign rights within the sphere of the League.

Now, more than ever, was needed that 'New International Order' for which the WILPF had laid down proposals as far back as its Washington Congress in 1924, and which was again to form the theme of the last pre-war International Congress in 1937. Since the 1934 Congress, the WILPF had celebrated its twentieth anniversary in April 1935—and mourned the death of its President Jane Addams only a month later. Three weeks before her death Jane Addams took part in an international radio programme on the work of the WILPF, together with statesmen and ambassadors speaking from Tokyo, Moscow, London, Paris and Geneva. The broadcast, arranged on the suggestion of Dr Sahlbom, was transmitted free of charge by the National Broadcasting Company of America from the League of Nations radio station in Geneva. In Washington, the anniversary was marked with a reception at the White House by Eleanor Roosevelt. Of the countless tributes to Jane Addams which poured in after her death from statesmen, fellow-workers and friends throughout the world, the personal recollection of Emily Balch may most suitably be mentioned here:

She was so unlike anyone else I have known—so utterly real and first-hand; so subtle, so simple and direct, so free from any preoccupation with self, as far from asceticism as from self-indulgence; full of compassion without weakness or sentimentality, loving merriment while carrying the world's woes in her heart . . . a great statesman, a great writer, one of the world's rare spirits, how can I or anyone evoke her? Go and read her books; they will bring her back as far as anything now can.

To commemorate her work for international peace, a Jane Addams Memorial Fund was set up, for which Sir George Paish consented to act as treasurer.

The living memorial to Jane Addams was the continued work of the Women's International League for Peace and Freedom. There was little time for repining. Not only world events but internal problems were pressing for settlement. The Zürich Congress had been marred by painful breaches, both personal and national. The next Congress, it was determined, should devote itself solely to world issues. Matters of WILPF policy and constitution must be settled by the Executive Committee preceding it. The upshot of this decision was an agreement in April 1937 to call a 'truce' on constitutional issues until after the Congress and until such time as the international situation was less critical.

The Ninth International Congress of the WILPF took place at Luhacovice in Czechoslovakia from July 27 to 31, 1937: a highly significant location, and one deliberately chosen, for the last pre-war Congress. The delegates, numbering 149 from 19 countries, were welcomed by the Czech Foreign Minister, Dr Krofta. Two visitors from countries without national sections were warmly greeted: the Begum Shareefah Hamid Ali, a founder of the All-India Women's Conference, who was noted for her pioneering work of community development in Indian villages; and Dr Margarita Camps from Spain, a biologist and the only woman professor at Barcelona University. The Congress unanimously elected Emily Greene Balch to follow Jane Addams as President of the WILPF. Clara Ragaz and Gertrude Baer were re-elected as International Chairmen, and were joined by Mrs Kathleen Innes as third chairman, in place of Mme Ramondt-Hirschmann. One new national section was admitted, from the newly-independent country of Egypt. Three sections had fallen out since the last Congress: Haiti, Ireland and Mexico.

The administration of the WILPF had undergone some changes since the return of Emily Balch to America in October 1935, when Gertrude Baer undertook a reorganization of the Maison Internationale. In March 1936 Lotti Birch was appointed Administrative Secretary, a post which she filled with outstanding ability. The monthly journal *Pax International* was now being edited in London by a British member, Karleen Baker.

In spite of international crises and internal difficulties, many of the national sections in reporting on their work over the past three years showed an upsurge in membership and activity. The Scandinavians continued to co-operate in joint study conferences, and on May 18, 1936, for the first time a common Peace Day took place simultaneously in the four northern countries. Sweden obtained over a million signatures for the People's Mandate and was co-operating in the International Peace Campaign. The small country of Denmark alone had 25,000 members—almost twice those in America. But the US section, with a paid staff of eleven and 120 branches, was undoubtedly the best organized and had an impressive record of achievement, notably:

Declaration by the US Government that it would never again intervene in foreign countries for the protection of property by military means—a policy worked for by the WIL since 1924.

Freedom for the Philippine Islands—worked for since 1921.

Withdrawal of marines from both Haiti and Nicaragua—worked for since troops were sent there.

Repeal of the Platt Amendment (Cuba)—worked for since 1930.

Recognition by the United States of the USSR—worked for since the Soviet Union attained a *de facto* government.

Passage of the Nye–Vandenberg Resolution which resulted in the investigation of the munitions industry—a leading point in WILPF policy.

Neutrality legislation.

In addition, one of the most important continuing projects of the American section was the work of the Inter-American Committee, established in 1934. Its chairman was Heloise Brainerd, whose experience included 26 years' service as Chief of the Education Division of the Pan-American Union. Under her able and enthusiastic leadership, the Committee recruited members in thirteen Latin American countries and circulated Spanish translations of WILPF literature.

The British section, in addition to its Disarmament campaigns, was working on the special problems of India, Palestine and the African colonies. The French section, maintaining its position in the vanguard of women's movements, had obtained the support of all the major women's organizations in France for the International Peace Campaign; it was also actively concerned with the situation in Spain and with attempts to democratize the League of Nations. The Dutch women were working on behalf of refugees, for the rights of conscientious objectors, and for the appointment of a Minister for Peace. New Zealand, unlike Australia, was enthusiastically supporting the IPC. The Polish section remained astonishingly active, with special commissions working on the problems of Minorities, the Baltic States, and Czechoslovakia. A memorandum on co-operation between sections in neighbouring states was jointly drawn up by the Czechoslovakian and Hungarian sections, with the support of Yugoslavia, and presented to the Congress.

Papers on the theme of A New International Order dealt with Colonies and Mandates; League of Nations Reform; Internationalization of Civil Aviation; Limitation and Regulation of State Sovereignty; Development and Extension of International Arbitration; Problems of International Economics; and Total and Universal Disarmament. This seems a comprehensive programme, but how could it be implemented in any one of these fields of study? Dr Schustleróva of Czechoslovakia

stressed the need for a 'moral law' between nations as between individuals, based on acceptance of an international ethos, as the first
requisite for any new order. Summarizing various schemes for League
of Nations reform, Thora Daugaard instanced four ways of strengthening the Covenant: international control of all production and traffic of
arms; internationalization of civil and military aircraft; a mandate system for all colonial territories; and free access to raw materials.

The political background to the Spanish War was outlined by Dr
Camps, while Miss Pye spoke of the plight of refugee children from
Spain and the one-sidedness of 'non-intervention'. A telegram was sent
from the Congress to the President of the Non-Intervention Committee again demanding the withdrawal of foreign troops, backed by a
resolution to the League of Nations Council. Other resolutions dealt
with Ethiopia, Right of Asylum, and Political Prisoners. A strong plea
was made for ratification by all governments of the 1933 Convention
on the international status of certain Refugees, and for a further Convention to cover refugees from Germany. An appeal was sent to the
League of Nations to set up a Commission, replacing the existing
Nansen Office and High Commission for Refugees from Germany, to
be responsible for the legal and juridical protection of all refugees.

The Congress also issued a statement on Neutrality, of which the
conclusion is worth quoting:

Though the Women's International League for Peace and Freedom
believes that it is unethical and unjust to treat both aggressor and
victim alike and stands always for solidarity as against isolation, it does
reiterate its firm and uncompromising stand against arming or financ-
ing either side, that is, against the shipments of munitions anywhere,
at any time, to any state, but rather urges that every moral, diplomatic,
political and economic means—except a food blockade—be applied to
the aggressor.

This represented a fair summing-up of the WILPF position not only
on Neutrality but on the use of sanctions against an aggressor. It could
scarcely have been more timely. At the very moment the Congress
was gathering, Japanese troops were invading north China in the first
moves towards full-scale, undeclared war. Immediately, on July 30th,
the Congress cabled a protest to the Japanese Government urging a
withdrawal from Chinese territory. Telegrams were also sent to the
League of Nations and to the British and French Governments, calling

for the immediate application of Article 17 of the Covenant (relating to aggression by a non-member of the League). Japan replied with the bombing of undefended cities and brutal atrocities against the fleeing civilian populations. The Sino-Japanese conflict marked a new downward turn of the spiral towards the twentieth-century barbarism of total war.

CHAPTER 14

THE ROUT OF REASON

Japan and the League of Nations—Anglo-Italian Agreement—Austrian 'Anschluss' 1938—Czechoslovakia —Munich Agreement 1938—WILPF Executive Committee 1939—Moves for a Peace Conference—Nazi-Soviet Pact—Outbreak of War

Two wars were now raging, in China and in Spain. Both were allowed to continue, although both could have been stopped. On the part of governments, not the means but the will to peace was lacking. The mass peace campaigns, though genuine enough, were too divided in their own forces to make any decisive impact.

The struggle continued, inside the WILPF, to contain within a harmony of accepted principle the sharply contrasting outlook of many of its members and sections, although the overall aim of the League never wavered and was never disputed: the need for total and universal disarmament as a condition of permanent peace. It was towards this aim that its two major campaigns of the 1930s had been directed: the World Disarmament Petition with its nine million signatures and the People's Mandate to Governments with fourteen million. Recalling this popular vote for disarmament, the WILPF Chairmen wrote to the Bureau of the Disarmament Conference in Geneva on May 28, 1937, urging that a fresh Conference be summoned and that it should include representatives not only of governments and military interests but of those organizations which had made a special study of the causes of war and the institutions of peace. 'If swift action is not taken,' they declared, 'the world cannot be saved from destruction.'

No action was taken by the League of Nations, either towards disarmament or towards the effective application of 'collective security' which was the excuse for retaining arms. Nor were the more realistic and less dangerous possibilities of non-military sanctions seriously explored. Gertrude Baer was working hard in this direction unofficially. Following the International Peace Campaign's conference in Stockholm in July 1937 she wrote to Malcolm Lilliehöok, who had given a lecture on 'Peace, Public Opinion and the League of Nations', to find out whether the Scandinavian countries would initiate an Emergency Conference to work out 'the machinery of non-military sanctions for the active and effective prevention of war and the establishment of real collective security'.

This initiative was not forthcoming, and the LON Assembly in September 1937 did no more than offer 'moral' support to China and condemn Japan's violation of the Kellogg Pact and the Nine-Power Treaty. The Nine-Power Conference which met in Brussels in November was boycotted by Germany and Japan and rendered impotent. In a letter to the President of the Conference the WILPF Chairmen demanded the withdrawal of Japanese troops and the restoration of Chinese sovereignty over Manchuria as conditions for a just settlement. A letter was also sent to President Roosevelt on October 7th, following his foreign policy speech in Chicago condemning Japan, expressing the hope that the United States would co-operate fully in any non-military measures to stop aggression.

The US section of the WILPF, however, was uneasy over the President's ambiguity regarding possible military action and critical of his failure to invoke the Neutrality Act. Emily Balch expressed the dilemma of 'peace-loving' Americans—and others—when she wrote to Gertrude Baer on December 1st:

It is a tragic dilemma that the world is in: To acquiesce is moral suicide and perhaps ultimately war. To resist is probably war and is almost impossible given the political morale, or lack of it, in England and France, each of them tied to a dying imperialism and divided between capitalism and conservatism and an unclear radicalism (Left).

The British and Dutch sections of the WILPF were prompt in demanding from their governments an immediate embargo on war materials to Japan, including oil, and all sections were urged by the International Chairmen to do the same. In January 1938 the Executive Committee decided to co-operate in promoting a Consumers' World Boycott of Japan under the sponsorship of the International Peace Campaign. In an appeal to the WILPF Mme Chiang Kai-Shek had written: 'Boycott is the most effective non-military weapon in the fight for peace and freedom'.

The question was raised by Gertrude Baer whether the WILPF should now send another private mission to China, as had been done in 1926. As it happened, a British member, Muriel Lester, was visiting both China and Japan on behalf of the Fellowship of Reconciliation at the end of 1937, and she readily agreed to act also as liaison for the WILPF. In China she found that the invasion was serving to unify the country as never before, and morale remained high in spite of the great sufferings inflicted by the war. But she was shocked to see the evil effects of the Japanese-controlled drug traffic. The mood in Japan was uneasy, with even the army divided about the merits of continuing the war, and Miss Lester spoke frankly with ministers and other officials. She was allowed to do this, she supposed (writing to Clara Ragaz on April 1, 1938), 'because of our WIL attitude against all war and our recognition that atrocities are inseparable from war'.

Muriel Lester completed her journey with a lecture tour in America, on which she wrote:

I shall try to make them see their own share of the guilt. They are making large profits out of supplying the means of death and torture. We women, being practical, must make the public see how ridiculous it is to be angry with people for a crime that would be impossible without our co-operation. A double standard indeed!

If only one statesman could have been found to speak in the voice of a Muriel Lester, how different the future course of history might have been!

One did, indeed, revolt against his Government's hypocritical policies, although he did not go so far as to offer any constructive alternative. The resignation of Anthony Eden as Foreign Minister on February 20, 1938, to make way for the more amenable Lord Halifax rent the last pretences of the British Government to support a League of Nations policy in Spain. The WILPF British section wrote to Mr Eden in appreciation of his stand on a matter of principle and to the Prime Minister, Neville Chamberlain, deploring the resignation:

under circumstances which gave the appearance of surrender to the campaign of vilification against him in Italy, and which suggest a reversal of the policy of support for the League of Nations obligations on which the Government was returned to power.

The new policy was quickly revealed. In April an agreement was negotiated with Mussolini, bartering the recognition of his conquest of Ethiopia for the withdrawal of Italian troops from Spain *after the*

war was over; scarcely a *quid pro quo*. The Italo-British agreement provoked a violent left-wing reaction and the demand for a Popular
Front Government in Britain. The WILPF joined in the protests, but
at the same time reaffirmed its opposition to the rearmament programme and stressed the need for positive action 'to secure general
economic appeasement'—a very different matter from the kind of
political 'appeasement' which the British Government's own action was
to bring into such disrepute. Now Britain proposed that the question
of recognition of Italian Ethiopia should come before the LON Council
in May. In vain, the WILPF International Chairmen protested to the
Council President that it was not within the competence of the League
thus to liquidate one of its own states members:

It cannot be the intention of the Council to sanction a breach of international law, committed by the violation of the territorial integrity and
political independence of a State Member of the League of Nations.

The conquest of certain other countries at present invaded or
threatened with invasion would thus be sanctioned in advance, and it
would be a fresh disillusionment for all those who still refuse to accept
the principle that 'might is right' to see a premium thus put upon
aggression.

It was not surprising, perhaps, seeing how the wind was blowing over
the Mediterranean, that Hitler now deemed it opportune to make the
first move in his expansionist policy outside Germany's own borders.
The unification of Austria with Germany had been a reasonable sup-
position ever since the destruction of the Austro-Hungarian Empire.
If the union had not been expressly forbidden by the Treaty of
Versailles it might have been accomplished peacefully and constitu-
tionally, to the benefit of both countries, long before the Nazi régime.
Instead, the *Anschluss* was accomplished by ultimatum and armed
threat, of a ferocity which shook even the most ardent sympathizers
with Germany's just grievances. The change of attitude in the WILPF
British section was at once apparent. Hitler crossed the Austrian border
on March 12, 1938. Two days later, the Annual Council of the British
section expressed its horror at this 'outrageous injustice' in no uncertain
terms. It urged HM Government to state that 'full economic and financial sanctions would immediately be applied in the event of a further
act of aggression in violation of the League Covenant'.

Pax International in April 1938 pointed to the increased danger to

Czechoslovakia from the Austrian *coup*: any 'trivial incident' in the German Minority area of Sudetenland might precipitate invasion, bloodshed and 'possibly a second world war'. German aggressiveness was encouraged, the article concluded, by the hesitating policy of the Western powers. France, it was true, had declared that she would uphold her pledges under the Franco-Czech alliance. But what of Britain? The British Government ignored not only the League of Nations—which did not even meet to consider the Austrian situation— but its own allies. No assurances were given to Czechoslovakia; Russia's offer of a Four-Power Conference to prevent further aggressions was refused. On September 4th, unable to withstand any longer the pressure from both enemy and friend, President Beneš capitulated to the Sudeten demands.

When the WILPF Executive Committee met in Geneva two days later, Czechoslovakia weighed heavily on both hearts and minds. Three members of the Czech section were present. There was the strongest feeling that no further concessions should be forced on the Prague Government. Cables to this effect were sent to Lord Halifax and President Roosevelt, and President Beneš was urged to stand firmly for the unity and independence of the Czechoslovakian state. The Committee also took this opportunity to reaffirm the abhorrence of the WILPF for all forms of dictatorship, 'whether it is practised in fascist, national socialist or bolshevist countries, or in countries where subject peoples or minorities are oppressed'. Clara Ragaz, in her opening address, raised the question of resistance without resort to arms. She was forced to conclude that, in the absence of peaceful pressure on Germany by the democratic powers through moral, political and economic means, the Czechoslovakian Government was right to take certain military measures against a German invasion. The British Quaker, Edith Pye, acknowledged her own dilemma. It seemed that the only way of stopping attacks on small countries was by a threat of armed force. It was a dreadful confession for a pacifist, said Miss Pye, but: 'The awful thing is that if I hear a sword rattle, I say thank God.' What was going on in Germany and Austria, she believed, was worse than war. Another British Quaker, Barbara Duncan Harris, corrected her: it was not worse than war, she said, it *was* war.

Madame Rudinger of Czechoslovakia agreed with Miss Pye that 'absolute pacifism' was powerless and said that Czech pacifists had abandoned it in favour of 'collective security'. Dr Gertrud Woker of Switzerland pointed out that a simple alternative to armed resistance or surrender would be the imposition of an oil embargo against Italy, Germany and Japan. Modern war could not be conducted without this fuel, and oil was almost entirely in the hands of the democracies. Gertrude Baer believed it was still not too late to explore the creation of a United States of Europe, from an economic basis, with the co-operation of the United States of America. She wrote to an American member, Mrs R. Klotsche, on September 5th:

I know that the WILPF is doing all in its power to have people see the problems of the hour on a large and international scale. Against the war scare everywhere we must put our firm and resolute decision to create something new and constructive, something which appeals to people of intelligence and good will and something which is worth-while to live and to work for.

But the democratic powers were otherwise engaged.

The feverish diplomatic activity leading up to the Munich Conference of September 29, 1938, cannot be detailed here. Between Neville Chamberlain's flights to Germany on September 15th and 22nd the Czechoslovakian Government, harassed also now by demands from Poland and Hungary, agreed to the peaceful transfer to Germany of the Sudeten territory and the abandonment of its alliances with France and Russia in return for an 'international guarantee' backed by Britain. The Czech offer was met by a further ultimatum and threat of military occupation.

The WILPF was no less active in these days. After consultation with the Czechoslovakian LON delegation in Geneva and with Lola Hanou-skova in Prague, a telegram was sent to the French Government on September 21st protesting against its vacillation in face of the attacks on Czechoslovakia. The French and British sections protested equally vigorously to their governments. A letter to the WILPF from the Czech section expressed gratitude for the action taken and gave some inkling of the situation there, with more than a thousand refugees from the Sudetenland passing through Prague each day: German democrats, socialists, Czechs and Jews, they could only create fresh minority and cultural problems for the harassed state. On September 23rd mobiliza-tion was ordered, although outwardly all was calm. A Czech member wrote to Geneva: 'These days of waiting are awful. Also my son has been called away. Where are the mothers of the world? Farewell to you all! What may be coming tomorrow?'

In despair, many people were looking to America for a way out. On September 28th Roosevelt's appeal for a general conference was warmly welcomed by the International Chairmen. Several national sections had already proposed such a step. But the Fascist governments, confident of success, were not to be deflected. In an effort to arouse the non-governmental forces, Gertrude Baer had an interview with M. Jézéquel, joint Vice-President with Philip Noel-Baker of the International Peace Campaign, and expressed the great disappointment of the WILPF that no meeting of the IPC Executive was called, or other consultation arranged, during the crisis and no action taken at the League of Nations. The Assembly was then meeting, turning down the Chinese appeal for help and ignoring the situation in Czechoslovakia; only Litvinoff demanded that it should be brought before the Council. Gertrude Baer also discussed with Dr Christian Lange, Chairman of the LON Disarmament Bureau, the question of Abolition of Air Warfare. The WILPF Executive Committee had issued an appeal to all LON delegations to support the convocation of the Air Commission and consider plans for internationalization of civil aviation and abolition of military and naval aircraft. Dr Lange expressed 'full agreement' with the appeal, but explained that nothing could then be done because efforts were being made for a 'Luftpakt' with Germany. 'It is the same old story all over the place,' Gertrude Baer wrote to her co-Chairmen on September 22nd. 'Negotiations with Germany on "chateaux en Espagne" handicap any international action.'

Only one week later, her worst fears were confirmed, as Hitler and Mussolini, Chamberlain and Daladier, conferred at Munich to 'save the peace'. A telegram was sent to the British and French statesmen on September 29th by the WILPF Chairmen, demanding the right of self-determination for Czechoslovakia on the basis of the Franco-British plan (for peaceful ceding of Sudetenland). None of these conditions was fulfilled in the terms of the agreement. Czechoslovakia was virtually dismembered, and on October 1st German troops marched into Sudetenland. Immediately, the International Chairmen circulated national sections with information and advice. The attitude of the WILPF to the Peace of Munich was clear and uncompromising:

It is a sham peace based on the violation of law, justice and right. It is a so-called 'peaceful change' dictated by four Powers and forced upon a young and small State, which was not represented when its dismemberment was finally decided upon.

Letters of sympathy to President Beneš and the Czech section were sent from the International Chairmen and many sections. The British, in particular, wrote that they were 'overwhelmed with shame'. The Czechs replied with an appeal for financial help to extend their relief work among Sudeten refugees, which met with an immediate response. The British Chairman, Mrs Barbara Duncan Harris, flew to Prague and arranged for twenty WILPF members to be given hospitality in England. Norway and Sweden also sent financial aid. Denmark proposed that President Beneš be nominated for the Nobel peace prize. Recommendations for practical action from the Chairmen to national sections included an international loan to Czechoslovakia; increasing Czech imports; and a careful study of the minority and frontier problems which would have to be solved by any genuine peace conference. The Chairmen ended with an appeal for the 'militant spirit' of the WILPF to be maintained:

Pacifism is *not* quietistic acceptance of betrayal and lies for the sake of 'Peace'. Pacifism is the struggle for truth, the struggle for right, the struggle for clear political aims, for firm political will and action. Pacifism is *not* weak acceptance of 'faits accomplis' achieved by brute force. Pacifism is courageous initiative for a constructive policy of just peace.

The International Chairmen met in London in February 1939 to consider proposals for a General Peace Conference. The Scandinavian sections were pressing for an initiative in response to President Roosevelt's appeals for a resumption of negotiations between the powers. The Chairmen were less sure that such a conference could serve any useful purpose. It should not be a means of confirming or stabilizing the Munich Agreement, they declared, and it must be conducted with full publicity. But the Munich Agreement itself was already a dead letter. On March 14th the independence of Slovakia was declared, thus nullifying Britain's guarantee of Czechoslovakia's existing frontiers. Germany was enjoying now the fruits of 'appeasement'. On March 15th, Hitler swept into Prague in triumph. One week later, Czechoslovakia was declared a German Protectorate. To round off the Axis victory, Germany also seized Memel from Lithuania, while Ruthenia was occupied by Hungary; and on April 8th, Mussolini annexed Albania.

In view of the critical situation, an emergency meeting of the WILPF

Executive Committee was called in Paris from April 22nd to 26th. It was the last international gathering of the League before the outbreak of war; thirteen national sections were represented. In all these countries, war preparations were being accelerated and were generally accepted as inevitable. Lida Gustava Heymann, reporting a rising discontent inside Germany and increasing repression, believed that war could still be averted by a strict, universal boycott of Italy and Germany. Gabrielle Duchêne appealed to the WILPF to come out in favour of co-operation with the Soviet Union to save the peace. Though reluctant to name the Soviet Union, in view of its record of internal violence against which the WILPF had directed protests since 1934, the Committee agreed that joint international action was necessary and that no state should be excluded which had adhered loyally to its obligations to the League of Nations; Russia was certainly no offender here. Had this pressure been exerted earlier by public opinion in the democracies, the Nazi-Soviet Pact of August 24, 1939, might have been forestalled.

The Executive Committee again demanded more economic aid for China and the cessation of war supplies to Japan—a plea that was cynically flouted by the British-Japanese Agreement of July 24th. It also protested strongly against any legal recognition of Hitler's annexation of Czechoslovakia. The Czech ambassador in Paris told Gertrude Baer that he had arranged for this resolution to be broadcast to Britain and the USA, and from there back to Czechoslovakia. An obvious way of helping Czechoslovakia was in caring for refugees, and this the WILPF was doing to the limit of its capacity. The British section secured the admission of 54 Czech members and their families, and Sweden admitted 25. The American section urged the President to increase the immigration quotas, and many members signed personal affidavits to accept financial responsibility for a refugee. At the same time, the Executive Committee appealed to all sections to press for the admittance of a number of Spanish refugees.

The Swedish section was still making proposals for an International Peace Conference, and after much discussion of pros and cons the Executive Committee issued 'A Call to Reason and Collective Consultation', urging the democratic countries to initiate an international conference, under clearly defined conditions, to consider the questions of access to raw materials; immigration and refugees; steps to disarmament; and resistance to aggression by diplomatic, economic and financial means. How, it might be wondered, could such a conference hope to succeed where the League of Nations—composed of the same governments, concerned with the same problems—had failed? Only, the WILPF believed, by direct action of the people. Along with the Call to Reason went an appeal to women's organizations for a world campaign in favour of President Roosevelt's peace proposals, with the slogan: the Peoples want Peace; the Peoples want Freedom; the Peoples want to Live.

The response was disappointing. It was true that the vast majority of the world's peoples wanted these ends, but—confused and paralysed by the pressure and horror of events—they were incapable of willing the means. The time for a People's Mandate was past. More and more, they were 'leaving it to the government' and accepting as inevitable the final disaster of war. Out of 32 women's organizations approached by the WILPF, eight replied; and only one, the French Ligue des Mères et des Educatrices, offered unconditional support. The Scandinavian sections, however, continued to campaign for a World Conference up to the last possible moment, and an appeal endorsed by 14 women's organizations was cabled to the meeting of the Oslo States in Brussels on August 20, 1939. In Britain, the WILPF supported the National Peace Council in a campaign for a Peace Conference to remedy economic grievances, for which over one million signatures were collected.

The United States section in May 1939 reaffirmed that the WILPF was 'unalterably opposed' to US participation in any foreign war and called for stronger neutrality legislation. At the same time it rejected an isolationist policy, proposing to President Roosevelt a World Convention to make plans for a democratic, non-military federation of nations. The Canadian section, too, urged its Government to take the lead in summoning a World Economic Conference and to prohibit the export of all war materials.

Gertrude Baer, for one, was sceptical about the value of an economic conference. She objected to Italy and Germany being treated as 'have-not' nations, when they belonged in fact among the 'haves'. It was not really a question of seeking a 'general settlement' between the powers, she said: 'there are quite different issues at stake'. Miss Baer had surely put her finger on the crux of the pacifist dilemma. The problem facing the world in 1939 was not so much how to remedy the natural injustices between nations by the exercise of reason and goodwill (which should have been done ten or twenty years earlier), but how to deal with an aggressive, totalitarian dictatorship without recourse to war.

And to this problem, no answer was forthcoming. German demands for Danzig and the Polish Corridor became more imperious; and with each concession by Poland, fresh humiliations were imposed. Hitler was not interested in a 'reasonable settlement'; it was perhaps the only thing he feared. As he is reported to have remarked to his generals on August 22nd, confident of the success of Ribbentrop's negotiations in Moscow: 'I am only afraid that at the last minute some swine or other will produce a plan of mediation' (Documents on German Foreign Policy, Series D, VII).

The Nazi-Soviet Pact knocked the last nail in the coffin of collective security. The authority of the League of Nations was dead. Alliances between sovereign states, designed solely for the protection of the most powerful, offered no alternative. Popular sentiment was divided between the desire for 'peace at any price' and a militant anti-Fascism, both to some extent spurious. For if the pacifists were the dupes of the dictators, the anti-Fascists were no less the dupes of Soviet self-interest, which had little to do with the wellbeing of peoples outside its own borders. Had popular sentiment been united in a mass movement of *resistance to violence*, within as well as between nations, what power on earth could have shaken it? But no such strategy of resistance existed; no union of peace and freedom existed; and so the enemies of peace and freedom were able to divide and rule.

It was a tragedy that the Western democracies wanted peace; Russia wanted peace; the German and Italian peoples wanted peace; even Mussolini wanted an absence of all-out war. Only Hitler was determined to march on Poland—and nobody could stop him. On September 1st, the order to attack was given. On September 3rd, this time honouring her commitments, Britain declared war. But by forcing Europe into a holocaust that nobody wanted, Hitlerism had triumphed before the first shot was fired.

On September 3rd also, the Executive Committee of the wILPF was due to meet in Zürich. There was no intention of cancelling the meeting, and the American representative had already reached Southampton, when at the last moment it had to be called off because troop movements made civilian transport impossible. Two British members, however—Barbara Duncan Harris and Kathleen Innes—travelled to Geneva for talks with Gertrude Baer; they were helped to obtain visas by the Foreign Secretary, Lord Halifax. It was agreed that the Executive Committee should meet as soon as could be arranged in a neutral country; but this did not prove possible for another three months.

On the outbreak of hostilities the British section issued a Statement on the Present Situation, which was widely distributed both in Britain and abroad. It reaffirmed the principles laid down at the Hague Congress in 1915, quoting again the concluding declaration from that Congress which seemed no less relevant in 1939:

We declare the doctrine that war is inevitable to be both a denial of the sovereignty of reason and a betrayal of the deepest instincts of the human heart. With a sense of our share in the failure to prevent the wars of the past and of the present, and in sorrow for the suffering, the desolate and the oppressed, we, the members of this Congress, urge the women of all nations to work for their own enfranchisement and unceasingly to strive for a just and lasting peace.

As the International Chairmen wrote in their circular letter to national sections on September 4th: 'WILPF work must go on—in spite of war.' The second great testing time had come.

CHAPTER 15

THE SECOND WORLD WAR

*Efforts for Mediation—WILPF Executive Committee
—Move to New York—International Circular Letters—
WILPF and Pacifism—Post-war Planning—UN Con-
ference at San Francisco 1945—Looking to the Future*

The technical state of war which existed in Europe from September 3, 1939, did not put an end to all efforts at mediation. On September 8th Louie Bennett proposed that the Women's International League for Peace and Freedom, as it had done in the First World War, should explore the possibilities of 'continuous mediation' by neutral states. She also approached the Bishop of Galway to plead that the Pope should intercede for peace. Other suggestions put to the WILPF as possible mediators were King Leopold of the Belgians, Queen Wilhelmina of the Netherlands and, of course, President Roosevelt in the still-neutral United States of America. Various unofficial moves were also being made in Scandinavia, where the WILPF held an emergency conference of Northern sections. On December 10th, the day on which the Nobel peace prize should have been awarded, a silent procession and mass meeting of women from more than twenty organizations took place in Norway. Amongst the speakers was Marie Lous-Mohr, Chairman of the WILPF Norwegian section. In December also a united Scandinavian women's appeal was sent to the President of the League of Nations asking for a suspension of hostilities and preparation of a general conference, at which women should be included amongst the delegates.

But Western statesmen, stunned by the speed of the German *Blitzkrieg* on Poland, remained unable or unwilling to respond to any whisper of peace. In fact the only positive gesture, in the early months of the war, came from Hitler himself who on October 8th, his Polish campaign successfully concluded, made a peace offer to the British and French premiers. With the wrongs of Versailles now righted, he saw no reason to prolong or extend the war. The reply of Messrs Chamberlain and Daladier was an uncompromising rejection of any peace terms based on a recognition of Germany's aggressions.

Writing to Louie Bennett on September 16th, Gertrude Baer discussed the difficulties of mediation in this situation, so different from that of 1915. The aims and principles worked out by the WILPF had been so thoroughly violated, she said—although she did not believe they had 'failed'—tht any proposals now must take into account 'the most fundamental conditions for political, social and economic justice'. It was no longer sufficient to proclaim aims: 'we must show possibilities of action, methods and means to carry them out'.

Gertrude Baer and Clara Ragaz were in almost daily contact at this time, gathering and disseminating information and trying desperately to maintain links between the national sections. *Pax International*, which could no longer be edited in Britain, was temporarily replaced by a duplicated news letter. In November 1939 this carried reports from the sections in Australia, Britain, Canada, Finland, Holland, New Zealand, Scandinavia, Switzerland and the USA, together with a statement by Clara Ragaz on the essential conditions of peace. The third International Chairman, Kathleen Innes, was writing in the British news sheet at the same time on similar lines—namely, that any peace terms must include provision for economic change and recognition of human rights. The National Peace Council in London was then launching a campaign to press the British Government to announce 'precise and constructive' peace terms.

The postponed meeting of the WILPF Executive Committee took place at Geneva from December 5 to 9, 1939. All three International Chairmen were present, together with the Vice-President, Lida Gustava Heymann, but there were sad gaps among the national sections. At the last moment, the Scandinavian and Dutch representatives failed to get the necessary transit visas; nor were Austrian and Czechoslovakian members living in England permitted to travel. British, French, Swiss and exiled German members were present, together with Dorothy Detzer, national secretary of the US section. Tributes were paid to three outstanding peace workers who had died during the past weeks: Mrs Charlotte Despard and Mrs H. M. Swanwick, pioneer members of the British section; and the American Quaker Dr William Hull.

The small Executive Committee made one firm decision for the future: echoing the wartime Congress of 1915, it resolved that an International Women's Congress should be held at the time and place of the peace conference. Discussion centred on the securing of a 'just and durable peace'. Both the Dutch and the Norwegian sections sent proposals for mobilizing the resources of science to prepare for such a peace; the Swedish section also submitted an eight-point programme for peace terms. These suggestions were circulated to national sections for further study. On the basis of a draft submitted by Gertrude Baer, a small committee was set up to promulgate an International Declaration of Human Rights. A memorandum on the situation in India by Agatha Harrison led to a resolution urging the British Government to recognize the claim of India to be a free and equal state. Other resolutions were concerned with the composition of the Peace Conference and the forcible transfer of populations. A letter was sent to President Beneš pledging support for the restoration of a free Czechoslovakia; a letter of sympathy was sent, via Sweden, to members in Finland, where the Soviet invasion had just been launched.

On the proposal of a British member, Barbara Duncan Harris, the Executive Committee issued 'A Recall to Reason', appealing to President Roosevelt to summon a conference of all neutral countries and reaffirming the conviction of the WILPF that the method of war could neither bring about justice nor lay the foundations of peace and freedom. In a further statement on Sovereign Rights, the Committee declared:

... if there is to be a peace which shall be just and durable, there must be a League or Association of countries which are prepared to surrender a part of their sovereign rights and to make concessions in the interest of the community of nations even if apparently opposed to their national interests.

If there is to be freedom, peace must be based on the acceptance by all countries concerned of the principle of individual human rights.

At this first and last wartime meeting of the WILPF Executive Committee, the United States section invited the League to transfer the international office to America for the duration of the war. It was decided, however, to carry on the international work in Geneva for as long as possible, but to ask Gertrude Baer to go to the USA to maintain contacts with the Economic section of the League of Nations, now established at Princeton, and the ILO transferred to Montreal. With typical generosity, the American representative reiterated that in the event of any danger of invasion of Switzerland, the US section would be prepared 'to send someone over by an American ship to facilitate the transfer of staff and files'. Happily, no such drastic action became necessary and the Maison Internationale remained open throughout the war, staffed by its faithful office secretary Louisa Jaques who also acted as manager of the Maison. Accommodation in the house was rented to the Association of Swiss returned from Abroad, under the wardenship of a pacifist pastor and his wife. The administrative secretary, Lotti Birch, whose work was inevitably halted by the war, had obtained a post with a pacifist youth group elsewhere in Switzerland. Her youth, vigour and efficiency had been greatly appreciated and her untimely death in a road accident in 1942 was felt as a tragic loss.

The last number of *Pax International* appeared in February 1940, but Circular Letters were issued from Geneva until August. Writing to the national sections in April 1940, Clara Ragaz transmitted news from the occupied territories of Finland, Denmark and Norway; from the still-active British section; from neutral Sweden, where 24 women's organizations held a mass demonstration and issued a peace appeal to Mrs Roosevelt; and from Switzerland, increasingly concerned with the plight and status of the thousands of refugees in the country.

At the end of May 1940, with the victorious German armies in command of Denmark, Norway, Holland and Belgium, with the withdrawal of the British Army at Dunkirk and the occupation of France only a matter of days, the International Chairmen agreed that a section of the international work of the WILPF should now be transferred to America. On a brilliant day in June 1940, accordingly, as the Germans were entering Paris and Italy flung in her support on what seemed to be the winning side, Gertrude Baer arrived in New York to establish an international outpost of the WILPF which was to be maintained throughout the war. In view of the unavoidable suspension of the Executive Committee and the impossibility of direct communication with certain national sections, a group of American members formed an International Advisory Council to share some of the responsibilities of administration, finance and policy-making. The International President, Emily Greene Balch, was of course also in the United States and in continuous consultation with Gertrude Baer. In Zürich, Clara Ragaz kept open the other end of the line of communication and sent out messages to all sections with which contact could be maintained. Her New Year greeting for 1941 contained news of Gabrielle Duchêne. She was safe in the south of France, separated from her family in the northern occupied zone, and maintaining herself with a market-garden and poultry-yard. There was also news from Hungary, where members still kept in touch although no active work for the League was possible.

The main channel of information during the Second World War, however, was provided by the International Circular Letters which Gertrude Baer compiled and distributed from New York. The first letter was dated March 1941 and four more were issued that year. Subsequently the letters appeared regularly four times a year until 1946, reaching a circulation of 1,200 copies in 35 countries. In many instances, where normal means of communication were closed, the letters were transmitted by diplomatic bag. In this way news of national sections, comments on world events, reports of current conferences and publications were relayed; and, not least in importance, an open forum was maintained for the formulation, discussion and modification of the aims and policies of the WILPF itself. Several national sections also continued to publish their own monthly news sheets—notably Australia, Britain, Denmark, Sweden and the USA.

A good example of the scope of the International Circular Letters is provided by the issue of June 1941. News from inside the movement included a report from France where, it was stated, majority opinion had not been opposed to the armistice with Germany. On the contrary, there was strong anti-English feeling following the destruction of the French fleet in North Africa by the British Navy in July 1940. But discontent was rapidly rising, due to food shortages, plundering by the occupying army, and the continued internment of French prisoners of war in German camps. In connection with post-war economic reconstruction—a topic already in the forefront of WILPF planning—the letter drew attention to the work of the International Industrial Relations Institute, founded at The Hague in 1925 and with an office also in New York. The pioneer WILPF member Louie Bennett, Secretary of the Irish Women Workers' Union, was a member of the governing board.

An Appendix to this letter contained a draft memorandum prepared by the Swedish section on the setting up of a democratic, non-military World Federation, in line with proposals which had been made by Rosika Schwimmer. Another Appendix analysed the shifts in the European export trade since the outbreak of war. Yet another discussed Hans Heymann's *Plan for Permanent Peace* (Harper, New York), an elaboration of a scheme first presented at the Genoa Reparation Conference in 1922 by the German Foreign Minister of the Weimar Republic, Walter Rathenau. The author traced the subsequent rise of the Nazi movement, on which Gertrude Baer commented that the régime would be overthrown from within, 'if the way to a higher socio-economic order is paved *from without*'. She continued: 'This war will not be won by ruthless warfare and power policies. This war will finally and eventually be won by the most just universal social order.'

The theme of 'a new international order' was to run strongly through the thinking of the WILPF throughout the war period, as it had indeed since 1915. Now it was echoed by the Allied powers in the Atlantic Charter of August 1941, and in the Axis counterblast for a European New Order. But how was any kind of 'new order' to come out of war? The pattern was being set, Gertrude Baer believed, in the countries of Occupied Europe by their practice of civilian non-co-operation. She pointed out that this was not a new method. It had been tried in Hungary in the nineteenth century and more recently in Egypt, Korea, Ireland and Germany. It was being successfully applied on a national scale in India. The significant factor now, however, was that the method was being demonstrated not by a pacifist minority but by the general population: by teachers, clergy, judges, industrial workers and peasants. She recalled the often-expressed hope of Jane Addams that methods of non-violent resistance should be devised 'in minute detail' to counteract bloodshed and tyranny. But in this field, Miss Baer added, the WILPF had failed completely. The working out of effective non-violent techniques was high in her priorities for future action. Emily Balch endorsed this view, in a letter to the World Jewish Congress in 1942:

We are all answerable in part for the development of a state of things where the moral insanity of Hitler Germany was possible. And for a state of things where the civilized world can find no better way out than competition in reciprocal slaughter and destruction. We were not ready in time with any other method than this slow and cruel one.

The attitude of the International President of the WILPF epitomized the inner struggle of the conscientious pacifist to reconcile the demands of both peace and justice. At the outbreak of war the United States section of the WILPF lost half its membership—equally, because it was 'too pacifist' and because it was 'not pacifist enough'. After Pearl Harbor in December 1941 and America's subsequent state of war with both Japan and Germany, the conflict of conscience became even more acute. In a message to the American members Miss Balch counselled them not to obstruct the war but to work against hatred and for world co-operation. She had never regarded herself as an 'absolute pacifist' in the Tolstoyan sense of rejecting all physical violence. To Emily Balch, relativism was itself the only fixed principle: an attitude that was sometimes an embarrassment to her more single-minded colleagues. 'I suppose', she is reported to have said early in 1942, 'I should resign from the WIL but I haven't the least intention of doing so.'

In May 1942 at a public luncheon in her honour—she had attained her 75th birthday the previous January—Miss Balch gave a lecture entitled 'Towards a Planetary Civilization'. Presaging the future United Nations, she envisaged the setting up not of a 'world government' but of 'international authorities' which would act as trustees of the common interests, for instance by administering the great airways and waterways of the world. Such authorities, she believed, would eliminate the need for national armed forces and reduce any international force to a minimum. But she also issued a warning that 'international unity' was not in itself a solution:

Unless this international unity has a moral quality, unless it accepts the discipline of moral standards and possesses the quality of humanity, it will not be the unity we are interested in. If it is autocratic and not co-operative in tone, it may be indeed a Frankenstein.

As the fateful year of 1942 ended, violence raged with unabated ferocity on a global scale: Japan victorious in South-East Asia; North Africa churned and re-churned by the *danse macabre* of the Allied and Axis armies; Britain and Germany pounded by ever-more indiscriminate bombing raids; the Jews of Europe driven mercilessly into extermination camps; Russia devastated by the German armies and now the German Sixth Army itself freezing and starving to death at Stalingrad. In January 1943 the battered remnant surrendered, and Hitler's defeat in Europe was assured: on the Russian front alone in that terrible winter, he had squandered more than a million men. But the promise of victory did not bring any real hope of peace. At Casablanca that same month the Western leaders promulgated their war aims, including the infamous demand for 'unconditional surrender' which destroyed any possibility of *rapprochement* with the German resistance movement and led to the murder of its heroic leaders by the Nazis.

The WILPF was not alone in condemning this criminally irresponsible declaration; it did not, however, like some peace groups, advocate instead a 'negotiated peace'. What the League demanded was a clear definition and expression of constructive and workable 'peace aims'. Towards this end, in 1943, Emily Balch and Gertrude Baer drew up a questionnaire to national sections with the object of obtaining a 'pool of opinion' on such questions as a 'People's Peace'; World Organization; International Law; Human Rights; Economic Planning; Disarmament and an International Police Force; Migration, Refugees and Minorities; the Axis Powers and Occupied Countries. At the same time Gertrude Baer put forward some concrete proposals for a Training Centre in Internationalism which, had they been taken up at high level, might have eased the solution of many post-war problems and provided a recruitment pool for the United Nations. The head of a New York university was ready to adopt the project, had funds been made available; but no financial support could be obtained for what was then regarded as a 'utopian' idea. Miss Baer hoped that embassies might provide the necessary sponsorship, 'so that students may be trained for International Service as they have been hitherto trained for the Foreign Diplomatic Service of their respective countries'. Amongst her Guiding Principles for the centre was the simple statement: To learn that the world is a unity. How few of us really believe this, even yet!

Discussion among the sections on the Pool of Opinion continued throughout 1943 and 1944, findings on the various questions being published in the International Circular Letters as they were received. The sections contributing to the 'pool' were Australia, Britain, Canada, Sweden, Switzerland and USA. It was recognized that this was an incomplete survey and that many of those most deeply affected by the war were not included. In September 1944, following the Allied invasion and subsequent liberation of much of occupied Europe, Emily Balch and Gertrude Baer issued additional questions to national sections on the future work and policies of the WILPF. A post-war generation, it was pointed out, would demand a clear-cut economic and social programme:

Merely to say that war is a crime and that our goal is a warless world is wittingly or unwittingly to ignore that war is only one element in a vast political, social and economic complex. A world without war might still be a very bad and cruel world. A new analysis and clarification of this whole complex and of the necessary prerequisites for a Constructive Peace are urgently needed.

Governments too, at this time, were in their own fashion laying the foundations of peace. At the Dumbarton Oaks Conference in September 1944 the Charter of the United Nations was drafted. Emily Balch made a characteristic comment: it was well to realize, she said, that

the success of the proposed organization will depend much less on the terms of any covenant or constitution than on how the Governments choose to behave. If they act like brigands dividing spoils, if they occupy themselves with jockeying for power, trying to get the better of one another, no document however well drawn can prevent them. If they honestly want to create a more co-operative world—and therefore one happier and more prosperous—they can do so under the proposed charter and could do so even under a much worse one.

The WILPF had always believed that one of the surest bases of peace lay in the strengthening of the international co-operative movement. As early as 1942 Gertrude Baer had urged that post-war relief should be channelled through co-operative agencies and not, as after the First World War, by private organizations. She recommended the setting up of four large-scale European co-operatives for Producing (mining, fishing, agriculture); Buying (importing of raw materials); Manufacturing (industry); and Distributing (transportation of goods). In July 1943 the International Circular Letter drew attention to a memorandum on post-war reconstruction prepared by the International Co-operative Women's Guild, of which the President was the former Austrian Member of Parliament and WILPF member, Emmy Freundlich. The ICL for March 1944 quoted proposals made by Howard A. Cowden at the Washington Conference on International Co-operative Reconstruction for setting up an International Co-operative Trading and Manufacturing Association for food and petroleum. Other reports published in the wartime ICLs dealt with co-operative developments in Canada, China, India and the USA.

But as the war in Europe ground to a standstill, the real question confronting the WILPF was its own future. Contact had been maintained almost unbroken with the Northern sections and Switzerland, Britain and the Commonwealth, and America, and with individuals in many other countries. During 1945 news began to trickle in also from Czechoslovakia, France, Holland and Hungary; and early in 1946, from Germany and Japan. The sections tell their own stories of courage, endurance and tragedy in the next chapter. Wartime activities showed no slackening of effort or enthusiasm for the long-term aims of the League: education for democracy, aid for refugees and war victims, the political status of women, the eradication of race discrimination and economic exploitation—all these aspects of the work were upheld and where possible developed.

In April 1945 the WILPF celebrated its thirtieth birthday—coinciding with the first United Nations Conference at San Francisco. A message to the UN President from the three International Chairmen recalled the long association of the WILPF with the League of Nations and offered four points for the consideration of the Conference:

World-wide education for a new association of nations.

An international Charter of Human Rights to safeguard individual freedoms in an era of large-scale planning.

Constructive measures of world co-operation to prevent aggression.

A new concept of 'security', not based on military power and prestige.

The WILPF maintained at this time, and continued to reiterate, that the headquarters of the United Nations should not be situated in the USA, or in the territory of any major power.

In September 1945, after nearly six years' separation, the three Chairmen met in England and laid plans for the first post-war International Congress. It was felt imperative that the national sections should be called together for consultation, and new international officers should be elected, without delay. It was decided to summon an 'Urgency Congress' and International Executive Committee in August 1946, the detailed arrangements being left in the hands of Clara Ragaz.

The Second World War was over—and a second chance had come to build that world of permanent peace in freedom towards which the WILPF had striven for thirty years. By September 1945 it was clear that the second chance would also be the last. On August 6th the first atomic bomb was dropped on Hiroshima, and a new epoch of human history began. As the British section wrote to their Prime Minister on August 20th:

The invention of the atomic bomb has rendered obsolete the weapons, conscript armies and strategic bases to which men cling. . . . Will not

His Majesty's Government make a dramatic appeal to the leaders of every country, to turn wholly from the preparation of men and machines for catastrophic destruction and to seek security in world-wide co-operation for the satisfaction of human need? We believe that such a step taken at this moment would awake a response from men and women everywhere which would carry the world forward into a new and happier era.

Had they been vouchsafed a glimpse into the future, and seen the destructive power of the atomic bomb magnified five hundred times within ten years, the British women might have spoken with less confidence in the power of governments to work miracles but not with less conviction in their own apprehension of the truth.

CHAPTER 16

RETROSPECT AND PROSPECT

Luxembourg Congress 1946—Reports of National Sections—Should the WILPF Continue?—WILPF and United Nations—Nobel Prize for Miss Balch

———————

The Tenth International Congress of the Women's International League for Peace and Freedom—and the second to be held in the aftermath of a world war—took place at Luxembourg from August 4 to 9, 1946. How different was the atmosphere from that of 1919! Zürich had seen the betrayal of many hopes, but not the destruction of the very ideals on which those hopes were founded. The second post-war mood was expressed by the International Chairmen in their letter of invitation to the national sections:

Do not let us forget that the phraseology formerly used to express the highest concepts of political life, national and international, the phraseology the WILPF itself has employed—such terms as freedom, democracy, justice, equality, peace and many others—has been abused and degraded to such an extent that these words have become hollow shams. Millions of men and women in every country have lost confidence in these terms and in those who use them.

This crisis of confidence was now facing the WILPF with an urgent problem: in such conditions, could the League continue? The Luxembourg Congress must answer that question before any other decisions for the future could be taken. But first of all, at this reunion of old friends and introduction of many new ones after long years of bitter separation, experiences must be exchanged and the lessons of the war digested. In all, thirteen sections were represented by 200 delegates, including one from the new section in Brazil; ten sections, including the new section in Cuba, were unable to send representatives. Emily Greene Balch presided, and all except one of the fourteen members of the Executive Committee elected at Luhacovice in 1937 were present. How fervent were the greetings after six years' separation—and how heart-warming was the welcome of 'little Luxembourg', with its well-stocked shops and gay cafés, after the drabness and stringency of war-time rations and post-war shortages. Local arrangements for the Congress were made by a committee of Luxembourg women, not themselves members of the League, whose generous service was greatly appreciated.

In 1919, delegates to Zürich from the 'victor' countries had been shocked by the physical evidence of starvation and other deprivations in their sisters from Central Europe. But these hardships were recognized as by-products of the war rather than deliberate acts of policy (though the Allied post-war blockade came dangerously near to a war against civilians). Now the Congress was to hear of women directly involved, no less than men, in all the violence and degradation of total war: victims of air-raids and concentration camps, partisans in the resistance movement, conscripts for war-service alongside their brothers, forced labourers in arms factories—how tragic was this culmination of the struggle for women's rights! And how essential, therefore, to carry on the fight and rectify the false values by which the new rights had been won! Listening to the 'splendours and miseries' of the past six years' history, delegates must already have been resolving that their work was not yet done. As Burgomaster Hamilius of Luxembourg symbolically expressed it at a civic reception for the League on August 5th: 'the eyes of all humanity are fixed on the important transactions of your Congress'. Women's qualities of heart and mind were desperately needed, he declared, to dissolve the 'cold calculations' of political men by which international affairs had hitherto been dominated.

Clara Ragaz, in her opening address, cited the roll of honour of war-time losses:

The two great pioneers from Germany, Anita Augspurg and Lida Gustava Heymann, died in exile in Switzerland. (In 1946, a street in Hamburg was named after L. G. Heymann.)

Eugénie Meller and Mélanie Vambery, President and Secretary of the Hungarian section, deported to extermination camps.

Frantiska Plaminkova, the outstanding Czech senator, brutally executed; as were Milena Illóva, Elsa Kalmus, and four other members of the Czechoslovakian section. Marie Schmolkova, formerly consultative member for her section, died in England.

Rosa Manus of Holland, co-organizer with Aletta Jacobs of the 1915 Hague Congress, died in a German concentration camp.

Other losses by death included Dr Helen Stöcker and Anna Hamburger-Ludwig, formerly of Germany; Marguerite Gobat of Switzerland; Mrs M. G. Thoday, founder of the Welsh branches of the British section; Dorothy Evans, pioneer feminist and first secretary of the British section; Mathilde Widegren, first President of the Swedish section; Lola Maverick Lloyd of the USA, close associate of Rosika Schwimmer in her campaigns for world government; Lucie Déjardin, Belgian delegate at the Hague Congress, who died shortly after her return home from England in 1945; and that revered associate member of the French section, Romain Rolland, to whom a tribute was paid at this Congress by Andrée Jouve. ('Our true country', he had told the WILPF in 1926, 'is life.')

Since it was laid down in the 1934 constitution of the WILPF that national sections must be consulted on matters of international policy, no concerted action by the Chairmen in the name of the League had been possible during the war. Communications were slow and hazardous and, although not entirely cut off from one another, sections had therefore to work largely as autonomous units. In these circumstances, the consistency and overall unity of their wartime activity was all the more astonishing—although the countries which had suffered most from the German occupation were marked off from the rest. The sections in Austria, Czechoslovakia, Holland, Hungary, Poland and Yugoslavia had virtually disappeared. Now, however, Yella Hertzka had returned to Austria from England and contact had been established with Mrs Szirmai in Hungary, so there was some possibility of groups being re-formed in these countries.

One Polish representative was present at Luxembourg: the section had been dissolved, she said, and all members went into the resistance movement. Many women had taken Jewish children into their own families. On one occasion a large crowd of women, 'like furies', flung themselves at a stationary deportation train and seized the children, in the presence of German soldiers. The work of reconstruction and social reform was now absorbing all their energies. A representative was also present from the Yugoslav National Front, who brought an appeal from the women of her country for 'a just and durable peace'. It was a great joy at Luxembourg to see six members of the Czecho-slovakian section: some had now returned to their own country from exile in England, others had remained steadfast throughout the occupation. They told how, although the section was dissolved after Munich, members continued to meet at the Women's Club in Prague and worked together to aid prisoners of war, internees and the underground resistance movement.

One of the great hopes of the Luxembourg Congress had been to receive back into the WILPF 'family'—as it was referred to, for censorship reasons, during the war—the remnant of the German section which had striven to maintain the principles of the League inside Germany throughout the Nazi régime and the war. But at the last moment, travel documents were refused and no delegates could be present. Contact had already been revived, however, and it was known that several groups were forming in the British and American zones of occupation, notably in Bremen, Munich and Stuttgart. The Women's Club of Bremen, founded in 1945, recalled the example of the Hague Congress of 1915 in an appeal to German women 'to help make the word "German" honourable again'.

In 1919 such an appeal would not have been necessary, inside or outside Germany. A notable feature of the years immediately after the First World War had been the successful co-operation of the French and German sections of the WILPF in working for the reconciliation of their countries. After the Second World War, this was not going to be so easy. The horror of the Nazi attempt at systematic extermination of Jews, Slavs and other 'inferior' races had seared all Europe. Andrée Jouve, reporting now from France, described the bitter hatred engendered by the German occupation and the impossibility of asking for 'forgiveness' of the Nazi war crimes. The French section had been dispersed, and all records destroyed; its rebuilding would be slow and difficult. Mme Jouve saw one hopeful portent, however, in the granting of parliamentary franchise to women and the election of the first woman deputy, Madeleine Braun, who was also Vice-President of the Constituent Assembly. (It may be noted here that the Liaison Committee of International Women's Organizations carried on its work from London during the war and never ceased to press the case for the equal status of women and their share in post-war reconstruction; during 1942–43 it sent some 40 delegations to Allied and Neutral governments represented in London. By 1945, in addition to France, six countries of Latin America and the Caribbean had granted the vote to women.)

Of all the occupied countries of Europe, the example of the Danish section—like the Danish nation as a whole—was unique. Its membership of 25,000 was maintained throughout the war. The monthly journal was published without a break. Educational and relief work continued and expanded. Between 1941 and 1943 a thousand meetings were held (mostly in private houses). Although plans were made for going underground, there was no interference by the Germans apart from one raid on the national office. Members even sold the WILPF 'peace flower' to German soldiers—who wore them inside their tunics. All this open activity did not mean that the Danish section in any way 'collaborated' with the army of occupation. The national policy of Denmark, with which the WILPF was in full accord, was one of strict non-co-operation with the invader; members only differed from some of their compatriots in maintaining their resistance solely by non-violent means. Strong protests were made to the Nazis against persecution of the Jews. A major effort of the section was the sending of food parcels, in the teeth of a Nazi prohibition, to Jews deported to the Theresienstadt concentration camp, thereby saving many lives. Three hundred Jewish children who had arrived in Denmark the day war broke out, destined for Palestine, remained and were cared for by members and almost every one of them survived. Another project of the WILPF was to initiate a united women's front for non-violent resistance; in this connection a questionnaire on democratic freedom, women's rights and international co-operation was circulated to 10,000 women. As the war ended, members spoke out against any revengeful treatment of Germany. Towards the end of the war the WILPF, in co-operation with Quakers and other peace workers, organized teams of young men and women Peace Volunteers to be trained for post-war relief work. In September 1945 an Inter-Scandinavian Conference of the WILPF took place in the Danish Parliament House. It was attended by delegates from the four Northern sections and attracted considerable press publicity; a guest speaker from the British section was the pacifist writer, Vera Brittain.

The strength of the smaller but active Finnish section had been weakened less than might be imagined from the country's encounters with the Soviet and German armies. The section was broken up by evacuation after the Russian attack, but members continued their work on behalf of war victims and, with the co-operation of the Danish and Swedish sections, arranged for many thousands of children to be sent to safety. Although all peace propaganda was forbidden after 1941, when Finland was fighting alongside Germany, WILPF meetings continued to be held. In the spring of 1945, an appeal to Finnish women to join the WILPF was issued and was published in all the national papers. Shortly afterwards, the section was awarded a government subsidy for its educational work—a recognition which perhaps owed something to the pacifist sympathies of the War Minister, Yrjo Kallinen!

Of all the Nordic countries, Norway suffered worst from the German occupation—no doubt because of the bitter fighting that had taken place on Norwegian soil. After the capitulation in June 1940, all political parties except the Nazis were closed down and the WILPF section was forcibly dissolved. Nevertheless, small groups continued to meet privately and to maintain activities: assisting in relief work, making illegal contacts with Sweden, organizing escape routes for Jews and young people, and generally contributing to the united, moral resistance by Norwegian teachers, judges and clergy which successfully undermined many of the Nazi decrees. In 1943 the WILPF Chairman, Marie Lous-Mohr, herself a teacher, was arrested by the Gestapo and sent to Grini concentration camp, where she was held for nearly two and a half years. The Vice-Chairman, Sigrid Lund, and two other members succeeded in escaping to Sweden. Living and working with the Norwegian section during the war was a British Quaker and WILPF member, Myrtle Wright, who also escaped to Sweden in 1944; in 1946 she was decorated by the King of Norway in recognition of her services to the resistance movement. The first post-war activity of the Norwegian section was to organize a series of public lectures at the Nobel Hall in Oslo on the theme of Education for Democracy and Peace. The opening lecture was given by Vera Brittain, to a packed hall. After five years of isolation, it seemed to the Scandinavians as if a window had opened on the world again.

The report of the Swedish section drew attention to the importance of the country's high standard of living and well-developed social services as a bulwark against Nazi propaganda, pointing out that these were a direct result of Sweden's immunity from war for 150 years. The WILPF not only maintained but increased its membership during the war, concentrating its efforts mainly on educational work. It initiated a Liaison Committee of Women's Organizations and launched a mass movement in favour of the United Nations which, with one and a half million members, grew into the Swedish branch of UNA. The section was continuously active on behalf of its sister sections in Scandinavia, and a weekly gathering for refugee women from Denmark and Norway was held in Stockholm throughout the war. Help for refugees and war-victims naturally absorbed a good deal of the section's energies; at one period, one in thirty of Sweden's population were refugees. One national event of some significance to the WILPF during the war was the election to the Swedish Academy of the second woman in its 158 years' existence: the writer Elin Wägner, co-founder of the Swedish section. The first woman elected had been the internationally famous writer Selma Lagerlöf, also of the WILPF.

In another neutral country of Europe, Switzerland, the WILPF section maintained its work under difficulties, but without persecution. It worked hard to improve the status of the many thousands of refugees in the country, and to combat any tendencies towards fascism or anti-semitism. Study courses were organized on the Jewish problem, European federation and on various aspects of post-war reconstruction. At the end of the war, the section strongly urged that Switzerland should join the United Nations and play an active part in the new international organization. But it was found much easier to interest Swiss women in practical, humanitarian work rather than in the study of war *prevention* which was felt to be the special task of the WILPF.

Although Britain was involved in the war as a belligerent from the start, the British section maintained its activities with a surprising degree of normality. Its isolation from the international fellowship of the League was lessened by the presence of many exiled members from Austria, Belgium, Czechoslovakia, Germany and Hungary. The national office in London suffered heavily from bombing and was evacuated to the country home of Mrs Innes, who besides being an International Chairman acted as honorary secretary of her section. Also evacuated with the office was its devoted administrative secretary Emily Horscroft, who retired from her post at the end of the war after thirty years' service. When the conscription of women was introduced in 1941 the British section petitioned the Minister of Labour to grant equal rights with men to women conscientious objectors; this recognition was subsequently given. In 1941 also, the section launched a 'penny a week' fund, to be set aside for the restoration of the international work of the League after the war—a generous gesture from a section which only a few years earlier was threatening to sever its links with the international body!

Considerable thought was given to planning for post-war reconstruction, both nationally and internationally, and the section organized joint conferences with other women's groups on the Atlantic Charter; the Sankey Charter of Human Rights; the Beveridge Report on social services; the Dumbarton Oaks conference; and international control of Atomic Energy. The worsening relations of Britain and India, due to India's refusal to support the British war-effort, naturally caused much concern to the WILPF, which increased its pressure for the early granting of Indian independence. Direct communication with India was maintained through Agatha Harrison and Grace Lankester in England; and through Mrs Pandit, herself an international member of the League, on the other side. As the war ended, measures of food relief for the occupied countries of Europe and also for ex-enemy countries were urged; it was no surprise to find Edith Pye again in action in France with the Friends' Relief Service. After the war, a memorial to the British Government signed by prominent women begged that German women should be encouraged to take part in the democratic revival of their country.

In America, too, in spite of heavy membership losses, the long-term aims of the WILPF were maintained unbroken and with no governmental suppression. Generous aid for all refugees included attempts to liberalize the immigration laws, which failed; and to provide an escape agency for Jews from Europe, which succeeded after two years' pressure and led finally to the establishment of the War Refugee Board. Similar pressure for a Bill to enable the feeding of children in occupied Europe was thwarted by the military invasion of Europe, but the strong demand by the WILPF and other organizations that the USA should contribute to the United Nations Relief and Rehabilitation Agency (UNRRA) rather than set up a national relief agency resulted in the passage of the necessary Bill. The section also protested vigorously, but without success, against the abolition of food rationing by the US Government *one week* after war ended.

On the national level, the section upheld the rights of conscientious objectors and helped to defeat a proposal to conscript women; worked for the release of Japanese Americans interned after Pearl Harbor, and for abrogation of the Oriental Exclusion Act; opposed the poll-tax for negroes in Southern states; and, after the horror of Hiroshima, co-operated with the Federation of Atomic Scientists for civilian control of atomic energy. Three WILPF representatives were present at the first United Nations conference in San Francisco and the section was recognized at the UN centre in New York as one of 25 consulting organizations. A new, and hopeful, factor in American public opinion, as distinct from that of 1919, was the keen interest in the United Nations and desire for its success.

Heloise Brainerd reported on the continuing work of the WILPF Committee on the Americas, which aimed to have a representative in every country of America. From the time of its mission to Haiti in

1926, the US section had consistently opposed American imperialist policies, more recently in connection with Mexico, Cuba and Puerto Rico. In May 1943, in conjunction with the Latin American Economic Institute of New York, the Committee held a public conference on Economic and Social Problems of the Caribbean, from which fourteen recommendations were sent to fifty governmental and other agencies. Miss Brainerd now asked the International Chairmen to appoint new members to the Committee, charged with the special task of training women for leadership in Latin American countries.

Of the remaining sections outside Europe, Canada was the least affected by the war, but its growth as a national organization was hampered by the vast distances between the branches in Toronto, Winnipeg and Vancouver. As in America, members were concerned to obtain fair treatment for citizens of Japanese origin, and to increase relief measures for war victims. They protested against military education in schools and against the shipping of arms to China. The sections in Australia and New Zealand, isolated for so long from Europe, had loosened their international links and tended to work more in co-operation with other peace groups inside their own countries. But the Australian honorary secretary, Eleanor Moore, remained a keen international member of the League, contributing reports to the wartime circular letters and publishing information about the WILPF in the Australian journal *Opportunity*. One issue of this paper referred to the Oslo 'health lunch' then enjoying a vogue amongst Australian youngsters. Passing on this information for the benefit of Scandinavian and Swiss friends, Gertrude Baer commented: 'What has the Oslo Health Lunch to do with Peace and Freedom? *Mens sana in corpore sano* has always remained our highest educational ideal.'

It was said earlier that the Dutch section of the WILPF was one of those in Europe which had 'virtually disappeared' during the war. Holland had suffered much from what Mme Ramondt-Hirschmann described as the 'moral wreckage' of the German occupation; a wreckage that was all the more devastating to a country of high international ideals and with a strongly-rooted pacifist tradition. There was a general exhaustion and disillusionment, with little enthusiasm for peace work. All peace organizations had been forbidden by the Nazis in May 1940 and, although small groups of pacifists continued to gather secretly, it was not until September 1945 that the WILPF board was able to meet again. The question at once was raised: should the League continue as a separate women's organization? No decision was made, and it was agreed that the motion should be put to the International Congress.

Now, therefore, it fell to the Dutch section, cradle of the League in 1915, to propose the dissolution of the organization. The main arguments, presented by Miss J. Repelaer van Driel, were that peace and freedom were not the special concern of women; that the war had proved the ability of women to work on an equal footing with men; and that all creative forces must be co-ordinated in a mass educational campaign. The case for continuation of the WILPF was stated by Mildred Olmsted (USA). She stressed the long international experience of the League and the strength of its influence—an influence out of all proportion to its numbers; the continued need for women's co-operation in building a world where 'children may grow up safely and happily'; the comprehensive programme of the WILPF for peace, freedom and non-violent change; and the importance of doing nothing that might weaken the peace movement at this crucial moment in world affairs. The motion for dissolution was overwhelmingly defeated. The Women's International League for Peace and Freedom was going forward into the atomic age. Perhaps delegates were influenced to some degree in their voting by the message to the Congress cabled by George Bernard Shaw: 'Convinced that the world would never be properly governed until 50 per cent of its rulers were women.'

With the decision to carry on the work of the WILPF into the postwar era, it was necessary to hold elections for international officers; the three wartime Chairmen did not wish to stand again. The Executive Committee elected by the Congress, as always on an individual and not a national basis, was as follows: Emily G. Balch (President, USA); Gertrude Bussey (Joint Chairman, USA); Marie Lous-Mohr (Joint Chairman, Norway); Gertrude Baer; Barbara Duncan Harris (Britain); Lola Hanouskova (Czechoslovakia); Signe Højer (Sweden); Andrée Jouve (France); Mildred S. Olmsted (USA); Dr Hélène Stähelin (Switzerland); Agnes Stapledon (Britain); Else Zeuthen (Denmark). Two veterans of the British section, Kathleen Innes and Edith Pye, were accorded the title of Vice-Presidents.

The Luxembourg Congress, as the Zürich Congress had done in 1919, sent recommendations to the Peace Conference meeting concurrently in Paris. The message from the President and Chairmen urged that all peace treaties should be based on human rights; that a Charter of Human Rights should be incorporated in the constitution of every state; that frontiers should not be drawn without regard to economic and social consequences; and that the decisions of the Conference should not be determined by national interests, economic advantage or prestige but in the interests of 'the human race as one unit'. Economically and socially, the 'united nations' had undoubtedly advanced a little in the direction of the WILPF's long-held principles 'for the ministration of human need'; but politically, the powers were farther apart than ever. The Paris conference of 1946 could not even conjure up a Versailles; no peace treaty of any kind was offered to Germany after the Second World War, although treaties with the lesser enemy states were concluded in a rather more liberal spirit.

The Congress surveyed and pronounced on many problems of peace and international relations, amongst them World Security; Atomic Energy; Non-Violent Resistance; Conscription; and attitudes towards Spain, Germany and the Soviet Union. But one issue remained unresolved: the revision of the League's own aims and constitution. Neither the ordeals of war nor the urgent need now to rebuild international co-operation had sufficed to bridge the divergences of opinion within the ranks of the WILPF. Broadly, this was the same cleavage that on the world stage was already threatening to disrupt the wartime alliances and precipitate new conflicts. In place of the promised 'Four Freedoms', the waiting peoples in 1946 were offered the chilling prospect of an East-West 'Cold War'.

But for the WILPF itself, the year ended on a note of jubilation which seemed to vindicate the decision to carry on its work. In December came the news that the International President, Emily Greene Balch (like her predecessor Jane Addams) had been awarded a Nobel peace prize, which she received jointly with the General Secretary of the World Student Christian Federation, John Mott. Miss Balch was unable to attend the ceremony in Oslo, but she would surely have approved the spirit of her commendation by the Chairman of the Nobel Committee, Mr Gunnar Jahn:

She has shown us that the reality we seek must be won through hard work in the world in which we live, but she has shown us more than this: that one does not become exhausted and that defeat gives new courage for the struggle to those who have within them the holy fire.

Of the organization which had provided the main channel for Emily Balch's international work, Mr Jahn said:

I can't repeat to you all the resolutions passed as amendments for the Peace Treaty from the Congress in 1919. But I want to say this: it would have been wise if the statesmen of the world had listened to the proposals from the women. But in the men's society in which we are living, proposals coming from women are not usually taken seriously.

This encouragement from the ranks of the 'men's society' must surely have strengthened the women of 1946 in their determination that the WILPF must go on making proposals for a saner and more humane world order until some statesmen, at least, did listen. One at least of its practical difficulties, the recurrent problem of finance, was eased by Miss Balch's donation of 10,000 dollars from her prize-money for the international work of the League.

CHAPTER 17

THE PRECARIOUS PEACE

*Marshall Aid—WILPF and NATO—Copenhagen
Congress 1949—German section—Eastern Europe—
Communist Peace Campaigns—NGOs at United Na-
tions—New Trends in WILPF*

By the time the next WILPF International Congress met at Christians-
borg Castle, Copenhagen, seat of the Danish Parliament, in August
1949, the promised 'Cold War' had hardened into a fact. Soviet penetration of the Balkans, and American counter-intervention under the
'Truman Doctrine' of March 1947 tore the last shreds of the wartime
alliance. In June the Marshall Plan for economic aid to Europe confirmed the worst suspicions of the Eastern bloc about American
'capitalist imperialism' and the worst suspicions of the Western bloc
about Soviet exploitation of the misery of Europe for political ends.

The question of Marshall Aid was not overlooked in WILPF discussions. The American section demanded from the start that aid
should be given 'without strings', and national sections were asked by
the International Chairmen to survey the working of Marshall Aid in
their own countries: most of them reported favourably. The Marshall
Plan, however, by its very nature laid itself open to manipulation by
business and political interests, as Gertrude Baer had warned when she
urged that all post-war reconstruction should be channelled through
a co-operative organization—or, since its institution, through the
United Nations, which in the Economic Commission for Europe had
the administrative machinery ready to hand. But Marshall Aid was
clearly very much better than no aid at all—as Czechoslovakia
acknowledged in accepting the programme before being rapped into
line by Soviet disapproval.

International relations rapidly worsened in the year preceding the
Congress, with four-power deadlock over the future of Germany; the
Soviet blockade of Berlin in July 1948, successfully countered by the
US airlift; and finally the signing of the Atlantic Pact and setting up of
the North Atlantic Treaty Organization (NATO) in April 1949. The
Atlantic Pact was a severe setback to the work of the WILPF, for

reasons stated by Else Zeuthen of Denmark in her paper to the Congress on Regional Pacts. Any military pact, even a 'defensive' one, was bound to harden divisions, accelerate the arms race and increase the distortions of propaganda. Against this background, could the Atlantic Pact really safeguard peace? There could be no doubt, said Mrs Zeuthen, that the answer must be No.

The Danish section had protested vigorously both against the substance of the Atlantic Pact as a breach of the country's 170 years' policy of neutrality and against the manner in which it was rushed through Parliament without consulting the electorate. In Norway, too, the WILPF petitioned the Government in January 1949 not to take a decision on joining the Pact until the public had been fully informed of the consequences. The British section, in a letter to the Foreign Secretary, Ernest Bevin, deplored the abandonment of the UN Charter which the Pact implied and called for a reorientation of foreign policy to seek means of co-operation with the USSR in the war on hunger, ignorance and want. The American section stated the case against the Pact in a letter to the *New York Times* on April 18, 1949: it would further divide and weaken the United Nations; it would hold up the constructive work of the European Recovery Programme; and, like other military alliances, it would make war more likely. As alternative policies the WILPF section proposed: social legislation to strengthen American democracy; support for world disarmament under international law; extension of the Point Four programme of economic aid by full utilization of UN specialized agencies.

This WILPF opposition to the Atlantic Pact was, as Else Zeuthen remarked, spontaneous and instinctive. Only in the French section, perhaps, was it also inspired by a sympathy with the policies of the Soviet Union. But it could not be denied that majority opinion in the NATO countries was solidly behind the Pact nor that the Second World War and its aftermath had strengthened rather than weakened popular belief in the efficacy of armed power.

Inevitably, then, during these years, the work of the League was restricted both in scope and in its international character. Only in parts of Western Europe and North America could it still claim to be an active force, although the international officers were well aware of the need for continued efforts to reach not only the women of Eastern Europe but also those in the new countries of the Far East and the unawakened countries of Latin America. One of the decisions of the 1949 Congress was to set up a New Sections Committee to assist the development of groups which had arisen since the war in Iceland, Italy and Palestine. In addition, steps were being taken to form a section in India, through the League's long-standing connection with the All-India Women's Conference; and the Japanese section was being revived with the help of two American members who had links with Japan, Mrs Gladys Walser and Mrs Elizabeth Weidemann.

A group of international members still existed in Holland, although it had been decided not to re-form the national section. In Sweden, a separate Baltic group was formed in January 1948 from amongst the 30,000 refugees who fled to Sweden from Estonia, Latvia and Lithuania in 1944; and in Paris, a Vietnamese group was working in co-operation with the French section with the intention of starting a section in Indo-China—where, it may be recalled, the WILPF had established links through Camille Drevet in 1926. The British section was trying to draw together some of the women of many nations living in London, including European 'displaced persons' brought over through government employment schemes, in an All-Nations Group which developed out of a refugee conference in 1949.

The political education of women in Latin America was being fostered by Heloise Brainerd through the Committee on the Americas, although of all the groups she had founded only Brazil retained the status of a national section. In August 1947 the WILPF initiated the first Inter-American Congress of Women at Guatemala City, out of which developed the Inter-American Federation of Women. From all this activity it can be seen that the outlook for future expansion of the WILPF was far from gloomy, even though in the immediate situation the division of Europe was a formidable block to progress.

Amongst the 13 countries represented at Copenhagen a special welcome was given to the eight delegates from the German section, now restored to the fellowship of the WILPF after an absence of 17 years. Legal recognition of the section by Allied Military Government was facilitated by the intervention of a British Member of Parliament and old supporter of the League, Ellen Wilkinson, and its reconstruction was aided by several other national sections. The post-war history of the German section to date may briefly be recounted here.

In 1946 Magda Hoppstock-Huth from Hamburg visited England at the invitation of the British section. (A member of the WILPF since 1916, Frau Hoppstock-Huth had worked on behalf of the Danish minority in the 1920s, against anti-semitism in the 1930s, and in 1944 was arrested by the Nazis under threat of execution. After the war she was elected to the Hamburg district Parliament as a Social Democrat.) A year later two British members, Barbara Duncan Harris and Mary Phillips, were granted permission to travel in the British and American zones of Germany, staying at Hamburg, Lübeck, Bremen and Hanover. They found strong WILPF groups in all four cities, in spite of food shortages and appalling living conditions, and were struck by the determination of the members to bring home to their compatriots a sense of individual responsibility for Nazism and war. The French zone was visited after the Luxembourg Congress by Gertrude Baer and Professor Gertrude Bussey of the American section, and in April 1947 Clara Ragaz arranged a gathering at Zürich for delegates who had been excluded from the Congress; fifteen Germans and two Austrians attended. The Swiss section also organized *Pax Jugendwerk*, a scheme for providing hospitality for French and German young people; under it, seven scholarships were granted for the WILPF summer school at Schiers in July 1948. The Swedish section sent several members to the German section's summer school in 1947, resulting in more exchange visits and the adoption of German groups by several Swedish branches.

One of the first concerns of the reconstituted German section had been to combat any signs of a renascence of anti-semitism. Nor was this evil confined to Germany and her former allies. In Sweden, the WILPF section found it necessary to conduct a vigorous campaign against racial and religious discrimination, resulting in a governmental investigation. It also instituted an enquiry amongst other WILPF sections on the extent of anti-semitism and measures to prevent it, the results showing 'a more or less latent anti-semitism' in the eight countries which responded.

Another immediate activity of the German section was to initiate an action committee against German rearmament and in favour of a neutralized Germany, in which 21 organizations joined. But with no central German Government and the country divided into four zones of foreign occupation, it was virtually impossible to build up a unified German section of the League. After the formal establishment of the West German Federal Republic and East German Democratic Republic in the autumn of 1949, the West German groups and the Berlin group suffered from a political as well as a geographical separation.

No Czechoslovakian delegates were present at the Copenhagen Congress, although an observer attended from the Czechoslovakian Women's Council and the Congress re-elected Lola Hanouskova as a member of the Executive Committee. But the revived Czech section was still functioning in a limited form as a Preparatory Committee for Peace attached to the Women's Club in Prague. In July 1947 the International Executive Committee was making arrangements for an East-West conference at Prague in the spring of 1948, in which it was hoped Russian women would participate, but this meeting never took place.

In February 1948 a report from the Czech section published in the International Circular Letter described its work among women's organizations and in co-operation with the Czech League of Human Rights. The Preparatory Committee, wrote Lola Hanouskova, was in constant touch with the women of the United States section 'and many misunderstandings have been cleared up'. At the beginning of February it organized the first joint meeting ever to take place in Czechoslovakia of all Christian Church organizations, from which a 'Peace and Friendship' proclamation signed by all the participating bodies was broadcast over the radio. But Communist pressure to gain control of the police force and labour unions was increasing, and that same month the democratic parties in the coalition government resigned in protest. For the second time in his country's short history President Beneš, now sick and ageing, was forced to bow to a show of force. But his Foreign Minister, Jan Masaryk, chose to take his own life rather than assist in the murder of the Czechoslovakian democratic state which his famous father had founded. From that time, official links between WILPF members and the International were weakened, and finally dissolved.

Under somewhat comparable conditions, the WILPF section in Hungary which had been reorganized in November 1946 was still actively functioning at the time of the 1949 Congress, although no delegates were present. The granting of equal rights to women—at least in theory—in 1946 gave an opportunity for the section, with its long feminist tradition, to renew the pressure for more women to be appointed to responsible positions. The death in New York of the former Hungarian member Rosika Schwimmer in the autumn of 1948 was marked by a memorial meeting addressed, amongst others, by Miss Edith Wynner, the American co-worker of Mme Schwimmer in the cause of world government. The section's report to the Congress distinguished, without comment, between the 'educational peace work' it had carried out through lecture-series addressed by scientists, psychologists and other expert speakers and the large-scale 'propaganda for peace' officially sponsored by the Communist régime. This section had always been outstanding in courage and initiative. Its spirit had survived both war and Fascism, and it was indeed tragic that the post-war 'People's Republic' could not find a place for it. The section was formally dissolved in November 1949, and continued contacts with former members were purely private.

An indication of the state of international tension during the years 1947–53 was the move in several Western countries to impose peacetime conscription for women. Sections of the WILPF were naturally amongst the first women's groups to protest, and on this issue received solid backing from sister organizations. So widespread was public hostility that the proposals were in all cases dropped. But the period of military service for men was lengthened throughout the Western alliance and Britain introduced compulsory service in peacetime, for the first time in her history, in January 1947.

The situation was further complicated by the Communist 'peace offensive' launched at the meeting of the World Peace Council in Stockholm in March 1950. The Stockholm Peace Appeal did not receive the official blessing of the WILPF, although many individual members saw no objection to signing the mass petition for unconditional prohibition of atomic weapons. But it must be acknowledged as a matter of history that the activities of the World Peace Council and its subsidiaries—Partisans for Peace and the Women's International Democratic Federation—often constituted as great a handicap to the established peace movement in the West as the Atlantic Pact. It was difficult, and sometimes painful, to cast doubts on expressions of solidarity in the cause of peace, freedom and democracy that claimed a mass following in the Eastern-bloc countries and sought to extend this following to the West; but impossible not to do so when these expressions were so at variance with the real conditions of life behind the Iron Curtain and so lacking in criticism of provocative actions by Communist governments. This kind of 'peace and freedom' was entirely foreign to the WILPF tradition of objective assessment of a situation and honest self-criticism on the part of all national sections.

The attempts of the Women's International Democratic Federation to use the older organization for its own partisan aims, even though unsuccessful, were a considerable embarrassment to WILPF national sections, particularly in Scandinavia, and caused a substantial loss of membership. On the other hand, there was a section of opinion in the WILPF which, sincerely anxious for co-operation with the women in

Communist countries, was continually pressing for closer collaboration with the WIDF. But did any such basis for collaboration at that time exist? Only by resisting what was spurious in the Communist appeal could the way be opened later for a genuine 'peaceful coexistence'. The Communists, on their side, did not lose any opportunity to expose the spurious elements in the propaganda of the 'free world'; and rightly so. Only thus could the areas of potential conflict be reduced. An example of this mutual misunderstanding occurred in connection with the most important post-war development in the work of the WILPF.

In May 1947 the Executive Committee had appointed Gertrude Baer as WILPF Consultant with the United Nations, and she immediately took steps to gain for the League as a non-governmental, international organization the 'consultative status' with the Economic and Social Council (ECOSOC) which was provided for in Article 71 of the Charter. Applications for consultative status were considered by the Committee on Non-Governmental Organizations (NGOs) of ECOSOC, consisting of representatives of the five Big Powers, which then made its recommendations to the full 18-nation Council.

The recommendation of the WILPF for consultative status B (only nine international organizations had status A and a few women's organizations were in category B) came before ECOSOC on March 3, 1948. Immediately, the Soviet delegate rose to object. Before voting on the recommendation, he asked for proof that certain charges made against the WILPF by another organization were 'unfounded'. The charges were that the League was a 'reactionary and pro-Fascist organization'; they were made by the Women's International Democratic Federation, which had already been granted consultative status. This was a strange way of expressing 'solidarity'—and a strange commentary on the pre-war accusations by right-wing extremists that the WILPF was a cloak for international Communism! The Soviet objection was overruled, on the ground that no charges had been made against the WILPF in the NGO Committee, and consultative status was granted.[1] In February 1949 the WILPF was admitted to consultative status also with UNESCO, for which Mme Andrée Jouve acted as the League's representative in Paris; and in January 1953, to specialized consultative status with the Food and Agriculture Organization in Rome.

[1] Gertrude Baer believed that the Soviet charge was due to a confusion of the WILPF with another organization, the International Alliance of Women.

In 1952, the Women's International Democratic Federation was refused renewal of its consultative status by ECOSOC, on the grounds that it did not adequately carry out the functions of an NGO. Miss Baer protested strongly at the exclusion of the WIDF without a hearing. She objected that the procedure was undemocratic and, if accepted as a precedent, could be applied to other NGOs in the future. She was anxious from the start that the WILPF should fulfil to the utmost the rights and duties of a non-governmental organization. For this to be done she depended on national sections to carry out her recommendations for action and to report back the results of their work. To facilitate this two-way link she started a bi-monthly circular letter in July 1947 and she recommended that every section should appoint a UN correspondent. Miss Baer's report to the 1949 Congress on her first three years' work as UN Consultant was a proof of the success of her methods. A model of clarity, and with scrupulous documentation, it must be studied in the original to be fully appreciated. (This and all subsequent reports are bound and obtainable by students from the UN Library at Geneva.)

The WILPF had naturally a deep interest in the UN Appeal for Children (UNAC), which was later merged in the UN International Children's Emergency Fund (UNICEF). The League was represented on the NGOs' Advisory Committee set up in 1949 and urged that UNICEF should be made a permanent agency for children's welfare: this step was taken by ECOSOC in 1950. Following a visit to Palestine by Gertrude Baer in June 1947, the WILPF exerted strong pressure to get UNICEF funds released to buy food and drugs for both Arab and Jewish children without discrimination: nearly 400,000 children of school age were estimated by UN officials to be in need. The political situation in Palestine was also a cause of concern. In October 1947 Emily Balch wrote to Judge Sandstrom, President of the UN Special Committee on Palestine (UNSCOP), suggesting the creation of an 'international constabulary', to be drawn from the nations represented on UNSCOP and to include women volunteers. No response was made to this suggestion, and the situation continued to deteriorate. (It took a big-power crisis, nearly ten years later, to conjure up a UN Emergency Force in 48 hours.) Other political activities during this period were concerned with East-West Relations, Franco Spain, Kashmir, Indonesia, Indians in South Africa, Former Italian Colonies and Trusteeship of the Polar Regions.

In addition, Gertrude Baer prepared a series of special study papers, including an analysis of actual co-operation and joint action between East and West; the role of ECOSOC as an instrument of international co-operation; and the advancement of indigenous populations under the Trusteeship system. A paper on matters covered by the UN Department of Social Affairs, the first such list to be compiled, was intended to encourage non-governmental organizations to make a division of their work according to their special interests and experience. Two subjects of particular interest to the WILPF were Human Rights and Status of Women. They are linked to the extent that Miss Baer herself had not favoured the setting up of a separate Status of Women Commission by the UN, believing that all questions of human rights—including discrimination on grounds of sex—should come under a general Human Rights Commission. But since both Commissions did exist, she worked diligently through both to further the principles and viewpoint of the WILPF.

In February 1948, she prepared a study paper for WILPF members on Women in the United Nations. No such survey had previously been made, and it showed that there had been no woman President of the General Assembly and there were no women among the members of the Security Council, Economic and Social Council and Trusteeship Council, i.e. 'not one woman on the highest level of the policy-shaping organs of the United Nations'. Gertrude Baer's survey, which was praised by many women's organizations and UN officials, was brought to the notice of the Status of Women Commission at its third session in Beirut in March 1949 by the US representative, Judge Dorothy Kenyon. A resolution adopted by the Commission requested the Secretary-General to prepare a report for its next session on the number of posts occupied by women in the Secretariat and the extent to which governments had included women in their UN delegations. According to Article 8 of the UN Charter, it was pointed out, 'the United Nations shall place no restrictions on the eligibility of men and women to participate in any capacity and under conditions of equality in its principal and subsidiary organs'.

Reports on the grades filled by women in the secretariat and delegations were subsequently issued, but they did not tell an encouraging story. In 1953 Gertrude Baer reported 'regress rather than progress' in the elimination of discrimination. The Secretary-General's report of January 1952 showed that in the highest grades of the UN service there were 1,148 men and 347 women. In none of the UN departments or agencies was there a woman Secretary-General, Assistant Secretary-

General, Principal Director or Deputy Director; there was one woman Director. As long as the UN Secretariat was itself violating the Charter in this respect, said Gertrude Baer, how could it effectively denounce violations from outside? But she conceded that the ultimate responsibility lay not with the UN but with national governments which failed to recruit and train sufficient numbers of women for their own foreign services; and with the women themselves, who were often too diffident to come forward.

The need for an International Declaration of Human Rights had been formulated by the WILPF as far back as 1939, but progress in the UN Human Rights Commission on drafting a Covenant was painfully slow. Although the Universal Declaration of Human Rights was unanimously adopted on December 10, 1948, by 1951 ECOSOC had been unable to enforce any of its articles. Miss Baer suggested that it was unwise to try and do so at a time of such political confusion, and still more unwise, as some delegates were proposing, to split the draft Covenant into two separate parts dealing respectively with (*a*) political and civil rights and (*b*) economic, social and cultural rights. The General Assembly in 1951 confirmed this view, but in 1952 ECOSOC decided to continue working on the basis of two draft Covenants.

For many years before a Human Rights Commission had ever been thought of, certain fundamental rights had been a special concern of the WILPF. The elimination of discrimination on grounds of race, sex or creed was built into its constitution as a prerequisite for social or political advancement. It had fought for the right of minorities to obtain a fair hearing under the League of Nations system of petitions, and was to continue to do so at the UN. In particular, the need for machinery to deal with petitions from individuals and groups was continuously pressed from 1949, and the WILPF closely co-operated with Rev. Michael Scott in his persistent campaign to obtain a hearing at the Trusteeship Council for the Herero people of South-West Africa. The League also urged in 1951 that the status of South-West Africa should be submitted to the decision, and not merely the advisory opinion, of the International Court of Justice. (The case of S.W. Africa was referred to the ICJ for judgment in 1961.)

In 1951 ECOSOC proposed on financial grounds to discontinue the Sub-Commission on the Prevention of Discrimination and Protection of Minorities and transfer its work to the Human Rights Commission, a decision which was strongly contested by the WILPF and other NGOs. Partly as a result of their pressure, the General Assembly in

February 1952 voted in favour of continuing the Sub-Commission's work. During 1948 the WILPF Consultant and national sections made strenuous efforts to secure adoption of the draft Convention on the Crime of Genocide, urging that the matter should be brought before the General Assembly that year. This was done and the Convention was adopted by the Assembly on December 9, 1948. The following year WILPF sections followed up the campaign by pressing their governments to ratify the Convention and so bring it into force: 14 states out of the required 20 had ratified it by 1953.

Another long-standing concern of the WILPF was the problem of Statelessness, on which it had organized an international conference in 1930. A second world war and wholesale displacements of populations brought fresh waves of refugees with little hope of re-settlement. The only effective solution, the WILPF maintained, was the complete elimination of statelessness by absorption and emigration, but until this could be achieved it called for a legal status and permanent protection for stateless persons. The decision of the International Refugee Organization to terminate its activities by June 30, 1950, caused Gertrude Baer to write to the President and members of ECOSOC in July 1949 requesting the Economic and Social Council to recommend the appointment of a UN High Commissioner whose office would become responsible for the large number of stateless refugees still existing. The High Commissioner's Office was established in January 1951. In July 1951 the WILPF and other NGOs participated in a plenipotentiary conference at Geneva at which the Convention on the Status of Refugees was drafted—the first time in the history of the United Nations, Miss Baer commented, 'or perhaps even in political history', that non-governmental organizations had assisted in the drafting of a convention and attended its signature by government representatives.

A Brazilian proposal in February 1948 for a United Nations Training Centre in international co-operation and administration was of special interest to Gertrude Baer, who had outlined her own plans for such a centre in 1943. She criticized the Brazilian draft for its lack of emphasis on the need for 'world-mindedness': without this consciousness, she said, even the best international administration would fail. In her 1949 Report she instanced positive achievements of the UN in ending or limiting conflicts without the use of force in Palestine, India, Indonesia and Berlin. The fact that crises leading to conflicts could be checked in time through methods of mediation, conciliation and arbitration she described as the crux of peacemaking. These were not sensational or dramatic methods:

For the active element that makes them effective is the patient give and take, the persistent finding, drafting and redrafting of formulas which, fully considering the sensibilities of prestige and national pride, are acceptable to all concerned.

This was the sort of work the WILPF had been persisting in since its founding members sat down at The Hague together in 1915. The proposals from that first Congress were cited by the Secretary of the NGOs Committee of ECOSOC, Mr Lyman White, as an example of the influence of private international organizations on governmental policy (in this case, the drafting of President Wilson's Fourteen Points for Peace) in an address to the American Academy of Political Science in April 1949.

One of the decisions of the Copenhagen Congress in 1949 was to revive the League's journal *Pax International*, which had last appeared in February 1940. Since Gertrude Baer's appointment as UN Consultant, the International Circular Letters had been compiled in London by two British members, Emily Horscroft and Alice Hyde. The production of *Pax International* was now transferred back to Geneva, being edited successively by Anne Bloch and Betty McCorkel, two able Americans who temporarily filled the position of International Secretary between 1948 and 1950. But obviously there was need for a more permanent and authoritative direction of the international headquarters. In June 1950 Gertrude Baer returned to Geneva, where the UN Economic and Social Council had established its permanent seat in the Palais des Nations, and at the request of the Executive Committee agreed to reorganize the international office and edit the journal, which she re-titled *Pax et Libertas*. The following year she assumed responsibility as Director of the International Headquarters of the WILPF; an arrangement which caused difficulties for the faithful Louisa Jaques who had remained continuously at her post in the Maison, often in sole charge, for more than thirty years. In February 1953 Mlle Jaques offered her resignation, to the very great regret of the many members in all sections who knew and appreciated her devoted service to the League.

In 1952 the Executive Committee made certain administrative changes, replacing the three International Co-Chairmen by one Chairman, Marie Lous-Mohr of Norway, and two Vice-Chairmen: Gertrude Bussey (USA) and Agnes Stapledon (Britain). Dr Bussey was also asked to act as observer for the WILPF at the UN General Assembly in New York, a pivotal role for which her personal qualities, academic distinction and long experience both as President of the US section and International Co-Chairman, admirably fitted her. Only the onset of chronic ill-health caused her to delegate some of this work to a fellow-American, Gladys Walser, who subsequently took over the UN assignment with outstanding success. Gertrude Baer was asked to take charge of the political work of the WILPF in Geneva, a task for which she was uniquely qualified, and to relinquish the office administration, which for the time being was undertaken on a voluntary basis by Agnes Stapledon.

By August 1953, when the Twelfth International Congress of the WILPF took place in Paris, new trends were emerging from the traditional pattern of work. These were conditioned by the technical and political developments which were taking place throughout the whole world on an unprecedented scale and at an unprecedented speed. The mass protests, manifestoes and petitions of the 1930s were no longer adequate, although they were still being used by some organizations. The need now was not so much to protest when an international crime had been committed, as to anticipate the crisis and offer an alternative, practicable policy. It was inevitable, therefore, that the International Congresses of the WILPF should decline in importance as the focus and stimulus of its work, and a greater value be given to the role of the Executive Committee with its constant attention to policy; the UN Consultants with their constant attendance at history-making Commissions and Assemblies; and the national sections as never-sleeping watchdogs of governmental policies which might make or break the world.

Two world-shocks contributed to this development: the Korean War which demonstrated that violence could still be used as an instrument of policy (whether or not in the name of police action); and the Hydrogen Bomb which demonstrated that it must never be used again.

CHAPTER 18

THE NUCLEAR WATERSHED

Korean War 1950—Disarmament Proposals—Paris
Congress 1953—Non-Violent Resistance—International
Education—Birmingham Congress 1956—Emily Balch
and China

———————

The special lesson of the Korean War for the Women's International League for Peace and Freedom was that the seat of China in the United Nations must be occupied by the Peking Government and not by the Nationalist rump on the island of Formosa which, propped up by the United States, still maintained the sham of 'big power' status as a member of the Security Council. This anomalous situation at the very heart of the UN was not only a gross injustice but a continual block to effective action in both the 'peace-keeping' and 'peace-making' functions of the international organization. The seating of the People's Republic of China was advocated by the WILPF in a letter to the President of the UN Assembly in December 1950 and reiterated at every subsequent Assembly.

The Executive Committee meeting in Liverpool on July 25, 1950, just one month after North Korean troops crossed the 38th parallel and touched off the first large-scale shooting war since 1939, had already called for this step and for an immediate cease-fire under the supervision of the UN Temporary Commission for Korea. It also urged the setting up of a Mediation Commission to secure a general settlement and the holding of free elections throughout Korea. Two resolutions on the situation were taken personally to embassies in London by the International Chairman and Vice-Chairman (Marie Lous-Mohr and Gertrude Bussey) and Lady Parmoor, President of the British section. Friendly talks were held at the Foreign Office and with American, French, Indian and Norwegian officials. At this stage, constructive action was still a practical possibility even though it was a deplorable feature of the Korean War that the United Nations was stampeded into military action by the USA without any prior attempt to make use of the existing machinery for mediation.

The WILPF, including the American section, firmly and unitedly opposed the war from the start. Far from being a 'holding action' by an international police force, it represented a flagrant extension of the East-West conflict to a new, and hotter, theatre of war. After the drive north of South Korean forces beyond the 38th parallel in October 1950—protected by a UN umbrella held firmly in the hands of the American General MacArthur—the last figment of 'police action' disappeared, as did any hope for a quick or easy peace. By November Chinese troops were in action in the North and a world clash—possibly involving atomic weapons—seemed imminent. Not only the WILPF was alarmed. The Asian members of the United Nations, under Indian leadership, were working feverishly for a truce. On December 3rd the British Prime Minister, Clement Attlee, flew to Washington to restrain President Truman and his military hotheads from dropping the atomic bomb on China. Letters were sent to both leaders by the WILPF urging an immediate conference of the Great Powers within a UN framework, in line with an Iraqi-Syrian resolution. Such efforts to find a solution, it was pointed out, 'are marks of statesmanship of the highest order and should not be stigmatized as appeasement'.

But by January 1951 the Chinese had swept into South Korea, and with the branding of China as an 'aggressor' by the UN General Assembly, under strong American pressure, peace seemed further away than ever. However, the pressure of world opinion did force the recall of General MacArthur by Truman in April, thus averting the worst dangers of an atomic holocaust. This was small comfort to the anguished Koreans, ground between rival armies and already familiar with the horrors of the American napalm bomb; or to the American families who were to mourn 25,000 dead, and to assuage their grief in a burning hatred of the People's Republic of China.

This ill-wind, however, did temporarily diminish American hostility towards the Soviet Union. Combined US-USSR pressure brought an opening of peace negotiations at Panmunjam on July 8th. The talks were to drag on, with breakdowns and intermittent fighting, for exactly two years, with intransigence on both sides. America's dubious ally in South Korea, Syngman Rhee, was recalcitrant on acceptance of a truce-line and free elections. The Chinese remained adamant on the forcible repatriation of prisoners of war. Throughout this period WILPF efforts to secure an armistice continued unceasingly through its UN Consultants in New York and Geneva, its international officers and its national sections. In New York Gertrude Bussey and Gladys Walser co-operated closely with the Quaker team of observers at the

UN, amongst whom was the British member Agatha Harrison; with the Indian delegation led by another WILPF member, Mrs V. J. Pandit; and with the Indian Government's special representative, Krishna Menon. The international mediation work which occupied Agatha Harrison during the last years of her life, following the granting of Indian independence in August 1947, was described by Mr Gerald Bailey of the Friends Peace Committee in the memorial booklet already referred to (page 110):

She was constantly seeking to bring people together. The Viceroy or the Secretary of State must see Mr Gandhi; Mr Malik should see Mr Eden; or Mr Dulles, Mr Chou En-lai. The North Korean and Chinese Communists must come to New York in person and be seen and heard. How else could we really sense and know what their purpose was or they ours? And incidentally when the Chinese Communists did come to New York in 1950 it was Agatha almost alone who penetrated the security guards at the Waldorf Astoria and met them face to face. It was all too simple, of course, for the wisdom of this world. But how right she was! Or if she was wrong, how deadly is our diplomacy and how grim the outlook for our times!

Agatha Harrison died 'in harness' at the Geneva Conference on Indo-China in April 1954.

In February 1953 Gertrude Baer addressed an urgent appeal to the President of the UN General Assembly to throw his whole weight into stopping the war in Korea. The first step, the WILPF reiterated, *must* be a cease-fire, followed by withdrawal of foreign troops; seating of the People's Republic of China; and a meeting of its representatives with Britain, France, India, USA and USSR. It was not until nearly six months later, on July 27th, that the Armistice Agreement was signed. The total casualties of both sides were estimated in an Associated Press survey at over two million; Korea, on whose behalf the war had ostensibly been fought, was in ruins. Visiting South Korea early in 1953 on behalf of the World Council of Churches, Dr Elfan Rees found 10 million refugees out of a total population of 21 million; 125,000 orphaned or abandoned children; 15,000 vagrant adolescents, running wild as shoe-shine boys and near-prostitutes; 294,000 widows with 517,000 children and no means of support. Social welfare, never more than rudimentary, had completely broken down. It was left to the United Nations to clean up the mess its own armies had helped to create, through the Korean Reconstruction Agency.

The WILPF International Congress, meeting in Paris in August 1953, was able to rejoice that the fighting had stopped; but had also to point out that no lasting peace could be established 'until the Peking Government is accorded its rightful place in the Security Council, the General Assembly and all other organs of the United Nations'.

The other great concern of the WILPF at this period was of course Disarmament—made ever more urgent with the development of nuclear weapons by both the USA and USSR in 1953. A proposal for a 'World Truce' had been put forward by the WILPF to the UN Secretary-General in February 1950 and an appeal for a two-year armaments truce was repeated in December 1951. During the period of the truce, states would pledge themselves to cease the use and production of all armaments and preparations would be made for a Disarmament Conference with the goal of 'simultaneous, total and universal disarmament'. As a first step, an international police force under UN control was proposed to replace national armies.

There was little or no chance of any such plan finding acceptance by any of the principal powers, although Gladys Walser continued to canvass it amongst delegates after the opening of the UN Disarmament Commission in March 1952. The initiative in making disarmament proposals at this time was certainly with the Soviet Union; but without the safeguards of inspection and control demanded by the West they were equally certain to be rejected. The WILPF consistently maintained that all disarmament proposals, from whatever source, should be considered on their merits and not dismissed out of hand. But as in the inter-war period, 'security' was still conceived solely in terms of military power and bi-lateral defence pacts were regarded as a safer insurance policy than reliance on an international organization. Two examples of this pre-war thinking carried over into the nuclear age were the US-Japanese Peace Treaty and Mutual Security Pact of September 1951 and the European Defence Community proposed in May 1952.

Japanese women, including WILPF members, were leading the campaign to safeguard the 'war-renouncing' clause of the post-war Constitution and to prevent any rearmament of their country. In February 1951, and again on the eve of the San Francisco Peace Conference, appeals were sent to the US Secretary of State, Mr Dulles, not to permit Japanese rearmament and to base world peace on the United Nations, 'our symbol of the conscience of the world'. A further appeal was sent from the Japanese Women's Disarmament Committee to every US Senator in January 1952. Amongst the signatories was Tano Jodai, President of the Japan Women's University and President of the revived Japanese section of the WILPF.

The question of German rearmament was of vital concern to all the national sections with memories going back as far as 1919. As in the 1920s, some of the strongest opposition to rearmament came from inside Germany itself. It was almost incredible that for a second time the chance to build a neutralized, disarmed Germany should be wilfully flung aside by the victorious Allies!—thus making a mockery of their own declared determination to show the German people that 'militarism' did not pay. The International Congress in 1953 called on national sections to work in their own countries against ratification of the Bonn and Paris Agreements, whereby West Germany would be integrated into the Western defence alliance. But the following October the Agreements were signed—and the German Federal Republic became a member of NATO with a permitted national army of twelve divisions (under NATO command). Only after the admission of Germany to NATO did the Eastern-bloc countries set up their own counter-defence organization under the Warsaw Pact, thus postponing any hope of a demilitarized disengaged Europe into an indefinite, and questionable, future.

Throughout its history, the WILPF had stressed the natural link between disarmament and economic development. The Executive Committee meeting after the Congress in August 1953 called for a UN Conference to take steps towards total disarmament, using the resources released from arms production to attack the problems of hunger, disease and illiteracy which were among the prime causes of war. One of the most promising initiatives reported by the United States section to the Congress was the setting up in New York in 1950 of a Committee on World Disarmament and World Development. Fifty-five organizations sent delegates to a two-day Workshop on Disarmament which the Committee organized in Washington, and after the first two and a half years' work the change in public attitudes to disarmament was described as 'remarkable'. Other factors, of course, were by this time contributing towards some diminution of tensions, notably the replacement of Truman by Eisenhower in November 1952 and the death of Stalin the following March.

But disarmament was not simply a matter of economic adjustment. Along with planning for the redeployment of resources there must be some consideration of an alternative security system. The League of

Nations had never succeeded in providing this. So far, the United Nations appeared to be doing no better: 'world law' was still a chimera. Was there yet another way? In May 1951 the WILPF President, Emily Greene Balch, submitted to the Executive Committee a memorandum on Governmental Non-Co-operation. This was a plan for non-violent resistance on Gandhian lines, to be *governmentally* organized throughout Europe as a means of deterring aggression without the disadvantages and dangers of rearmament. The scheme, Miss Balch admitted, would be difficult and costly. But 'the sacrifices would be infinitely less costly than those of war and would be morally rejuvenating, as they proved in India'. It seems a pity that this proposal never received a wider hearing, but the WILPF set up its own committee to study non-violent techniques and especially to investigate war-time resistance in Norway and Denmark. Its findings, as reported to the 1953 Congress, were not very encouraging.

Elin Appel of Denmark concluded that, although the majority of the population favoured passive resistance, the liberation of the country was achieved by outside forces and not through the efforts of any of the resistance groups, violent or non-violent. The case of Norway, said Sigrid Larsen, showed that non-violent defence could never succeed where an occupied nation was dependent on the occupier for the means of subsistence; while violent resistance only increased the number of victims without helping either the nation or the course of the war. Both *rapporteurs* agreed that in neither country was there any real understanding of non-violent principles. The need for prior acceptance of these principles before there could be any chance of influencing policies was stressed by Else Zeuthen (Denmark) in her paper on Non-Violence and Current Politics. She enumerated some of them as follows: Recognition that violence breeds violence; upholding truth before prestige; acceptance of the principle of equal rights; freedom of conscience and of information; strengthening of altruistic rather than materialistic values.

All these recommendations were wholly in line with the WILPF's own long-standing work, but it was clear that the advancement of non-violence both as a means of defence and in the promotion of necessary social change would demand a great deal more study and a massive educational campaign. The WILPF Consultant at UNESCO, Mme Andrée Jouve, took every opportunity both in speech and writing to further the ideal of a humane internationalism. Her work in this field had of course started long before UNESCO, as the moving force for over thirty years behind the League's international summer schools. It was almost entirely her own personal achievement that in 1955 a UNESCO grant was awarded for the WILPF summer school at Barsbüttel near Hamburg, enabling students to be present not only from Europe but from Asian, African, Caribbean and North American countries. Grants were subsequently awarded for seminars which took place in Denmark in 1959; Norway in 1961; and again Denmark in 1963.

Education from the grass-roots of childhood had always been seen as a vital factor in WILPF work: the inculcation of an attitude of 'reverence for life' could not begin too early, and obviously must largely be in the hands of women. This aspect of their work was a particular concern of the Scandinavian sections. For schoolchildren, however, an original educational development came from the United States in 1946. Following up an idea put forward at a UNESCO conference, a WILPF group in Delaware, Pennsylvania, started an international exchange of children's drawings. Thanks largely to the dedicated enthusiasm of Mrs Maude Muller, 'Art for World Friendship' grew rapidly into an international movement, cutting across frontiers and ideologies. By 1953 more than 20,000 pictures were being circulated in 32 countries (on both sides of the 'iron curtain') and Art for World Friendship was accepted in the state schools of Denmark, Holland, India, Israel, Italy and Norway; in 1956 40 countries were co-operating in the exchange.

At adult level, 'reverence for life' implied a minimum right to life for every human being—a right which was incompatible with the traditional right of the state to take life, not only in war but by means of capital punishment. Shocked by political death sentences in Czechoslovakia, and by the much-publicized case of the Rosenbergs in the USA, the WILPF International Chairmen in January 1953 addressed an appeal to every government of the world—97 in all—to eliminate capital punishment from their constitutions. The response from governments was negligible, but the appeal received wide publicity and much favourable comment. The WILPF Congress in 1953 called for amendment of the draft Covenant on Civil and Political Rights to include abolition of the death sentence, and in July 1954 Gertrude Baer made a statement on behalf of the League in the NGOs Committee of ECOSOC. She pointed out that, in an epoch of mass destruction by 'the most perfected devices of death', the taking of one man's life would not seem to be a very powerful 'deterrent'. The question was also taken up by Gladys Walser in New York, who in consultation with various delegations tried, unsuccessfully, to get capital punishment included in a series of special studies by the Human Rights Commission in March 1956.

At the Thirteenth International Congress of the WILPF in July 1956 the Norwegian section introduced a resolution, which was adopted, on 'The Sacredness of Human Life'. To take the life of a human being, it maintained, should be declared a crime against humanity—whether by a private individual (murder); by a state against one of its citizens (capital punishment); by a government against citizens of another state (war) or between citizens of the same state (civil war). This seemed a comprehensive statement of principle which covered all categories and degrees of man-slaughter. But one new factor was omitted. To these time-honoured devices for taking life, the governments of the nuclear powers in the 1950s added the novelty of destroying *future* life through the genetic effects of atomic radiation released by the testing of hydrogen bombs.

It was appropriate that the theme of the 1956 Congress should be 'The WILPF in the Atomic Age'; doubly appropriate that it should be held, for the first time, in Britain—just moving into the nuclear class— and that the President of the British section should be the distinguished atomic scientist, Professor Dame Kathleen Lonsdale, FRS. The Congress, housed in the five Selly Oak Colleges outside Birmingham, was a large one, with 250 delegates from 14 countries. It marked a revitalizing of the League after the inevitable depression of the war-time and cold-war years; a revitalizing that was also a reflection of growing public concern about the terrifying potentialities of nuclear power.

This concern—which sprang not only from fear but from a moral revulsion, particularly on the part of the post-war generation—was first made vocal after the testing of the American 'superbomb' at Bikini in the Marshall Islands in March 1954, and the consequent contamination of Japanese fishing boats many miles from the explosions. The WILPF was not alone in its immediate protests and appeals from national sections and international headquarters. It was, perhaps, unique in linking its demand for the abolition of nuclear weapons and weapons-testing to the need for total and universal disarmament, as the only realistic means of 'security' in the nuclear age. Writing in the British news sheet *Peace and Freedom* on 'The Hydrogen Bomb and International Control' in May 1954, Professor Lonsdale stressed that 'partial disarmament' would not solve the problem: 'if future atomic wars are to be avoided, the reduction of armaments must be not a one-third or a two-thirds reduction, but a genuine disarmament down to police levels of an agreed standard'.

Gertrude Baer was working hard to get an investigation of the effects of atomic radiation from weapon tests under the *aegis* of the World Health Organization, which refused to discuss 'political' questions. At the WHO Assembly in Mexico City in May 1955, however, Dr Evang of Norway referred to the problem of radioactive 'fall-out' and urged delegates to speak out concerning both the effects of contamination and the genetic effects. Miss Baer immediately wrote to Dr Evang, recalling the WILPF conference on scientific warfare held in 1929, and received a helpful reply. It was gratifying that one year later WHO adopted a resolution to study 'public health problems related to somatic and genetic action of radiation'.

But meanwhile, nuclear tests continued. Nor were the dangers from atomic radiation confined to—or even mainly due to—nuclear tests. Gertrude Baer was concerned that the use of other sources of power than the atom for industrial purposes should not be neglected, particularly by underdeveloped countries. She first proposed that a study should be made of the utilization of Solar Energy at an NGO Conference of the Food and Agriculture Organization in November 1955 and her suggestion was included in the conference report. The following year the French delegation at ECOSOC brought forward a resolution, which was unanimously adopted, requesting the UN Secretary-General to make a report on new sources of energy other than the atom as a factor in economic development, with a view to convening an international conference. Conferences on Solar Energy had already taken place in India and the USA.

Three members of the WILPF Committee on Scientific Warfare attended the UN Conference on Peaceful Uses of Atomic Energy at Geneva in August 1955: Dr Gertrud Woker, who had been crusading against the misapplication of science for military purposes since 1924; Dr Stähelin of Switzerland and Mlle Pontheil of France. A letter was sent to the President of the conference, Dr J. H. Bhabha, welcoming this beneficial co-operation but urging that all destructive experiments should cease. Reporting on the conference to the Birmingham Congress, Dr Woker stated that although the dangers of radioactivity were thoroughly discussed, a paper by Professor J. J. Muller of Indiana University was excluded because it referred to the genetic effects of the Hiroshima and Nagasaki bombs. She believed the ban was due to fears of the American Atomic Energy Commission that this information would strengthen the 'world-wide agitation' against further nuclear tests; but thanks to the insistence of many of the experts present, the paper was included in the official publications of the conference and was later published in the American *Bulletin of Atomic Scientists*.

The WILPF Congress in a resolution strongly urged the cessation of nuclear tests, finding eight good reasons for doing so and concluding that an agreement to suspend further tests 'would create a new climate of hope and confidence and would prove to be a first step towards a genuine universal and total disarmament'. This was a decidedly optimistic conclusion, although it in no way invalidated the case against nuclear tests. But the question of disarmament was surely in a different category altogether.

In her masterly survey of Disarmament Negotiations since 1946, the WILPF Consultant at the United Nations in New York, Gladys Walser, put her finger on the crux of the problem:

For those who have followed the disarmament discussions in the United Nations for the past ten years, it is revealing and at the same time frustrating to observe the reversals of positions of the two sides. For example, in 1946 and thereafter, Mr Gromyko contended unsuccessfully that atomic and non-atomic disarmament were inseparable. The Western powers after dismissing this claim, accepted it in 1951. Now, in 1956, the same Mr Gromyko insists there are no cogent reasons for linking the two. In 1952 the United States proposed a ceiling on armed forces of one and a half million for the Big Three. This was revived by the British and French in their joint proposal in 1954 and accepted by the USSR in 1955. In 1956 it was rejected by the US which had changed the figure to two and a half million.

The pattern of subsequent negotiations has shown little change. The major powers, in short, did not want disarmament. They wanted 'security'; and security, as this History has illustrated time and again, could not be conceived of apart from military power. It was useless for the WILPF to appeal for 'a new system of security', when the basis for such a system did not exist.

Which way, then, did progress lie? In the statements of its three Commissions—concerned respectively with the scientific consequences of nuclear power; with power politics and the United Nations; and with disarmament and its consequences—the Congress reiterated many of the long-term programmes of the WILPF: More and better education, as Andrée Jouve had indicated in her paper on humanist values. Strengthening of UN agencies for economic development. Acceptance of international law. Continued study of non-violent techniques. The reports from national sections showed also that the WILPF, unlike some organizations, had not been stampeded into dropping all its established activities for the sake of a feverish anti-nuclear campaign. (Some of the younger members might have wished that it did, but this was undoubtedly a shortsighted view. The nuclear disarmament movement soon discovered that it must look beyond the bomb if it was ever to get rid of it.) So at this time the French section was naturally concerned with the independence movements in North Africa; the British, with its Government's policies in Central and Southern Africa, Kenya and Cyprus; the United States, with civil liberties and civil rights for negroes.

In Australia, where the section had been successfully reorganized by Mrs A. L. Abbott after the death of Eleanor Moore in 1949, the WILPF was not only the first organization to protest publicly against nuclear tests at Monte Bello and against the Woomera rocket range, but was pressing for full citizens' rights for the aboriginal peoples. The section's new secretary, Anna Vroland, took a leading part in this work. Austria and Germany, having unsuccessfully opposed the re-creation of national armies in their countries, were upholding the rights of conscientious objectors. The German section appealed to the WILPF Executive Committee, the (East German) Women's Democratic Federation and the World Peace Council to urge that the right of conscientious objection be included in the Universal Declaration of Human Rights. A member of the Swedish section, the well-known journalist Barbro Alving, was gaoled in January 1956 for refusing to undertake civil defence duties. The resulting public outcry led to legislation providing for exemption from these duties on conscientious grounds.

These and other reports seemed to indicate that by 1956 the worst effects of the Cold War were over as far as the WILPF was concerned. The Congress could look more confidently to the future. In Europe, rifts caused by the Communist peace campaigns which had halved the membership in Scandinavia and Switzerland, now began to heal. Britain and America, though likewise shaken to a lesser extent, had a solid basis of constructive activity that resisted extremist pressures.

The new Indian section was welcomed into membership at Birmingham through its representative, Mrs Narayanaswami. (During a two-year stay in Travancore a Swedish member, Signe Højer, had initiated two WILPF branches. Dr Axel Højer was serving as a World Health Organization expert, while Mrs Højer was engaged in the training of nursery school teachers; she also started a branch of the Family Planning Association. On her return in 1954 Signe Højer became President of the Swedish section.) Only in Latin America was progress disappointing, due to reactionary régimes, poverty and violent unrest. Elsewhere, promising new groups were emerging. New Zealand was reviving its national section. Two African countries, Nigeria and the Gold Coast (later Ghana), were eager to form sections. New members were joining in Indonesia. Israel, which was admitted as a new section at the 1953 Congress, now had five active groups, working in conditions of incredible difficulty and tension.

A notable feature of the Birmingham Congress was the presence not only of Mrs Hannah Rosenzweig from Israel but of a visitor from an Arab state. The young Syrian lawyer, Talat Rifai, was quite adamant in rejecting the Jewish claim to a national home in Palestine; but her refusal, or inability, to compromise must have influenced the Congress in deciding that the WILPF, with its tradition of fact-finding and reconciling missions, must itself send a personal emissary to the Middle East. The representative chosen was Dr Madeleine Sylvain Bouchereau of Haiti, wife of the Haitian consul in Hamburg. She was an active member of the WILPF group there, and had lectured at two summer schools.

An honoured visitor at Birmingham was the British founder-member, Catherine Marshall, still—in spite of physical handicaps—taking a keen interest in the League's work. But the ranks of the pioneers were thinning. In 1948 Yella Hertzka had died, followed in 1951 by Thora Daugaard and Benny Cederfeld of Denmark. Britain had lost its former President, Lady Parmoor, Agatha Harrison and Dr Hilda Clark; Norway, its founder Marta Larsen Jahn, wife of the Chairman of the Nobel Committee. The French section in 1955 mourned that outstanding personality, Gabrielle Duchêne, loved even by those who most strongly differed from her.

The resignation of Marie Lous-Mohr as International Chairman, after ten most difficult years in office, was regretfully received now. She was replaced by Else Zeuthen, formerly Chairman of the Danish section and a Member of Parliament since 1953. Andrée Jouve and

Emily Parker Simon (USA) were elected International Vice-Chairmen. The editorship of *Pax et Libertas* passed from Gertrude Baer to Mrs Phoebe Cusden, one of the most active of the post-war British members, a magistrate and one-time mayor of Reading. It was also decided at Birmingham to revert to the pre-war practice of appointing a full-time administrative secretary at Geneva to ensure the efficient functioning of the international headquarters: this post was now taken up by Elizabeth Tapper, an Englishwoman with many years' experience in Geneva.

One other feature of the Birmingham Congress must not be over-looked: a happening which arose directly out of the WILPF tradition of bringing to intractable problems a human and personal warmth. Early in 1955 the International President, Emily Greene Balch, troubled by the great wall of isolation and hostility surrounding the People's Republic of China, wrote a poem To the People of China. This was translated into Chinese and published in September 1955 in the national newspaper *Ta Kung Pao*. Appealing for patience and understanding, and a surmounting of ideological barriers, Emily Balch wrote:

> Men and women with your patient faces,
> Little children with your bright eyes,
> How could I not love you?

So moved were some of the Chinese women reading this message that Miss Balch received a personal invitation to visit China from Madame Li Teh-Chuan, Minister of Health of the People's Republic and Chairman of the Chinese Red Cross. Now nearly 90 years of age, she had regretfully to decline the invitation. But the link with the WILPF, already established during a visit to China by the Danish Chairman, Else Zeuthen, in 1952, was further consolidated. Amongst subsequent visitors were two from Britain, Professor Kathleen Lonsdale and Mrs Phoebe Cusden. And now, here in Birmingham, was Mme Li herself, having flown to England to attend the WILPF Congress! In her one brief speech to the delegates she said that the work of the League was by no means unknown to the women of China, who eagerly followed its efforts for peace. For the remainder of the Congress, Mme Li with her interpreter sat quietly through all the sessions, following with close attention the speeches and discussion. Her reciprocal invitation to the retiring Chairman led to a six-weeks' tour of China by Marie Lous-Mohr in 1958.

As so often before, it seemed here that the give and take of a personal interchange was a more effective method of peace-making than the formal approaches to governments and the formulation of statements and resolutions; although each method was bound to reinforce the other. But at this nuclear watershed of history, an almost instinctive movement towards world co-operation was so far ahead of official thinking that the old-world postures of governments in their straitjackets of 'national interest' seemed scarcely relevant to the real issues at stake. Before the end of 1956, however, two new international crises were once again to threaten the precarious peace.

CHAPTER 19

CONVULSIONS OF A DYING AGE

Suez and Hungary 1956—Middle East Mission 1958—
Nuclear Tests and International Law—Stockholm Con-
gress 1959—WILPF and UNESCO—Congo Crisis
1960—Berlin Wall 1961—Cuba Crisis 1962

The violent explosions in the Middle East and Hungary in October 1956 were scarcely happy auguries for the nuclear age. But they represented the death-rattle of an old order rather than the birth-pangs of a new. The Anglo-French intervention in Egypt could not avert the decline of Britain's influence in the Middle East or France's in North Africa, and had the positive outcome of permitting a genuine United Nations police force to demonstrate its usefulness. The ruthless Soviet suppression of the Hungarian revolution did not, in the long run, turn back the tide of liberalization in the East European satellites. Stalin was still dead; and Mr Khrushchev, for one, showed no inclination to disinter him. Above all, the Suez-Hungary crises marked an advance from power politics towards a supra-national loyalty. In the United Nations, the USA led the opposition to her premier ally, Britain; while Poland withheld support from the USSR by abstaining on the Three-Power resolution (India-Ceylon-Indonesia) calling for the admission of UN observers into Hungary.

In both crises, the WILPF acted promptly through its International Chairman, UN observers and national sections. Already on October 31st, as the Anglo-French attack on Egypt was launched, the International Chairman wrote to the Secretary-General in support of the US cease-fire resolution in the Security Council; a further letter on November 2nd urged the withdrawal of foreign troops as a preliminary to negotiations. In line with WILPF tradition, the British and French sections were amongst the first to condemn their governments' actions in the strongest terms. The British section cited this protest to its own Government in pressing on the Soviet Embassy in London the withdrawal of Russian troops from Hungary. The smaller countries of Europe were naturally the most deeply shocked and alarmed by the Soviet intervention. In Sweden, the WILPF joined with 60 women's organizations and representatives of political parties in a resolution to the President of the UN Assembly. The Danish section, in a sharply-worded statement, deplored Russia's bad faith in flouting thus the principles of peaceful co-existence.

In a circular letter to the Executive Committee and national sections the International Chairman, Else Zeuthen, explained why the WILPF did not issue any official condemnation of the Soviet Union. She pointed out, as the Western powers themselves were aware, that no military help could be given without risking a major war and that any increase of tension in Europe at that point could only worsen the plight of the Hungarians themselves. She saw the only chance of greater political freedom for Eastern Europe in mutual concessions from both sides, and for this to happen a climate of *détente* must be preserved. On October 28th she had cabled to Gladys Walser at the United Nations the bones of the WILPF position: an immediate armistice; a UN investigating commission; consideration of an 'Austrian' status for Hungary; and a general amnesty. Reporting on the atmosphere of the Eleventh Assembly as the Hungarian question was debated, Gladys Walser wrote that never, even in the worst days of the Cold War, had emotions run so high. She regretted the vociferous denunciation of Russia by 'rightist dictatorships', such as Cuba and Spain, which made all the more impossible any attempt to find a solution in the interests of the Hungarian people. Backed by communications from WILPF sections in Australia, Britain, Canada, Denmark, France, Norway and USA, she interviewed delegates and put forward the League's viewpoint. She also made friendly contacts with the former Hungarian member Anna Kethly, Minister of State in the Nagy Government, who had travelled to New York to put her country's case; but by the time she arrived at the Assembly Imre Nagy had been deposed and the Kadar régime installed. Anna Kethly appealed for moral, political and economic pressure on the Soviet Union; she did not seek military intervention, 'because it would lead to a world war'.

The United Nations was impotent to act in Hungary not because it lacked military forces but because it lacked an overwhelming pressure of public opinion in favour of non-military intervention. There was no public outcry inside the Soviet Union, as there had been in the Western democracies against the Suez adventure; nor, regrettably, was there the same enthusiasm among the Afro-Asian members to condemn the Soviet brand of imperialism. But in the Middle East, the UN 'presence' seemed to be achieving its object. The WILPF had now to consider its attitude to the UN Emergency Force (UNEF). It had hitherto opposed the establishment of an international armed force, whether by the League of Nations or the United Nations. It had also to remember what had happened, under a UN flag, in Korea. Gladys Walser believed that the UN had learnt its lesson. 'No longer will the UN allow itself to be used', she wrote on November 10, 1956, 'to bless the military operations of its members.' UNEF had grown out of the Truce Supervision observer corps, and recruitment from the great powers was excluded. The Secretary-General had said that although UNEF was 'para-military' in nature, it was 'not a force with military objectives'. The WILPF was disposed to trust the integrity and essential non-violence of Dag Hammarskjöld and the Executive Committee in 1957 accepted the desirability of an international police force, provided that:

its police purpose and power is ensured, as in the present Emergency Force, by the moral weight of world opinion and not by the possession of any kind of offensive military weapon.

The Suez crisis had delayed the WILPF's own projected mission to the Middle East, but this was not forgotten. Owing much to the personal initiative of one of the International Vice-Chairmen, Emily Parker Simon, the mission eventually took place in the spring of 1958. Between April and June, Dr Bouchereau travelled in Egypt, Lebanon, Syria, Iraq, Iran, Jordan and Israel. In all the Arab countries, with the exception of Jordan, she found amongst the leading women a degree of willingness to co-operate with the WILPF in seeking a non-violent settlement with Israel; and even in Jordan, there was some eagerness to know the views of the Israeli section on a compromise agreement. In Israel itself, Dr Bouchereau's mission was facilitated by the active WILPF section, with help from the Foreign Ministry. One of her objects was to investigate the condition of the Arab minority, on which she reported that although the official policy was to offer economic justice to Arab citizens, in practice some inequalities of treatment did exist. But her main purpose was to place before the WILPF section the four conditions for a settlement laid down to her by the Arab women. The chief points from the Israeli reply were as follows:

1. Internationalization of Jerusalem: Jordan refused to sign the 1952 agreement; Israel was willing.

2. Implementation of UN Partition Plan: The plan was nullified by Arab invasion of territory allotted to the Jews and refusal to set up a separate Arab state, as envisaged by the UN.

3. Full compensation for abandoned property: Israel was willing to pay full compensation if the Arabs would drop their total economic boycott.

4. Resettlement in Israel of all Arab refugees so desiring: Israel had offered to pay for settlement of Palestinian refugees in Arab countries and to accept any groups remaining. The WILPF section would ask for resettlement of Arab refugees willing to live as Israeli citizens and selected under UN supervision. The section made a counter-proposal to the Arab women: would they persuade their governments to hand over to a quarter of a million Arab refugees the abandoned property of a quarter of million Jewish refugees from Yemen and Iraq who had been absorbed into Israel?

Further proposals to the Arab women for easing tension were: Stop hate propaganda against Israel; lift the economic boycott; join with Israel in membership of a Middle East Confederation to co-operate in raising the living standards of all.

Dr Bouchereau herself enumerated eleven factors bearing on the whole Middle East situation:

1. Misery of the Arab masses.
2. Impact of the Moslem religion.
3. Gathering ferment against feudal régimes.
4. Distrust of the West because of past colonialism.
5. Hatred of Israel due to Arab refugees and fear of expansion.
6. Middle East oil.
7. Recognition of Russian interests.
8. Arab nationalism.
9. Aggressive Egyptian leadership under Nasser.
10. Right of self-determination.
11. Desire for neutralization and disarmament.

The Israeli section urged the WILPF internationally to encourage the formation of Arab groups. A section had existed in Egypt before the Second World War and during Dr Bouchereau's visit the nucleus of a new group was formed. In 1958 the Israeli section itself started a mixed Jewish-Arab group of students and graduates of the Hebrew

University in Jerusalem, and in 1959 the first Arab group of the section was formed in Nazareth. The importance of including Arab sections in the WILPF was not overlooked by the international officers; progress was necessarily slow and tentative, but it did continue to be made.

Following the crisis in Jordan and Lebanon in July 1958 (when big power intervention was again circumvented by a UN presence), the WILPF stressed the necessity for a 'total solution' to the whole Middle Eastern situation. The Executive Committee meeting in August recommended large-scale international assistance for development; international guarantees of neutrality for countries desiring it; and recognition of the right of Middle East countries to form a federation.

But there was little hope of any such solution to Middle East problems so long as the East-West arms race continued. This moved into a new dimension with the launching of the first Russian *sputnik* in October 1957 and American counter-moves to establish missile bases in Europe. The WILPF made urgent representations to NATO in December 1957 and May 1958 not to proceed with these plans, and particularly not to station atomic weapons in West Germany. On the initiative of the Israeli section, an international Appeal to the Nuclear Powers was issued that spring, signed by well-known women in all countries with national sections, and submitted to the Foreign Ministers of the USA, USSR and UK. Favourable acknowledgment was received from all three.

Another concerted activity by the WILPF during 1958 took place in connection with the Conference on Law of the Sea which opened in London on February 24th. Gertrude Baer had already made efforts through the International Law Commission to have inserted in the draft Convention on Freedom of the High Seas a clause prohibiting nuclear tests as a violation of this freedom. The international jurists did not go as far as this, but they added a commentary to Article 27 that 'States are bound to refrain from any acts which might adversely affect the use of the high seas by nationals of other States'. In addition, Article 48 on Pollution of the High Seas requested states to co-operate in preventing pollution by the dumping of radio-active waste or 'resulting from experiments or activities with radio-active materials or other harmful agents'. To reinforce these draft articles, the WILPF International Chairman sent a letter to all governments represented at the Conference asking for a definite provision in Article 27 to prohibit nuclear tests; in addition, a statement of WILPF policy and proposals was circulated by the Conference secretariat to all the 850 delegates.

National sections in twelve countries backed up this activity by approaches to their own governments. The ILC Commentary to Article 27 was not adopted by the Conference and the proposals on pollution under Article 48 were lost by one vote. However, this latter decision was subsequently reversed and the new Convention on the High Seas bound states to take measures against pollution from dumping and from 'any activities with radio-active materials', although nuclear weapons experiments as such were not specified.

On October 31, 1958, the three-power Conference on Cessation of Nuclear Weapon Tests opened in Geneva; and on November 10th, the second Conference on Measures against Surprise Attacks, comprising five western and five eastern bloc countries. During the course of November, Gertrude Baer obtained interviews with the leaders of all delegations at both conferences and presented to each of them a letter signed by Emily Balch, Else Zeuthen and herself. This reiterated the WILPF conviction 'that war has become obsolete as a lawful instrument in international relations and that the use of brute force must no longer be regarded as a proper means for settling international conflicts . . . and that total and universal disarmament is the only effective means of setting the world free from war'. The Conference on Surprise Attacks adjourned after thirty sessions without tangible result; the Nuclear Tests Conference sat until August 1959, when it adjourned until October having achieved the unanimous adoption of 17 articles towards a Treaty.

The WILPF insistence on the need for 'total and universal disarmament' was not voiced as a magic formula that could somehow wish away the obstacles to an agreement. The means to its achievement demanded a persistent effort and analysis, a selection and careful tending of 'growing points' that would not wither in the bud. The League's Fourteenth International Congress, meeting at Stockholm in July 1959, took as its theme 'Alternatives to Violence'. It was realized that new and better policies *must* be formulated before real progress could come.

The 250 delegates from 16 countries gathered in the Parliament House and were welcomed by the Swedish Minister for United Nations Affairs, Mrs Ulla Lindstrom, herself a WILPF member for 25 years. Many visitors, observers and fraternal delegates were present, amongst them a representative from the League of Polish Women and the East German Frauenrat; and, from the Soviet Women's Committee, Maria Ovajanikova, editor of *Soviet Woman*. An honoured guest speaker was Professor Linus Pauling, a good friend of the US section in which his wife was an active member. Three revived national sections were readmitted to the League, with great rejoicing: Italy, Netherlands and New Zealand. The much-loved Andrée Jouve resigned as an International Vice-Chairman at this Congress, and was replaced by Mrs Agnes Stapledon of Britain. Since the last Congress, death had taken a heavy toll of the League's oldest members: Louie Bennett in 1956; Clara Ragaz, Cor Ramondt-Hirschmann and Naima Sahlbom in 1957; Barbara Duncan Harris, Magda Hoppstock-Huth and Irma Szirmai in 1959. But younger women were coming forward to revivify the movement. Three new members were elected to the Executive Committee in 1959: Mrs Ellen Holmgaard (Denmark), Professor Flemmie Kittrell (USA) and Dr Sushila Nayar, MP (India).

As at Birmingham in 1956, the Congress divided into three Commissions for detailed discussions on policy, concerned respectively with Human Rights; Political Settlements; and World Disarmament and World Development. In her background paper for the Political Commission, Dr Dorothy Hutchinson (USA) expressed the broad aim of the Congress:

WILPF sets its sights far higher than the mere prevention of World War III. Our concern is for positive human wellbeing and for a peace which is not simply the absence of war but the presence of justice, freedom and a richer life for all men. We envisage political settlements, not only as relieving the present intolerable tensions and dangers but as setting free the material resources of the world and the minds of men to serve the physical and spiritual needs of mankind.

To this end, the Political Commission made certain specific recommendations:

Seating the Peking Government of China at the UN—'perhaps the most important first step in the direction of world peace'. Reform of the voting system in the UN.

Extension of international law from nations to individuals; prior consent to judgments of the International Court of Justice, without reservations.

Pilot projects for UN administration of uncontrolled areas, e.g. Antarctica, Outer Space.

Settlement of the German question by East and West Germany themselves, rather than by the big powers.

Recognition of Israel by the Arab states.

Study of non-violent resistance as the only effective means of national defence.

The Human Rights Commission, under the guidance of Andrée Jouve, made the point that Human Rights are not 'self-perpetuating' but must constantly be renewed, and the importance of *dissent* was emphasized:

Blind conformity, of which the world has seen far too much in recent years, is destructive of initiative and creativity. The tyranny of the majority must not be permitted to stifle new ideas, even when these raise fundamental questions as to the established order. If change does not come by peaceful means through the interchange of ideas in the market place of world public opinion, it will eventually come by violence, to which we in the Women's International League for Peace and Freedom are unalterably opposed.

The Disarmament Commission based its findings on a paper by Gladys Walser, bearing in mind her warning:

that the chief source of peril posed by the arms race lies not in the weapons but in the human beings behind them and that therefore the danger can only be resolved by changes in human attitudes.

Amongst the recommendations of the Commission were:

Replacement of conscription by international voluntary service.

Establishment of an International Institute for research into the deeper causes of international tension and war.

Discontinuance of military research.

Transfer of funds from military spending to development.

Encouragement of family planning centres.

A comprehensive Policy Statement, incorporating the main findings of all three Commissions, was issued from the Congress. Its conclusion had a wider perspective:

In formulating these policies we have tried to take a world point of view, without regard to the national interests of the countries from which our 16 delegations come. That we have been able to agree upon specific alternatives to the use of violence to solve the world's problems affords hope that representatives of nations could likewise reach such agreement, if solutions were sought in the spirit of goodwill which has characterized this Congress.

In United Nations matters, the WILPF Consultants were able to report some encouraging developments. Mrs Adelaide Baker, who replaced Gladys Walser as the League's representative in New York in 1957, referred to some positive gains since her appointment. The long-promised Disarmament Commission had been set up—although it had not so far met. An Atomic Energy Agency and a Committee on Peaceful Uses of Outer Space—both called for by the WILPF—were in operation. In May 1959, the UN Special Fund began a survey of basic development projects in 16 countries. In May also, the Committee on South-West Africa granted a hearing to the representative of the Herero people: a victory for the patient and persistent campaign of the Rev. Michael Scott, in which the WILPF had actively participated. Another step welcomed by the WILPF was the adoption by UNICEF in 1959 of a Declaration on the Rights of the Child: a document, said Adelaide Baker, which must not be left 'as a fine scroll with beautiful but empty words'.

Recalling the campaigns of the WILPF since the first session of the League of Nations in 1920 to have more women included in national delegations, it is of interest that in 1958 (as Adelaide Baker reported in *Pax et Libertas*, January 1959) forty women were participating at the United Nations as delegates or alternates. Amongst them were three WILPF members: Marian Anderson (USA), Taki Fugita (Japan) and Else Zeuthen (Denmark).

Gertrude Baer in her report to Congress mentioned progress in the Status of Women Commission concerning political rights of women, nationality of married women, equal pay, and equal educational opportunities. The Supplementary Convention on Slavery adopted in September 1956 marked an advance in another field; by May 1959 it had been ratified by 27 states. In January 1957 the WILPF was amongst the 28 non-governmental organizations granted 'special consultative relations' with the International Labour Organization; only six large-scale NGOs had full consultative status.

In June 1959 the WILPF sent three representatives to an NGOS' Conference in Geneva on Eradication of Prejudice and Discrimination: Gertrude Baer took part in the Legal Commission; Flemmie Kittrell and Sushila Nayar in the Educational Commission. Two British members attended a UNESCO seminar in London on Methods and Techniques of Adult Education in April 1959. The reports of the national sections showed a continuation of the common efforts for disarmament and stopping of nuclear tests, for refugees and international education, as well as some special projects of their own: Aborigines (Australia); Africa and Race Relations (Britain); immigration laws (Canada); help for a Greek refugee camp (Denmark); Algeria (France); Arab-Israeli co-operation (Israel); war toys (Italy); democratic education (Japan); broadcasts on peace work (Norway); children's television and radio programmes (Sweden); legality of nuclear tests on the high seas (Switzerland); intensive legislative work (USA).

One special achievement of the Stockholm Congress must be mentioned. After postponements in 1937, 1946, 1949 and 1953, a revised Statement of Aims of the WILPF was at last unanimously adopted, and remains in force. (See Appendix 4.)

But in the wider world outside, hopes of achieving a genuine thaw in the 'spirit of goodwill' of the WILPF Congress still seemed remote. The brief USA-USSR honeymoon, following the death of John Foster Dulles in May 1959 and Mr Khrushchev's visit to the United States in September, marked a respite rather than a reconciliation. A short-term gain was the unanimous resolution of the UN Fourteenth Assembly on General and Complete Disarmament, coupled with strong protests against nuclear testing and the spread of atomic weapons. But set against this was the unsettled state of South-East Asia, still a cockpit of the Cold War. To the recurring crises in Laos was now added the Sino-Indian border dispute. China had already shocked world opinion that year, and diminished her chances of acceptance into the world community, by her armed intervention in Tibet. But to isolate her further was not the road to peace.

At least as important as a settlement of the political divisions of Europe was the fostering of better understanding in the relations of Occident and Orient. This object was the theme of a major UNESCO project adopted at its General Conference in New Delhi in 1956 as a ten-year study. The co-operation of NGOS was invited, and in the summer of 1959 the WILPF Danish section organized a seminar on

East-West Cultural Relations. This section was already represented on the Danish Commission for UNESCO, and urged other sections to apply for membership of their national UNESCO Commissions. The Danish seminar proposed to UNESCO that the People's Republic of China should be included in the East-West project, and recommended the organization of international youth seminars in co-operation with NGOs. A second highly successful seminar on the East-West project was organized by the Norwegian section of the WILPF in 1961, with students from 20 countries including many from Africa and Asia. This seminar was commended in the UNESCO publication *Orient-Occident*, which also drew attention to the WILPF's long record of education for international understanding since its first summer school in 1921. (See Appendix 5.)

Andrée Jouve herself, however, was a little uneasy about some of the ways in which UNESCO was developing. Internationalism was spreading so rapidly that it was in danger of being spread too thin, and in too poor a quality. In her report to the Stockholm Congress she referred to the problems arising out of the vastly increased membership of the United Nations—then exactly doubled since its foundation—and the unequal development of member states. She wrote some time later:

I asked myself whether institutions on a planetary scale were not too vast for the capacities of the human body and spirit to compass. I wondered whether, after having ambitiously dreamed of the unity of the world, we were not going to be compelled to lower our sights to a more modest range, to decentralize our international institutions in order to accomplish our work 'in depth', to a human scale, 'à l'échelle humaine', according to the fine phrase of Léon Blum.

One is reminded of Emily Balch's thoughts on a 'planetary civilization', nearly twenty years earlier, and the need for 'the discipline of moral standards'.

But the new world was already battering at the ramparts of the old, and would not be gainsaid. At the 1960 General Conference of UNESCO, twelve newly-independent African states were admitted.

If the year 1960 seemed to bring new hope with the opening of the ten-nation Disarmament Conference in Geneva on March 15th, and the USA-USSR agreement for a moratorium on nuclear tests on the 30th, fresh crises were soon to follow. In March came the Sharpeville shootings in South Africa; in April, the abortive US invasion of Cuba; in May, the shooting down of an American spy-plane over Russia and abandonment of the Paris Summit Conference; in July, a threat of civil war in the newly-independent Congo.

The launching of the United Nations Congo Operation in August, at the request of the Lumumba Government, brought a new dimension to the existing complex of East-West rivalry, racial hatreds, and the machinations of international finance. That the UN 'presence' appeared to triumph over all these pressures was little short of a miracle. Mr Khrushchev's violent attack on Dag Hammarskjöld at the 1960 Assembly, and the Soviet demand for replacement of the Secretary-General by a 'troika' administration, was checked by the solidity of the Afro-Asians in favour of the UN. Efforts by some Western powers to obstruct the Assembly's resolutions were similarly foiled. The UN force in the Congo was certainly a very different animal from the lamb-like UNEF. It resorted to military measures, with loss of life on both sides, at least three times in the course of the two and a half year struggle to prevent civil war and eliminate foreign mercenaries. Nevertheless, the overall view of the WILPF was that the Congo operation must be supported. The choices were well summed up by a British member, Mary Phillips, at the section's 1963 Annual Council:

We can surely say that the UN force has prevented what might have been a blood bath, has stopped the cold war extending into a hot war, and has given a breathing space for other UN personnel to carry out their job of building up the health, education and other services of the country.

In July 1961 the division of Europe was hardened with the erection by East Germany of the Berlin Wall, thus sealing off the exit route for the thousands of defectors who were pouring into the West. The WILPF Executive Committee, meeting in London the same day, sent a letter to the UN Secretary-General, the Four Powers concerned, and the West and East German governments, calling for a new international status for West Berlin, under UN supervision and guaranteed by the Four Powers.

In September, the world was faced with the tragic death of Dag Hammarskjöld in the Congo, the resumption of nuclear testing by the USSR, and threatened resumption by the USA. Letters were immediately sent by the WILPF International Chairman to both Mr Khrushchev and Mr Kennedy, appealing for a return to the voluntary moratorium on tests and for negotiations to be reopened towards the achievement of total and universal disarmament in accordance with the unanimous resolution of the UN Fourteenth Assembly. Demonstrations and protests were simultaneously taking place in the national sections. But all these appeals, and many others from concerned public opinion, went unheeded. The Soviet 50-megaton bomb was exploded on October 30th, and testing by both sides continued throughout 1962. The old international order, it seemed, was determined to go out with a bang.

In October 1962, as Russian ships sailed towards Cuba carrying arms for the Castro régime and American ships closed in to enforce the island's blockade, the final *coup* all but fell. In this strangely hypnotic crisis—when the single voice of one elderly Englishman, Bertrand Russell, seemed more potent on the side of reason than all the resources of diplomacy—the United States section of the WILPF rose to the challenge in the highest traditions of its own and the whole League's history. Already on October 9th, alternative policies were being offered to the US Government's threats of blockade and invasion: adherence to non-intervention; normalization of relations with Cuba through the offered mediation of Mexico or Brazil; settlement of the immediate crisis through the UN and the Organization of American States. On October 26th, when violent confrontation seemed almost inevitable, telegrams were sent to President Kennedy and to every member of the Senate Foreign Relations Committee urging restraint and acceptance of U Thant's proposal for immediate negotiations. On October 27th, a further telegram to the President called for acceptance of the Soviet proposal to 'trade' bases in Cuba and Turkey. On October 28th, the WILPF National Board issued the following statement:

WILPF notes with deep regret that by responding to the Soviet challenge of the establishment of offensive missile bases in Cuba with the imposition of a quarantine, our Government violated its treaty commitments under the Charters of the Organization of American States and of the United Nations. We strongly believe that scrupulous compliance with international law and treaty obligations is an indispensable prerequisite to the maintenance of world peace. A situation having been created in Cuba which our Government felt threatened its vital security interests, it should have exhausted every possibility of peaceful settlement through negotiation, and by bringing the matter before the United Nations, rather than resorting to unilateral action calculated to bring the world to the brink of destruction.

The immediate goal sought by our Government in this instance may possibly be achieved by the policy adopted. But the long-term goal of the world's peoples to live in a world free from nuclear war is jeopardized by a policy dependent upon one side yielding to the threats of the other. With leaders of each side believing that the other, if rational, must give way rather than resort to thermo-nuclear war, the path is open for the fatal collision when neither yields.

The WILPF takes encouragement from the fact that both the US and the USSR have shown some measure of restraint in the current crisis. That the US has, to this date, stopped short of invasion and/or bombing of the Cuban bases represents a victory for the forces of moderation within the Government over those who would return to that shameful period of US history when sending in the Marines was the typical response to any hemispheric crisis. That Chairman Khrushchev first ordered his ships not to run the blockade, then directed their return to the Soviet Union and, finally, offered to dismantle the missile bases, has demonstrated both restraint and a willingness to make substantial concessions in the interest of peaceful settlement of the present dispute.

We welcome the announced willingness of both the US and the USSR to negotiate their differences under UN auspices, and their apparent recognition that the Cuban crisis, if resolved, can result in general negotiations leading to a *détente* between the NATO and Warsaw Pact countries. We believe that the opportunity here presented to negotiate a mutually advantageous military disengagement and territorial disarmament not only in Cuba but also in Turkey and elsewhere, should be of tremendous significance in reversing the present arms spiral and in bringing about the general and complete disarmament to which both countries have committed themselves in principle, though not yet in practice.

The world did not destroy itself over Cuba; nor over the almost simultaneous Sino-Indian clash. The voice of reason, if only by a narrow margin, did prevail. The WILPF continued its efforts to bring the long-awaited 'world community' to a painless and tranquil birth. And the omens for this happy event were not all so inauspicious as the convulsions that started this chapter might suggest.

APPENDIX 4

STATEMENT OF AIMS OF WILPF
as revised at Stockholm Congress, 1959

1. The WILPF aims at bringing together women of different political and philosophical tendencies united in their determination to study, make known and help abolish the political, social, economic and psychological causes of war, and to work for a constructive peace.

2. The primary objects of the WILPF continue to be total and universal disarmament, the abolition of violent means of coercion for the settlement of all conflicts, the substitution in every case of some form of peaceful settlement, and the strengthening of a world organization for the prevention of war, the institution of international law, and for the political, social and economic co-operation of peoples.

3. In order to promote these aims, the WILPF seeks to remove such restrictions on freedom as impair human dignity and to establish by nonviolent means the conditions under which men and women may live in peace and justice free from the fear of war and of want and of discrimination on grounds of sex, race, colour, language, national, ethnical or social origin, property, birth, or other status, political, religious or other belief.

4. The work of all the National Sections is based upon the statements adopted and the resolutions passed by the International Congresses of the League.

APPENDIX 5

WILPF INTERNATIONAL SUMMER SCHOOLS
1921–63

1921. Salzburg: *Education and Internationalism.*
    Hosts: Stefan and Fredericka Zweig.
1922. Lugano: *The International Idea in Civilization.*
Mme Andrée Jouve described this historic school in an address to the Seminar at Leangkollen, Norway, in 1961:

'John Keynes Holmes spoke of the American contribution to the International idea; Kalidas Nag, Professor of History in the University of Calcutta—and a disciple of Tagore—spoke of the Indian, and Ayusawa of the Japanese points of view; while Bertrand Russell dealt with that of Modern China and Paul Birukoff, secretary of Tolstoy, spoke of Pacifism in Russia.

'The speakers envisaged that the work of internationalization begun by the League of Nations would continue in various directions. The international protection of labour was treated by André de Maday, a Swiss professor; international public health by the Italian Dr Ettore Levi; while Pierre Cérésole, himself the creator of the idea of an International Civil

Service to replace military service, spoke of its possibilities for the future. The role of women, of youth, and the education of children in the development of the international idea were expounded by the Dutch writer Frederic van Elden and by Austrian, German, French and Hungarian speakers, among the last of whom was our Vilma Glücklich.

'Finally the arts had their turn, introducing the most human and universal elements. The Italian poet Francesco Chiesa spoke on Dante and Giovanni di Casamichele on St Francis of Assisi. Mme Bianche Albane-Duhamel gave a fine reading of French poetry citing the tragedy of war, Felicien Challaye commented on the pictures of the ruins of Angkor (Cambodia). Hermann Hesse read a chapter of his unpublished book "Siddharta" full of the wisdom of the East, and Dillip Roy, taking up the history of Hindu music, one night sang old Hindu hymns while rowing on the Lake!'

1923. Poděbrady, Czechoslovakia: *Social Peace.*
Kalidas Nag on Indian thought; Bulgachov on Tolstoy; Bishop Velmirovic (Yugoslavia) on Christianity; Pierre Hamp (France) on Economic Questions; E. W. Wilton (Britain) on Guild Socialism; P. Hodza (Czech Ministry of Agriculture) on the Agrarian Problem; the Belgian specialist Decroly on the education of abnormal children.

1924. Chicago: Follow-up of Washington Congress and Pax Special tour.

1925. Thonon, France: *Co-operation in its Economic and International Applications.*
Claude Gignoux on the Co-operative Movement in France; W. James Warbasse on Co-operation in the USA; Co-operation of Races and Nations by Professor Radl (Prague) and W. Arnold Forster (London); Intellectual Co-operation by Dr Wilhelm Friedmann (Leipzig) and Anderson Naxo (Copenhagen).

1926. Gland, Switzerland: Six-weeks school for peace workers attending sessions of League of Nations.

1927. Gland, Switzerland: *Relations between White and Coloured Races.*
Discussions led by Felicien Challaye, expert on Indo-China and Equatorial Africa. Participants from LON Mandates Commission: John H. Harris, Henri Junod, William Rappard, Salvador de Madariaga. Also present: Romain Rolland, Roger Baldwin (USA), J. C. Bose (India), Dr Albert Schweitzer, J. L. Nehru, Mrs Roland-Holst (Holland), Dr Leo Frobenius (Germany); Wong van Giao (Indo-China), Mohammed Hatta (Indonesia), S. Stefani (Madagascar), Mukerji (India) and Sia Ting (China).

1928. Birmingham: Organized by British Section. *New Governmental Theories* (Socialism, Bolshevism, Fascism): their relation to international peace.
Professor Salvemini on Fascism; C. Roden Buxton on Socialism; E. F. Wise on Bolshevism (economic aspect). Discussions led by Mrs H. M. Swanwick.

1928, 1930 and 1931: Schools on *Minority Problems* held at Visegrad (Hungary), Sofia (Bulgaria), Ribeauvillé (Alsace) and Lowenberg (Silesia).

1938. Paris: Organized by French Section. *The True Face of Contemporary France.*

1948. Schiers, Switzerland: *Democracy.*

Professor R. H. Pender (British zone, Germany), André Ribard (France), Frank Hardie (Britain), Mrs Alva Myrdal (Sweden), Dr A. Gasser and Dr Elisabeth Rotten (Switzerland)

1949. Gripsholm, Sweden: *Peace and Freedom.*
Discussion leader: Dr Elisabeth Rotten.

1950. Beauvallon-Dieulefit, France: *Planning and Individual Liberty; Peace and Independence.*

Gertrude Baer, Jaques Duboin, André Ribard, Agnes and Olaf Stapledon.

1951. Filzbach, Switzerland: *Freedom and Responsibility.*

Professor Pender, Professor Mieville, Dr Friedemann, Dr E. Rotten.

1952. Cavigliano, Locarno: *The Young Generation and the Modern World.*

Professor Hubert Deschamps (Paris), Professor Pender, Professor Sigerist.

1954. Magleaas, Copenhagen: *A Peace Civilization in the Making*—(1) International Agencies.

Mme Sylvain Bouchereau and lecturers on UN Specialized Agencies.

1955. Barsbüttel, Hamburg: *A Peace Civilization in the Making*—(2) Peaceful Uses of Atomic Energy; Racial Co-operation.
Grant received from UNESCO.

Dr R. Chastel (Paris) and Dr Obourn (UNESCO) on atomic energy. Dr Erich Luth (Germany) on Anti-Semitism; Mme Sylvain Bouchereau, Frau Hoppstock-Huth.

1959. Holte, Copenhagen: *East and West—Towards Mutual Understanding.* (UNESCO Major Project).
Organized by Danish section with grant from UNESCO.

1961. Leangkollen, Oslo: *East and West—Cultural Co-existence?*
Organized by Norwegian section with grants from UNESCO, Nobel Committee and Norwegian Ministry of Foreign Affairs.

Dr Højer (Sweden); Professor J. Galtung, Professor G. Gjessing, Dr A. M. Klausen, D. Lund (Norway); Dr Sushila Nayar (India); Mrs Fujiko Isono (Japan).

1963. Holte, Copenhagen: *Economic and Social Consequences of Disarmament; Peace Research.*
Organized by Danish section with grant from UNESCO.

Professor K. Boulding (USA), Professor J. Pajestka (Poland), Mrs M. H. Ruge (Norway), Christel Küpper (Germany), Peter Lengyl (UNESCO).

Opened by Danish Minister of Education, Mr Helveg Petersen.

CHAPTER 20

TOWARDS A WORLD COMMUNITY

World Refugee Year—Jane Addams House—Freedom from Hunger Campaign—Development Decade—Asilomar Congress 1962—Danish Seminar 1963—Test Ban Treaty—Soviet-American Co-operation—WILPF at its 50th Anniversary—International Co-operation Year.

During 1959–60, 97 countries participated in World Refugee Year, the main object of which was to arouse the public conscience to the shame and misery of the refugee camps which still existed in Europe and to resettle their 140,000 inhabitants as members of the normal community. The campaign was an outstanding success, and one to which the Women's International League for Peace and Freedom made its own special contribution. World Refugee Year coincided with the centenary of the birth of Jane Addams in September 1960, and the WILPF was quick to sense the appropriateness of linking these events. Jane Addams, founder of Hull House—that haven for nineteenth-century immigrants to the USA—should be commemorated in a house for the new victims of man's inhumanity to man, the 'displaced persons' of the Second World War. On a proposal first put to the Executive Committee by Adelaide Baker in 1958, plans were laid for the Jane Addams House, to be built at Spittal-Drau in Austria as part of a new village rising from the ashes of the Spittal refugee camp. In consultation with the UN High Commissioner for Refugees, Dr Auguste Lindt, the WILPF promised to raise 20,000 dollars towards the building costs, the balance to be met by the UN and the Austrian authorities.

Ten national sections of the League co-operated in this effort, surpassing the target figure by fifty per cent. This fine result was a tribute to the devotion and enthusiasm of Adelaide Baker in promoting and guiding the project through all its stages. The final 10,000 dollars was presented to Dr Lindt in Geneva by the International Chairman on August 24, 1960. On August 28th, Jane Addams House was formally opened, many of the occupants of its 32 apartments already being in residence. A four-storey, pink-washed building, situated at No. 2 Fridtjof Nansen Street in the Van Heuven Goedhart district, Jane

Addams House thus commemorated in one humanitarian enterprise two great Refugee Commissioners and three Nobel prize-winners! Many WILPF members travelled to Spittal for the ceremony. They were welcomed by the Burgomeister and a boys' brass band drawn from a refugee training school, its fourteen nationalities welded in a vociferous harmony. Speeches were made by the former and the present International Chairmen—Marie Lous-Mohr and Else Zeuthen —who presented an illuminated scroll listing the sections of the WILPF which had contributed to the House. This now hangs in the entrance hall. On an outer wall is a large mural, painted by the Austrian artist Bränstetter from a design by the American muralist Robert Lamdin, showing the PAX symbol of the WILPF and a family group, together with an inscription, in German, from Jane Addams' *Newer Ideals of Peace*:

Not the heroism connected with warfare and destruction but that which pertains to labour and the nourishing of human life.

The connection of the WILPF with Jane Addams House did not end with the opening ceremony; it would be truer to say that it only began at that point. Members have continued to visit Spittal, to send gifts to the residents, and to contribute towards other amenities for the environment, such as gardens, seats and fencing, and towards a Community Centre for the whole new village.

As World Refugee Year ended, another great international effort for human betterment was launched. The Freedom from Hunger Campaign was initiated by FAO in June 1960. Its aim was to solve the problems of world hunger by means of education, increased food production and improved distribution; in short, 'to help the hungry to help themselves'. At an NGOs Conference the previous month, the WILPF was represented by Gertrude Baer on behalf of the international and Mrs Elizabeth A. Campbell on behalf of the British section; members of the Rome branch also attended some of the sessions. Amongst suggestions for projects was one made by Gertrude Baer, which aroused much interest, on rural education by means of Farm Broadcasting; a scheme about which she had been informed by the WILPF Australian section.

The WILPF decided to make the provision of transistor radios for farm broadcasting its own international project for the Freedom from Hunger Campaign. Gertrude Baer and Elizabeth Campbell were appointed to co-ordinate the campaign. The area selected was the

Kaira District Milk Co-operative, covering 250 villages, at Anand in Gujerat, India, where community instruction by radio would be given under the direction of FAO. The Japanese section of the League worked hard to obtain an offer of transistors at a much reduced cost and the Indian section secured duty-free import; seven other national sections also contributed to the project. Anand was described by the British economist Barbara Ward Jackson as 'an example of everything that one can hope for in a development programme'. In addition, several sections started their own national FFHC projects. The Toronto group's 'Share a Loaf' appeal was praised by the FFHC Co-ordinator in Rome and recommended to other organizations and national committees as an example of a simple but effective initiative. The British section in less than two years raised £3,500 to buy farm tools for a new agricultural college in Swaziland.

In December 1961 the UN General Assembly called for a UN 'Development Decade': a ten-year, combined effort to raise the living standards of the underdeveloped countries and check the widening gap between rich and poor. At once the need became apparent for the kind of training in international administration about which Gertrude Baer had dreamed—and acted—since 1943. She had persistently raised the matter with delegates at the UN and with successive Secretary-Generals. In 1958, on a suggestion of Lester Pearson of Canada, Dag Hammarskjöld initiated 'Operation Executive' (OPEX), an experimental scheme to supply administrators and executives to governments requesting them. OPEX was put on a continuing basis in 1960; but merely to supply trained personnel did not meet the demand Miss Baer, for one, had foreseen. In December 1962 the General Assembly instructed the Secretary-General to look into the question of a United Nations Training Institute. The following December, having received U Thant's report and a favourable recommendation by ECOSOC, Resolution 1934 of the Eighteenth General Assembly requested the Secretary-General to take steps to set up a training and research institute, with the hope that it would be established in 1964. The resolution noted—as the WILPF had been observing for nearly fifty years—'the close inter-relationship between economic and social development and the achievement of peace and security, and the dependence of both of these on international co-operation'. It further stated that

the provision and training of personnel of the highest calibre from the developing Member States for national service and service with the

United Nations and the specialized agencies are important in order to fulfil the objectives of the United Nations, especially in the context of the United Nations Development Decade.

The interrelationship between peace and economic devlopment, for so long ignored by governments, was again brought home in the report of a UN Consultative Group on the Economic and Social Consequences of Disarmament. The ten experts, from USA, USSR, UK, France, Czechoslovakia, Poland, India, Pakistan, Sudan and Venezuela, issued their report just prior to the opening of the 18-nation Disarmament Conference at Geneva in March 1962. They reached the unanimous conclusion that 'the achievement of general and complete disarmament would be an unqualified blessing to all mankind' and that all the problems of transition to disarmament *could* be met by appropriate national and international measures.

When the report of this study group was discussed at the plenary session of the Economic Commission for Europe in May 1962, Gertrude Baer asked for the floor and was granted permission to make a statement on behalf of the WILPF—the first time a representative of a women's international organization had done so in the plenary meeting. The text of the statement was included in the Summary Record ECE (XVII), SR 15, May 1962. Its concluding paragraph may be quoted here:

Considering the Study as of greatest import for promoting a worldwide enlightened public opinion in favour of the present negotiations on total and universal disarmament to which our international organization has been pledged ever since 1915, we seriously hope that this research will be further pursued. We venture to suggest that the membership of the coming Study Group or Groups be such as to allow them considerably to enlarge upon the 'Social Consequences of Disarmament'. It is these very social and socio-psychological aspects together with the all-important economic factors which will determine human relations within the national community as well as between countries and continents in a world without war which must be based on an entirely new concept of peace, on a new *worldwide* and universally and totally disarmed economic and social structure of peace.

In the light of the UN Report, it was perhaps not entirely utopian that the WILPF should choose for the theme of its Fifteenth International

Congress 'Total and Universal Disarmament—Now'. The political, economic, social and psychological aspects of Disarmament were to come under review. For this Congress the WILPF returned to America, after an absence of 38 years. All five continents of the world were represented amongst the 250 members from 15 countries who gathered at Asilomar, California, from July 8 to 13, 1962. Greetings were received from President Kennedy, Eleanor Roosevelt, U Thant, Pandit Nehru and many other world figures. Fraternal delegates and visitors included representatives of the Women's International Democratic Federation and World Peace Council; a member of the Polish Senate; and observers from Iraq, Lebanon, Kuwait and Syria. Two new national sections were admitted: Lebanon, represented by Mme Anissa Najjaer, and Nigeria. Both had developed from personal contact—by Dr Bouchereau and others in the Middle East and by Emily Parker Simon in Africa. A special welcome was given to Mme Lucila Rubio de Laverde of Colombia, Chairman of the WILPF Committee on Latin America. Since the last Congress the League had suffered two sad losses amongst its officers: Emily Greene Balch had died on January 9, 1961, the day after her 94th birthday; to be followed in March by an International Vice-President, Gertrude Bussey. The last three years had also seen the passing of Mary Sheepshanks of the British section; Madeleine Rolland of France; and Mrs Wulfften-Palthe, a founder-member of the Dutch section.

The Political aspects of Disarmament were dealt with by Dr E. Raymond Wilson, Executive Secretary emeritus of the Friends' Committee on National Legislation, and Dorothy Hutchinson, President of the US section; Social and Economic aspects by Dr Frances W. Herring, of Berkeley, California; Psychological and Cultural aspects in a paper submitted by the French section. The text of the addresses by Raymond Wilson and Dorothy Hutchinson and a summary of Frances Herring's paper were inserted into the US Congressional Record on Thursday, September 20, 1962, together with a commendatory note on the work of the WILPF since its foundation, on the proposal of Senator Hubert Humphrey.

In her summary of work with the United Nations Gertrude Baer reported on the progress of the Geneva Disarmament talks. The original eighteen nations were reduced to seventeen since France refused to participate, but the presence of eight non-aligned countries was a new and hopeful factor. She had interviews with the non-aligned delegations, calling attention to the many Disarmament campaigns undertaken by the WILPF and in particular to the work of the Committee against Scientific Warfare, which had submitted a memorandum to all seventeen heads of delegations at the opening of the conference.

In addition, Gertrude Baer was continuing her efforts in the Human Rights Commission in favour of the Right of Asylum and for abolition of Capital Punishment. The problems of the stateless had moved a little nearer to solution with the Convention on Reduction of Future Statelessness of August 1961, but only three governments had signed it. All national sections were asked to press for ratification. There was encouraging progress in the Status of Women Commission, and a global study was planned on the 'occupational outlook' of women, to promote the access of women to technical and professional training and employment. National sections were asked to co-operate in supplying authentic information to the Commission in New York.

Further reports on Status of Women and Human Rights were given by Adelaide Baker. In connection with the draft principles of the HRC on freedom and non-discrimination in religious rights and practices, she submitted a statement urging that the principle of conscientious objection should be recognized in stronger terms, namely: 'Exemption from military service shall be granted to genuine objectors to military service in a manner ensuring no adverse distinction based on religion or belief.' The Congress recommended that national sections should investigate the treatment of conscientious objectors in their various countries and report their findings to the Executive Committee. The Congress further urged ratification of the Human Rights Covenant to strengthen efforts against Capital Punishment, Slavery, Genocide, Prostitution and infringements of the Right of Asylum; and in favour of the political and national equality of women, equal rights in labour and education, and rights of refugees and stateless persons.

The question of slavery, and its increasing practice during recent years, had been taken up by the WILPF on the prompting of a British member, Mrs Mary Nuttall, working in association with the Anti-Slavery Society and the Society of Friends. She appealed to national sections to press for ratification of the Slavery Conventions of 1926 and 1956, and also stressed the need for implementation of the Conventions by a UN Committee of Experts. In Denmark, the WILPF International Chairman, Else Zeuthen, raised the matter in Parliament and in July 1962 a joint Danish-UK resolution was adopted by ECOSOC, asking for the question of slavery to be brought to the General Assembly and calling on all governments to ratify the Conventions.

At this same session of ECOSOC, thanks largely to the persistence of Mary Nuttall and Mr C. W. W. Greenidge of the Anti-Slavery Society, six NGOs submitted statements asking for a Committee of Experts to be set up. The culmination of their campaign came in February 1964, with the appointment by the UN Secretary-General of Mohamed Awad of Giza (United Arab Republic) as Special Rapporteur on Slavery, as authorized by ECOSOC in 1963. ECOSOC had turned down the demand for a Committee, but NGOs were satisfied that the decision to appoint a Rapporteur represented a step in the right direction.

A common theme among many speakers at the Asilomar Congress was the danger of Accidental War, a danger that was daily becoming more acute with the increasing numbers and complexity of nuclear weapons. National sections were asked to make a co-ordinated effort on November 11, 1962, to bring home the dangers as dramatically and forcefully as possible. Linked with this emotional appeal, it was suggested, should be a positive vision of the benefits of a disarmed world. Out of these discussions came a new development of WILPF work, although one well in line with its earliest traditions. It was recognized that, in the era of nuclear weapons, peace work too must be given a 'scientific' status through the setting up of many more institutes for fundamental Peace Research. All national sections were asked to encourage the formation of such institutes, if these did not exist, in their own countries. In addition, a resolution was sent to UNESCO asking for an international conference of scholars working in this field.

Following the Congress, the WILPF set up its own International Consultative Committee on Peace Research, with the following members: Convener, Johanne Gjermoe (Norway), economist; Chairman: Elise Boulding (USA), sociologist, of the Michigan University Center for Research on Conflict Resolution; Ingrid Galtung (Norway), Oslo Institute for Social Research; Sushila Nayar (India), Minister of Health; Fujiko Isono (Japan), anthropologist; and Sheila Young (Canada). The following winter the first issue appeared of the International Newsletter on Peace Research, edited by Elise Boulding. This subsequently became the official organ of the international peace research movement, and in 1964 its sponsorship was taken over by UNESCO.

In July 1963 the WILPF, with a grant from UNESCO, organized a seminar in Denmark which explored further the two major concerns of the 1962 Congress: Economic and Social Consequences of Disarmament and Peace Research. Unlike previous summer schools, it was planned for the benefit of members of the League, rather than for young students from outside. Sixteen countries were represented by nearly 50 participants. The lecturing staff consisted of Professor Jozef Pajestka, a member of the Polish Economic Council; Professor Kenneth Boulding, Director of the Center for Research on Conflict Resolution, Michigan; Peter Lengyl, UNESCO Social Sciences department; Mrs Mari Holmboe Ruge, Norwegian Peace Research Institute; and from the WILPF, Andrée Jouve of France, Christel Küpper of Germany, and Emily Parker Simon, International Vice-Chairman. The final report of the seminar stressed the need for 'a social vision of the kind of world we want', and concluded:

The WILPF must make the best possible use of its resources and the gifts of its members to create a picture in the minds of the world publics, and their opinion leaders, of a stable, prosperous, disarmed, international community as an achievable reality.

In practical terms, this meant that the positive rather than the negative case should be emphasized. In the economic sphere, the process of Disarmament must be presented 'as a positive releasing of resources for world development instead of a negative process of producing economic insecurity'. Politically, the WILPF must foster a sense of world community and the development of an international moral consensus: 'Education for politically-wise policies must go hand in hand with the development of a moral framework within which decisions must be made'.

The WILPF Executive Committee, meeting immediately before the seminar, had reiterated the need for total and universal disarmament, opposed the arming of NATO forces with nuclear weapons, and expressed approval of the revised Rapacki Plan for demilitarization of all Germany, Poland and Czechoslovakia. With the signing of a Test Ban Treaty an imminent possibility, the Committee also issued a statement on the WILPF attitude to such a treaty. Expressing the belief that a comprehensive test ban agreement with adequate safeguards was now technically feasible, the statement continued:

If, however, the governments are able to agree to ban tests only in the atmosphere, outer space and under water, the WILPF will not oppose such a partial ban, recognizing that even a partial ban would protect the world's people from the greatest hazards to their health and heredity, would inhibit the spread of nuclear weapons to many more nations, and would break the prolonged deadlock, opening the way for further negotiations on underground tests and on disarmament.

On August 5, 1963, the Partial Test Ban Treaty was signed in Moscow by the UK, USA and USSR. With the majority of the world's peoples, the WILPF welcomed this East-West *rapprochement*, but it also noted the dangers arising out of the further isolation of China. The International Chairman was requested by the Executive Committee to send an appeal to all governments which did not support the seating of the Peking Government at the United Nations to reconsider their decision. At the 1963 Assembly 57 votes were cast in favour of China's admission and 41 against, with 12 abstentions.

Meanwhile, unofficial contacts with the women of Eastern Europe, which had been maintained throughout the Cold War, were beginning to yield more concrete results. In November 1961, the first conference of American and Soviet women ever held in the USA took place at Bryn Mawr College, initiated by the WILPF. After a week of intensive private discussions, the nine Russian and twelve American women issued an unanimously agreed statement expressing the belief:

that despite the differences in social and economic systems, our two countries must find a way to grow and develop in an atmosphere of peace between ourselves and with the other peoples of the world.

It was further recognized:

that our two tremendously powerful countries have a special responsibility to initiate a system of necessary concrete measures for general and complete disarmament and vigorously to carry them out.

Here reference was made to the agreed principles for disarmament signed by Mr Zorin and Mr Stevenson at the UN on September 20, 1961. An original recommendation of the women's conference was that the USA and USSR should set up a joint research centre on problems of peace, under formal international auspices.

In March 1963, six American WILPF members visited Poland at the invitation of the League of Polish Women, during the course of which Dorothy Hutchinson was asked to lecture at the Warsaw Institute of International Relations on Disarmament and US Public Opinion. In

April 1964, after several unavoidable delays, nine American women paid a return visit to Moscow for a second conference with Soviet women. The atmosphere was described as one of 'growing hopefulness', with a general reduction of tensions due to the Test Ban Treaty; the agreement not to put vehicles carrying nuclear weapons in Outer Space; and the direct, 'hot-line' communication between Washington and Moscow. These advances, the agreed statement of the conference declared, must be followed up by others:

While nothing less than general and complete disarmament must be the goal, we will welcome any measures for partial disarmament which can be agreed upon as interim steps.

The role of the United Nations in facilitating disarmament was stressed—and the UN must include 'all the nations of the world'. The Americans in Moscow emphasized that 'peaceful co-existence'—a favourite Soviet phrase—was not enough; there must be 'peaceful co-operation' between countries with differing systems. This point was included in the final statement, which also acknowledged (as the Bryn Mawr statement had not) that there were still disagreements between the two sides on the best means of achieving their objectives.

These differences of opinion were not confined to East-West relations. As the Soviet women sometimes found it difficult to understand, there were many disagreements among Western peace groups about their aims and methods of working. It was evident at the Asilomar Congress that some of the younger WILPF members wished to co-operate more closely with the new women's peace groups which had sprung up during the past few years, mainly as an expression of women's concern about the effects of nuclear tests. Was the WILPF being overtaken and out-distanced by the more immediate, dynamic appeal of such movements as the Canadian Voice of Women (VOW) or the American Women's International Strike for Peace (WISP)? Both VOW and WISP grew rapidly and spontaneously into popular, international movements, giving an impression of youth and vitality that captured the public imagination in a way that the WILPF had not done since its earliest days—when it too was a youthful, pioneer movement. The question was much debated and on the whole closer co-operation with the new groups was favoured.

But the WILPF officers were quite clear that the League itself should not seek to become a mass, popular movement on the same lines as its younger sisters. The fantastic rate of technical development, both civil and military, and the ever-present threat of instant global destruction, brought a fresh urgency to the task of creating a peaceful world, but did not fundamentally change the nature of the problems to be solved. These problems the WILPF had been facing for 47 years and would continue to face, equipped with the well-tried tools of education, investigation, personal confrontation of issues, and action always from a basis of reasoned argument and conviction. It was gratifying to the WILPF that many of the leaders of the newer groups, having explored the possibilities and limits of the method of public demonstration, then turned to the older body for guidance in the next steps; although, at the same time, other new recruits became impatient with the 'traditionalism' and 'top-heaviness' of the WILPF, and drifted away.

These faults, an inevitable accretion to any well-established organization, must be squarely faced as the WILPF approaches its fiftieth anniversary. Losses sustained during the Second World War and the Cold War were undoubtedly being made up in the 1960s, but there is still some way to go to recapture the pre-war peak of a 50,000 membership (not a large figure for a world organization, even on a quality basis). In 1964, there were 20 affiliated national sections: Australia, Austria, Canada, Denmark, Finland, France, Germany, Great Britain, India, Israel, Italy, Japan, Lebanon, Netherlands, New Zealand, Nigeria, Norway, Sweden, Switzerland, United States. In addition smaller groups existed in Ghana and Korea; and a new section was forming in the Federal Republic of Cameroon. The international office was also in touch with corresponding members in Burma, Colombia, Ethiopia, Gambia, Haiti, Ireland, Kuwait, Philippines, Singapore, Syria and Tanganyika. Elizabeth Tapper appealed strongly for a committee to follow up and encourage new sections, if possible through personal visits. The world tour undertaken by the International Chairman, Else Zeuthen, immediately after the Asilomar Congress was an example of the value of such personal contacts. In five months, she toured through California, Australia, New Zealand, Philippines, Japan, Hong Kong, Thailand, India, Ceylon and the Middle East (Arab countries and Israel), talking to WILPF groups and extending the League's influence through TV and radio broadcasts and public meetings.

For its fiftieth anniversary, the WILPF returns to its birthplace, The Hague, where the Sixteenth International Congress will take place in July 1965, on the theme 'Towards a World without War'. The cen-

tenary of Jane Addams' birth had coincided with one great international effort—World Refugee Year. The half-century after the
League's birth coincides with another which is perhaps even more
appropriate to the occasion—International Co-operation Year. The
idea for such a year grew out of a suggestion first made by Voice of
Women in Canada in 1961, which was taken up by Pandit Nehru of
India and adopted by the UN General Assembly in 1963. It is not, like
World Refugee Year and the Freedom from Hunger Campaign, an
appeal primarily for money. It is an appeal for fresh thinking, imagination and effort to translate the One World of modern technology into
a human reality. Its success or failure depends above all on the response
of the non-governmental organizations in consultative status with the
United Nations, which itself reaches its twentieth year in 1965 and
must reconsider its Charter. Amongst these NGOs, the WILPF is
particular well-equipped to meet the challenge. It has been working
for 'international co-operation' not for one year only but for fifty. It
has explored the conditions for permanent peace in the light both of
institutions and of the human beings who must make them effective.
Peace, the WILPF saw from the start, must be related to freedom.
Jane Addams perceived also the link between 'peace and bread'; Emily
Greene Balch, between 'peace and morality'; Gertrude Baer, between
'peace and social justice'. The leaders of the WILPF, though differing
in their emphases, were always united in their belief that peace must
be envisaged as a total situation, in a global world. One special project of the League for International Co-operation Year is a seminar on
Community Development, intended primarily for Asian and African
women, to take place in India at the invitation of the Indian section.
In addition, the Danish section has secured a grant from UNESCO for
a Danish-Polish seminar.

The current thinking of the WILPF has been concerned with the
development of the United Nations organization into a genuine world
political community—as the 1963 Executive Committee expressed it:

with effective international machinery to settle political as well as
legal conflicts and facilitate, where needed, radical social and economic
change without the use of violence.

No study could be more relevant than this to the aims of International
Co-operation Year, aims which will surely be most effectively achieved
by increasing the power and influence of the non-governmental

organizations from whose ranks the first world citizens of the future will spring. The 'voice of the people' is a cliché which governments can well afford to ignore, since more often than not it may only be the voice of ignorance, prejudice and demagogery. The voice of an informed, concerned and articulate public opinion, united in the conviction that a common basis of self-interest exists for all humanity, has yet to make itself heard. The basis of common interest has still to be formulated, and is far from being accepted. It is the particular task of our century to find it. In this great educational and social, non-violent revolution, the voice of the Women's International League for Peace and Freedom will surely be heard in the second half-century of its existence, as it has been in the first.

INDEX